Georgetown University Round Table on Languages and Linguistics 1975

Developmental Psycholinguistics: Theory and Applications

Daniel P. Dato
Editor

Georgetown University Press, Washington, D.C. 20057

BIBLIOGRAPHIC NOTICE

Since this series has been variously, and confusingly, cited as: Georgetown University Monograph Series on Languages and Linguistics, Monograph Series on Languages and Linguistics, Reports of the Annual Round Table Meetings on Linguistics and Language Study, etc., beginning with the 1973 volume, the title of the series was changed.

The new title of the series includes the year of a Round Table and omits both the monograph number and the meeting number, thus: Georgetown University Round Table on Languages and Linguistics 1975, with the regular abbreviation GURT 1975. Full bibliographical references should show the form:

Ferguson, Charles A. 1975. Sound patterns in language acquisition. In: Georgetown University Round Table on Languages and Linguistics 1975. Edited by Daniel P. Dato. Washington, D.C., Georgetown University Press. 1-16.

Library of Congress Catalog Card Number: 58-31607
ISBN 0-87840-110-5

CONTENTS

PANEL II. CHILDREN'S LANGUAGE ACQUISITION
          AND COMMUNICATIVE DISORDERS

Chairman: James W. Hillis, The George Washington University

PANEL III. DEVELOPMENTAL PSYCHOLINGUISTICS
           AND SECOND LANGUAGE LEARNING

Chairman: Irene Thompson, The George Washington University

PANEL IV. DEVELOPMENTAL PSYCHOLINGUISTICS
          AND EDUCATION

Chairman: Roger W. Shuy, Georgetown University

WELCOMING REMARKS

JAMES E. ALATIS

Dean, School of Languages and Linguistics
Georgetown University

Good evening, ladies and gentlemen! It gives me much pleasure, indeed, to welcome you, on behalf of Georgetown University and its School of Languages and Linguistics, to this, the 26th Annual Georgetown University Round Table.

The theme of this year's program--Developmental Psycholinguistics: Theory and Applications--gives us the opportunity to consider, in some depth, one of the most important 'hyphenated interdisciplines' that have grown around the field of linguistics in recent years. The growth of such hyphenated interdisciplines as psycholinguistics, sociolinguistics, neurolinguistics, etc. (though I realize that in writing they are not usually hyphenated), is just another indication of the vitality and constant state of development of our most exciting field.

We all know that the nature of linguistics, and with it some of the interests and goals of second language teaching, has changed considerably since 1954. Among the most important psycholinguistic developments have been those which have centered around the study of the nature and developmental stages of 'first' language acquisition. These developments, in my opinion, hold great promise for a better understanding of second language learning, and as a result, for the improvement of second language teaching. The research methodology for the study of first language acquisition has great relevance and applicability to investigations of the second language learning process. This interrelationship between first language and second language acquisition has been explored by some of the most outstanding scholars in the country. This important interrelationship has also been discussed at a most successful convention in Los Angeles of the TESOL Organization.

I am very much impressed with the complete roster of speakers that Dr. Daniel P. Dato has selected to speak and share their wisdom with us, and I congratulate him on the very special care with which I know he has organized and arranged the presentations, including the special interest groups. Each of the participants in the Georgetown University Round Table this year is, in his own way, a leader in psycholinguistic research and teaching, and I am very happy to extend a very special welcome to each of them.

In my opinion, work in psycholinguistics is the most exciting work going on in linguistics today. It has a great deal to offer the language teacher, and specifically, I have noted because of my special involvement in that field, the teacher of English as a foreign language. However, we must remember that the appropriate and effective use of this work assumes the existence of a basic linguistic sophistication and an ability to handle linguistic concepts and follow linguistic argumentation. Unfortunately, the record of linguists in communicating a linguistic way of thinking to non-specialist outsiders, and to the general educated public, has not been good. I fervently hope that this situation will improve, and I am confident that the proceedings of this conference will contribute greatly toward such improvement. I am confident, also, that the views of distinguished linguists and language teachers, working together on this subject, will receive wide attention within our profession and without, will help all of us come to grips with our most pressing language-education problems, and perhaps help us find solutions to them, not so much through esoteric debates as to what constitutes 'real linguistics', but rather by exploring ways in which linguistics and any of its branches, sub-disciplines, peripheral disciplines, or 'hyphenated' disciplines can contribute to our understanding of the 'real world'.

The School of Languages and Linguistics takes pride in its twenty-six years of sponsorship of these meetings and extends its thanks to all of you who have come to participate in, and help us celebrate this 26th anniversary of the Georgetown University Round Table.

INTRODUCTION

This volume represents the proceedings of the <u>Georgetown University Round Table on Languages and Linguistics 1975</u>. This, the twenty-sixth annual meeting, was held at Georgetown University in Washington, D.C., March 13-15, 1975. 'Developmental Psycholinguistics: Theory and Applications' was selected as the theme for the conference because of the significant role language acquisition plays today not only in linguistics and psychology, but also in foreign language teaching, education, communicative disorders, and other fields as well. The conference consisted of four plenary sessions, each showing the relationship between native-language acquisition, or developmental psycholinguistics, as it is sometimes called, and some other area. The panels were entitled: (1) Children's language acquisition: Linguistic and psycholinguistic theory; (2) Children's language acquisition and communicative disorders; (3) Developmental psycholinguistics and second-language learning; (4) Developmental psycholinguistics and education. Some of the papers relate to more than one panel, thereby showing how these areas overlap. In effect, certain papers were intended to form a transition from one panel to the next.

The relationship between children's language development and psycholinguistic and linguistic theory can be seen in two important ways: (1) the recent surge of research activity in children's language acquisition is to a great extent attributable to advances in linguistic theory during the past two decades, notably to the advent of transformational grammar; (2) on the other hand, insightful descriptions of the language acquisition process of many languages, done mostly by psychologists, have given linguists a better understanding of how children manipulate grammatical structures and a greater perspective of the nature and function of language itself. Essentially, the aims of the conference were to present the most sophisticated research in developmental psycholinguistics and to show how it either supports or contradicts some theory involving universals. Furthermore, the scholars reporting here were encouraged to demonstrate, where possible, how their research findings might be applied to some of the language problems in our society. Representing some of these theoretical issues are papers by Charles Ferguson, who argues for the importance of child phonology research for general phonological theory; by William O. Dingwall, who deals with some of the biological aspects of language including evolutionary, neurological, and ontogenetic factors; by Thomas G. Bever, who discusses the psychological role that a grammar plays in language learning; by Eve V. Clark, who relates language and nonlinguistic knowledge in the acquisition of word meanings; and by David Ingram, who describes the acquisition of transformations by children between the ages of six and twelve. Ingram's paper deals with psycholinguistic theory as well as with the implications that this type of linguistic description has for the assessment of children's language that is delayed or deviant in some way. Thus it forms a bridge between the first and second plenary sessions.

In the plenary session on children's language acquisition and communicative disorders Paula Menyuk discusses the question of qualitative and quantitative differences in normally developing children as compared to those children with disorders of the central nervous system. She states certain implications that this issue has for both the researcher and clinician remediating the language behavior of children with language problems. Co-authors Susan Curtiss, Victoria Fromkin (who made the presentation at the conference), David Rigler, Marilyn Rigler, and Stephen Krashen update the linguistic development of Genie, a child who suffered extreme cruelty and social and psychological deprivation for most of her childhood years. Carolyn Kessler discusses data on children undergoing therapy for deviant language and compares it with both the first- and second-language learning situations. This paper also serves as a transition between the second and third panels.

In the plenary session on developmental psycholinguistics and second-language learning Stephen Krashen discusses various theories concerning cerebral dominance as they pertain to both first- and second-language learning. Kenji Hakuta describes certain aspects of the process by which a Japanese child learned English. Heidi Dulay and Marina Burt discuss creative construction, complexity, and learning strategy in second-language acquisition. This presentation, made at the conference, was an updating of an earlier version of their topic 'A new perspective on the creative construction process in child second language acquisition', which may be found in Language Learning, volume 24, number 2.

Daniel P. Dato compares children's second-language learning of Spanish with the acquisition of Spanish as a native language. Using noun phrase structures and verb tenses as the basis for comparison, he argues that similarities in the two learning processes suggest the existence of certain universal psycholinguistic strategies used by children in language learning, regardless of whether it is the native language or a second language. Furthermore, he discusses the implications that second-language learning research has for the field of education which is the theme of the last panel.

In the final panel on developmental psycholinguistics and education, Ruth Tremaine presents a paper on the comprehension of syntax in bilingual children learning English and French and discusses its relationship to the development of Piagetian operational intelligence. G. Richard Tucker examines the mastery of content material by native speakers of English in kindergarten to grade five while studying arithmetic, science, and social studies in French, their second language. Elizabeth Shipley treats certain linguistic concepts that have a role in the assessment of cognitive competence, specifically in what is known as the class-inclusion task, involving comparisons of classes and subclasses. In the final paper of the conference Jean Berko-Gleason discusses the nature of the language used with children by fathers at home and by male teachers at day care centers.

In planning this conference, I hoped to bring together people from the fields of psychology, speech pathology, audiology, foreign language teaching, education, and linguistics. I also had another objective--that of suggesting to our own students here at Georgetown University and to the linguistic community in general that there are many ways in which they may serve the needs of society.

I want to express my appreciation to Dr. James E. Alatis, Dean of the School of Languages and Linguistics, for asking me to be the chairman of this year's Round Table and for making helpful suggestions about its planning. For much fruitful discussion on the topics considered for this conference and for their generous offering of time and reading materials, I want to thank Carolyn Kessler and Bill Dingwall. I am also grateful to my colleagues at Georgetown University who participated as panel chairmen and interest group leaders, for helping to make the Round Table a success. Finally, I express my gratitude to the host of students, to Dorea Saxon and Mrs. Marian Higgins for their help in arranging for the countless details that make possible a worthwhile conference.

Daniel P. Dato

SOUND PATTERNS IN LANGUAGE ACQUISITION[1]

CHARLES A. FERGUSON

Stanford University

Abstract. The paper argues for the importance of child phonology research for general phonological theory. Two examples are examined, (a) a proposed universal on relative stability among stop consonants, and (b) the phonological equivalence of nasal assimilation within a word and across word boundary. Evidence from phonological development of English-speaking and Spanish-speaking children is offered in support of the claim that /g/ and /p/ are the least stable of the core stop inventory /p t k b d g/ in human languages. Evidence from phonological development of Spanish-speaking and Greek-speaking children is offered in support of the claim that internal and external nasal assimilation are different processes in spite of the formal similarity of rules representing them. English and Spanish data are from the Stanford Child Phonology Project; stop inventory data from 570 languages are taken from the Stanford Phonology Archive.

0. Introduction. This Round Table is devoted to both Theory and Applications. Usually at past Round Tables I have found myself arguing for the application of the findings of linguistics to the solution of language problems or else arguing for the position that there is no sharp line between theory and application. This year I would like to argue for the relevance of developmental psycholinguistics to linguistic theory.

In 1925 Edward Sapir published his paper 'Sound patterns in language', and nearly fifty years later Noam Chomsky and Morris Halle published their book The Sound Pattern of English (SPE). The two publications reflect essentially the same goals: to improve the linguist's ability to characterize the phonologies of languages and to discover the general properties shared by all phonologies, including the ways

1

they change through time. Sapir's article was short, discursive rather than formalized, and drew examples from a variety of languages, giving only a few from English. The Chomsky-Halle book was long, highly formalized in places, and drew primarily on English, but from a variety of other languages as well. For the student of child phonology the book represented only a slight improvement over the article. Sapir did not mention child language development at all, even though he sought evidence for sound patterns in many kinds of behavior, whereas Chomsky and Halle discussed child language acquisition specifically in a number of places and acknowledged its relevance for phonological theory. Actually, however, SPE speculates or makes claims about phonological development but does not really report on empirical investigations, so that neither the article nor the book seems to take the study of child phonology very seriously.

I would prefer to adopt the views of two other linguists--Jespersen, who wrote before Sapir, and Jakobson, whose key work came halfway between Sapir and SPE (Jespersen 1922:161-88; Jakobson 1968). They both felt that the study of child language behavior was of central importance in understanding the nature of human language, and Jakobson was quite explicit in his claims about child phonology. He took the position that the phonology of child language is structured in exactly the same sense as adult phonology, no matter how much the two may differ in detail and level of development; and he also claimed that the basic principles which account for the properties of sound systems and the way they change through time are clearly exemplified in child language by such phenomena as the order of acquisition of phonological elements. Jakobson's views may be inadequate or even just plain wrong in detail, but we must agree with the main thrust of his arguments, and the two points I want to make in this report are both findings of recent research in phonological development which teach us something about phonology in general.

1. Gaps in the stop series. First let me report on a proposed phonological universal and the way child language research has contributed to its formulation and has found evidence relevant to it. Almost five years ago, in doing a longitudinal study of initial consonants in English with a group of young children, Carol Farwell and I noticed a phenomenon in the acquisition of velar stops that we had not expected. Two children of our study showed a strong preference for voiceless [k] over voiced [g] in initial position, just the opposite of what the process of initial voicing (Ingram 1974) would predict and, indeed, the opposite of what we found for labial and alveolar initial stops, for which the voiced varieties were preferred. This unexpected fact, for which additional support could be found in Leopold's

study of his daughter (Leopold 1942) and a recent statistical study of the phonological errors of a hundred children (Olmsted 1971), we mentioned in a 1972 working paper which is due to appear in Language this year (Ferguson and Farwell 1975). We noted at that time that the phenomenon was probably related to Greenberg's observation of the general weakness of voiced velar obstruents, and we let the matter rest there while other questions in the acquisition of English and Spanish consonant systems were under investigation.

Last year the Soviet linguist Gamkrelidze published a study of markedness in stops and fricatives (Gamkrelidze 1974) and this re-opened the issue for us. [2] Gamkrelidze, among a number of other points, makes the claim that if a language has stops in the labial, dental/alveolar and velar places of articulation, has a voiced–voiceless distinction in the stops, and has one or more gaps in this basic stop inventory, then it is highly likely that either the voiced velar /g/ or the voiceless labial /p/ will be lacking. He interprets this as evidence for his view that with voiced stops it is the labial end of the place of articulation dimension which is least marked, whereas with voiceless stops it is the velar/post-velar end which is least marked.

Our immediate reaction on reading this was to check it out with the Stanford Phonology Archive. At that moment the segment inventories of 106 languages had been entered into the computer Archive, but worksheets of an additional 464 languages were available for manual inspection. The Archive strongly confirmed the proposed universal. Out of the total number of 570 languages 377 meet the two criteria of a voicing distinction and stops in the three places of articulation. Of these, 88 languages have at least one gap in the series /p t k b ɑ g/; of these, 40 lack /g/ and 36 lack /p/, the remaining cases being scattered. [3] The list of languages with their stop inventories appears in Figure 1, which also includes two little diagrams representing a stability scale among stops. The first is taken directly from Gamkrelidze (1974:13) and was intended to show his view of the opposite directions of the markedness scale in voiceless and voiced stops. The second is a combined scale in the style of James Foley. At the stable end of the scale, /t/ is present in every language which has stops in three places and a voicing distinction; at the other end is /g/, which is absent in 40 of the 88 languages with gaps. The score is t 0, k 5, b 11, d 21, p 36, g 40. If we limit the count to languages which have only a single gap in the stop series the result is identical except for the exchange of /p/ and /g/: t 0, k 1, b 4, d 10, g 23, p 27. The /g/ remains at the bottom of the combined scale because of additional evidence from child phonology and other inventory data (Sherman, forthcoming).

A statistical tendency as pronounced as this in a cross-language comparison should turn up in some way in child language development.

FIGURE 1. Gaps in the stop series /p t k b d g/.

Languages meeting the criteria	377		g
Languages with at least one gap	88	↑b p	p
Languages lacking /g/	40	d t	d
Languages lacking /p/	36	g k↓	b
			k
			t ↓

Languages lacking /g/

Alabaman	Huastec	Secoya
Arawak	Ifugao	Siriono
Byelorussian	Istrorumanian	Sko
Cambodian	Itonama	Tacana
Cashinawa	Kazakh	Tairora
Cavinena	Ket	Tamazight
Cayuvava	Khasi	Tegali
Chama	Kru	Telefol
Chol	Kumyk	Tzeltal
Cubeo	Maya	Ubyx
Efik	Nasioi	Uighur
Finnish	Pomo	Yai
Gadsup	Sa'ban	Yurak
Guahibo		

Languages lacking /p/

Aleut	Ewondo	Nyimang
Amharic	Galice	Oirat
Arabic (Egyptian)	Galla	Pomo
Arabic (Moroccan)	Hausa	Shilha
Arabic (Syrian)	Kalagan	Somali
Arawak	Katla	Tama
Barya	Kunama	Tamazight
Bedawiye	Maba	Tegali
Bilin	Murui	Telefol
Buryat	Ngemba	Tolowa
Chuave	Nubian (Hill)	Yareba
Efik	Nubian (Nobiin)	Yoruba

The question is, How? The most obvious evidence would be a child who just matched the conditions--stops in three places, voicing distinction, and one gap. But for many children the voicing opposition is late, and many children at some point in their development show the initial voicing process already mentioned, which may override the voicing opposition. Also, patterns of consonant acquisition typically differ depending on the position in the syllable or word.

Finally, there is the problem of the distribution and frequency patterns of the child's input language. In Spanish, for example, the
number of words beginning with /g/ is small, final /g/ is nonexistent,
intervocalic /g/ is normally spirantized, and in some varieties of
Mexican Spanish even initial /g/ is a spirant. In spite of all these
obstacles we were still able to find some supporting evidence, even
in Spanish. [4]

Much of our Spanish child language data is from specific investigations of perception and imitation of nonsense stimuli, not directly
related to the question, but we have several batches of data from
eight young children (ages 1;4-1;10) which consist of spontaneous
speech and repetitions of Spanish words said by an experimenter. In
one set of data from four of the children, recorded at monthly intervals over a four-month period, we found 226 items clearly identifiable
as productions of words that in the adult model contain at least one of
the stop series. A simple examination of the substitutions yields the
figures of Table 1.

TABLE 1. Productions of adult stops by children (Spanish).

Model	Replica	# of Tokens	Model	Replica	# of Tokens
/p/	[p]	53	/b/	[p]	1
	[b]	26		[b]	9
	Other	7		Other	9
	∅	–		∅	–
/t/	[t]	58	/d/	[t]	–
	[d]	11		[d]	2
	Other	22		Other	2
	∅	3		∅	–
/k/	[k]	8	/g/	[k]	3
	[g]	1		[g]	1
	Other	5		Other	4
	∅	–		∅	1

More voiceless stops than voiced were attempted (194 to 32), as
one might expect from the widely held assumption that the unmarked
series will be of higher frequency than the marked series in the adult
language and will be acquired earlier by children. But beyond this,
it is clear that b is preferred to p, and k is preferred to g, in substitutions. The substitution p → b is common, 26 out of 86 attempts,
while b → p occurs only once in 19 attempts, and g → k occurs 3 out
of 9 attempts while k → g is only once in 15. Even though the numbers
are very small, the trend is unmistakable: /p/ in spite of its relatively high frequency of occurrence is reproduced as voiced [b] about
half as often as it is reproduced correctly as voiceless [p], and the

velar stops are the reverse, /k/ reproduced correctly 8 to 1 and /g/ reproduced as [k] 3 to 1.

We examined another batch of Spanish data from the eight children, recorded over a three-month period, which included some of the previous data and additional items whose models were uncertain. In these productions we simply counted occurrences of stop phones in initial position regardless of the adult model. The productions of one child, R, were so dramatically in agreement with the hypothesis, largely because she had a favorite word [kukui] 'spooky animal' which she kept repeating, that we separated her data from the others'. But even the other seven children consistently favored /b/ and /k/ over /p/ and /g/ in spite of the effect of the markedness factor. The count is given in Table 2.

TABLE 2. Children's productions of initial stop phones (Spanish).

Seven Children					Child R			
Nov.	Dec.	Jan.	Total		Nov.	Dec.	Jan.	Total
17	30	37	84	[p]	2	4	3	9
19	29	35	83	[b]	11	1	0	12
6	20	25	51	[t]	1	5	0	6
10	13	16	39	[d]	2	0	2	4
11	18	11	40	[k]	38	9	5	52

The figures for [t] and [d] are about what one might expect from the assumption about markedness, namely [t] is about a third again as frequent as [d], but the labials and velars are shifted in the direction of the hypothesis: [p] and [b] are about equal and [k] is over twice as frequent as [g].

The Spanish data are tantalizing in that there is not enough solid information to see the processes at work. Fortunately we have abundant longitudinal data from seven children learning English. The data were collected at approximately weekly intervals for seven to ten months and are available now in tape recordings and transcripts in relatively narrow transcription (cf. Johnson and Bush 1972). The information is substantial enough to illustrate the hypothesized differences in stability among the stops. Two of the children are the ones who originally directed our attention to the question; of the remaining five, two also provide useful evidence, and the other three are following a developmental path of late acquisition of the voice distinction and hence are inconclusive for our purposes during the period of data collection.

There are probably many such children who show no early evidence of voicing contrasts in their development, typically showing at first a range of free variation regardless of the model.[5] The

phonology of such children may also be affected by the initial voicing
process, which is manifested in greater frequency of voiced phones
in initial position and voiceless phones in final position, even to the
point that [± voice] pairs seem to function as positional variants of the
same phonological units (cf. Velten 1943, Ferguson 1968). It may be
assumed that such children are able to discriminate between voiceless
and voiced obstruents, but do not yet have 'phonemic perception'
(Shvachkin 1973, Garnica 1973) of the contrast, i.e. do not use the
sound difference to identify, store, and recognize lexical items.

Other children, such as the four to be described, show early evidence of the voicing contrast even though they may not have full productive use of it until much later. The evidence is of two kinds:
their selection of words and their actual pronunciations. Thus, for
a number of months a child may produce almost exclusively b̲-words
as opposed to p̲- words (i.e. words with b̲ or p̲ respectively in the
adult model). Also such children may pronounce p̲-words more frequently with voiceless phones and b̲-words with voiced phones, at the
level of whole word shapes (so-called 'phonological idioms' Moskowitz 1972) and not yet organized into a systematic segmental contrast
(for discussion of word distinctions as opposed to phonological opposi-
tions in the usual sense, cf. Ferguson and Farwell 1975). The
phonology of these children may also be affected at some point by
the initial voicing process, which may then change correct initial
p̲'s to b̲ even though the voicing distinction is apparently already used
to identify, store, and recognize words. In current phonological
terminology these children have an underlying /p/ which a phonological rule changes to [b].

The phonological development of the four children who showed early
evidence of the voicing distinction (T, K, JB, JJ) differs considerably
in detail, but they seem to share a common sound pattern of acquisition in important respects. They all have at an early stage a voicing
distinction of some sort in initial position in their speech, usually with
/p b t d/ at first and then /k g/. Sometime later the voicing distinction
is temporarily abandoned in the labials and velars. Early p̲-words and
g̲-words are dropped, and the repertoire of b̲-words and k̲-words is
expanded. One child, K, did this for velars only, maintaining the
voice distinction throughout in initial labials. Next the children add
initial /p/ to their active repertoires and then /g/. The development
in medial position is harder to follow because of the few examples and
the effects of reduplication. K's case is interesting; she had no period
of a p̲-gap in initial position, but she went through a period when her
medial inventory was b (←p, b), t, d, k (←k, g). The force of the
constraint is apparently somewhat different medially: two children
(JB, K) reversed the order of acquisition medially to /g/ before /p/,
and the other two gave some evidence of this tendency as well.

In sum, we have enough evidence from sound patterns in language acquisition and from phonological gaps in the world's languages to assert that the voiced velar and the voiceless labial are the least stable of the central core of stop consonants used in human language. This phonological universal--if we may call it that--is of particular interest because no current phonological theory explains it or would predict it. I have used it here as an example of the way child phonology exemplifies the underlying principles of phonological organization and phonological processes, and the way research in child language can itself lead to new discoveries or can test hypotheses generated by other lines of research. As with many phonological universals, the explanation of g-p instability is probably to be sought in the physiology of the vocal tract. Also, like many language universals, the explanation is probably multiple, rather than a single 'law' or causal factor. Even the two halves of our universal--the /g/ instability and the /p/ instability--may be relatively independent. [b] All these questions are now under investigation, as well as the possibility suggested by Gamkrelidze that fricatives may sometimes function as a kind of compensation for the missing stops. But here my point is simply the role of child phonology research in discovering and verifying the phenomenon itself.

2. Nasal assimilation. As a second example, let me report on the theoretical issue of a morpheme (rather, word) structure condition versus a phonological rule, as seen in the acquisition of Spanish.

For several decades phonological analysis has given high value to notions of simplicity, generality, and the elimination of redundancy in weighing alternative analyses of a language. In particular, most contemporary analysts would attempt to subsume under a single rule two phonological processes in a language which have identical or nearly identical inputs, environments, and outputs. People do not like to write essentially the same rule twice in the grammar. However, one of the main points of Sapir's 'Sound patterns' was that things which seem alike may not really be the same in linguistic function or as he called it elsewhere 'psychological reality'. We would all agree with his obvious example of the [hw] used to blow out a flame versus word-initial [hw] in American English, but the principle may well be extended to other apparent sames whose functional or psychological difference is less obvious. Spanish phonology offers a good example in its patterns of nasal assimilation. In consonant clusters of nasal plus obstruent the nasal is assimilated to the obstruent in place of articulation so that there is complete neutralization of nasal segments in this position. This pattern of assimilation holds both within words and across word boundaries in the same phonological phrase. Linguists' passion for simplicity and economy has led them to consider the assimilation within words and the assimilation across word boundaries to be the same phonological fact. Trager, epitome of American structuralism, Alarcos Llorach, the eminent neo-Praguian, and James Harris, generative phonologist, have all, in their varied ways, identified the two as a single process (Trager 1939, Alarcos 1943, Harris 1969).

Last summer Ed Hernandez, Irene Vogel, and Harold Clumeck, in a special study of the Stanford Child Phonology Project, investigated the acquisition of these assimilation patterns by Chicano children learning Spanish as their mother tongue. One of the assumptions of their study was that identical phonological processes will be acquired in identical ways and different phonological processes will be acquired in different ways. The study, which involved testing of perception, imitation, and spontaneous production by 18 children between the ages of 2;5 and 5;10, was very clear on the nasal assimilation patterns. The children do not learn the two patterns in the same way or at the same time (for details of the study cf. Hernandez et al. 1974).

In the acquisition of the internal assimilation pattern the children normally make a difference between clusters with voiceless obstruent and clusters with voiced obstruent. At the earliest stage children omit the nasal completely in the voiceless obstruent cluster but omit the obstruent in the voiced obstruent cluster, sometimes lengthening the nasal. Thus an adult model sequence of the shape anta would appear in the child's replica sequence ata, whereas anda would appear as ana. [7]

In the second stage in the acquisition of the internal nasal clusters the children have a nasal vowel with the voiceless obstruent and in the final stage both clusters are made correctly. At no point are there errors in place of articulation of the nasal. This sound pattern is summarized in Figure 2.

The developmental pattern of the assimilation across word boundary is quite different. The earliest stage has an alveolar nasal in word-final position, unassimilated to the initial consonant of the following word. In the second stage the nasal segment is dropped, and the nasality is either lost completely or remains in the nasalization of the preceding vowel. Next an assimilated nasal segment is inserted as a brief transitional segment between the vowel and the following obstruent. In this stage, possibly as an alternative strategy followed by some children, the following consonant, if voiced, may be replaced by the assimilated nasal segment. Finally the child reaches the adult stage. This pattern of acquisition is summarized in Figure 3.

As can be seen from the tables the children overall seem to acquire the internal assimilation pattern first and then the assimilation across

FIGURE 2. Acquisition of nasal and obstruent clusters in Spanish.

N = assimilated nasal. X = dominant pronunciation i. e. over 2/3 of the child's productions. (X) = minor pronunciation i. e. under 1/3 of the child's productions.					
Voiceless stop				Voiced stop	
Child Age	VCV	ṼCV	VNC	VNV	VNCV
1. 2;5	X			X	
2. 2;10	X			X	
3. 2;11		X			X
4. 3;1			X		X
5. 3;3		X			X
6. 3;4	(X)	(X)	(X)		X
7. 4;1			X		X
8, 4;4	(X)	(X)	X	(X)	X
9. 4;7		(X)	X	(X)	X
10. 4;9		(X)	X		X
11. 4;9		X	(X)		X
12. 4;11		X	(X)		X
13. 5;2		X	(X)	(X)	X
14. 5;5			X		X
15. 5;5					X
16. 5;10		(X)	X		X

word boundaries. Also, in both patterns the children seem to master the voiced clusters before the voiceless.

Many languages have extensive assimilation or neutralization patterns which tend toward homorganic nasal-obstruent clusters as opposed to nonhomorganic clusters. In fact, the tendency toward homorganic nasal clusters is probably universal in the sense that any language which has sequences of nasal + consonant shows at least some evidence of the tendency. Studies of universal hierarchies of consonant clusters invariably note this tendency (Greenberg 1965: 13-14; Pertz and Bever 1974; Anderson 1974:295). Also, non-universalistic treatments of phonology often call attention to the phenomenon in particular languages. In order to understand this tendency and the explanatory principles which underlie it, we must not look on it as a global process or a simplex universal. We must focus on the different ways it works in different positions in the word or syllable, with different consonants, and with different configurations of nasal contrast. One striking fact is that nasal cluster assimilation in languages works at different rates and with different outcomes in medial position and at word boundaries. Typically, the processes are simpler and neater internally than at word boundaries. Brian

FIGURE 3.   Acquisition of nasal assimilation with following
obstruent across word boundary.

N = assimilated nasal. X = dominant pronunciation i. e. over 2/3 of the child's productions; two checks in one row indicate over 1/3 each. (X) = minor production i. e. less than 1/3 of the child's productions.

		Voiceless obstruents			Voiced obstruents			
Child	Age	Vn#C	V#C	VN#C	Vn#C	V#C	(V#N)	VN#C
1.	2;5	X			X			
2.	2;10							
3.	2;11					X		
4.	3;1		X	(X)	(X)	X		
5.	3;3	(X)	X	(X)				
6.	3;4	X	X	(X)		X	(X)	
7.	4;1	X	X		X			
8.	4;4	X	(X)	(X)		(X)		X
9.	4;7							
10.	4;9	(X)	X	(X)		X		(X)
11.	4;9							
12.	4;11	(X)	X	(X)		X		
13.	5;2	(X)	X	(X)			X	X
14.	5;5	(X)	X	(X)		X		(X)
15.	5;5	X	X			X		
16.	5;10	(X)	X			X		X

Newton, after analyzing the internal assimilation in his very informative generative phonology of modern Greek dialects, notes 'A further dimension of complexity is introduced when we consider nasal-initial clusters at word boundaries' (Newton 1972:96). Thus, we might have expected the two processes to be independent even in a language like Spanish in which the two seem very similar.

   In medial position nasal clusters are among the commonest of consonant cluster types and they are the locus for three common types of consonant assimilation processes: place of articulation, voicing, and manner of articulation. The place assimilation typically takes the form of the nasal assimilating to the following consonant. The voice assimilation takes two forms: either the voiceless consonants become voiced or the nasal segment is reduced or deleted. Manner assimilation appears either as the preservation of stops which are elsewhere spirantizing, or as the full assimilation or deletion of the nasal before continuants. In our Spanish child phonology data the most interesting of the three types is voice assimilation. The children delete the nasal rather than voice the following voiceless consonant. This pattern is at least a candidate for the 'typical' or 'universal' tendency; it is well attested in English-learning children (e.g. Smith 1973; cf. Ingram 1974:58-59), and we are now able to report it also for Spanish. An ideal language for testing this hypothesis is Modern Greek, where the other pattern, the voicing of consonants after nasals, has played an important role diachronically and remains a widespread, productive synchronic process. In Modern Greek, clusters of nasal + voiceless stop are all in foreign loan words or learned borrowings from Classical Greek and hence relatively rare; but the Drachmans' study (Drachman and Malikouti-Drachman 1973) found that at least some Greek children in acquiring words of this kind tend to drop the nasal segment while the voicing process is learned step by step as a morphophonemic alternation.

Assimilation in nasal clusters across word boundary in many languages seems to involve at least two processes: the tendency to reduce contrast among nasals in final position, and the tendency to reduce the phonological marking of grammatical boundaries. In Spanish the first of these specifies the alveolar quality (or in some dialects velar quality) of the final nasal, and the other assimilates the final nasal as though it had no boundary after it. The Spanish children in our nasal assimilation study seem to reflect the adult processes very well: they learn the internal assimilated clusters and acquire the final neutralization in [n], and then add the assimilation across word boundary. Thus, an assimilated nasal segment at word boundary alternates with phrase-final unassimilated [n] while an internal assimilated nasal segment has no such regular alternation.

In summary, the Spanish-learning children give convincing evidence that the two assimilation patterns are distinct in spite of the similarity between them, [8] and the word boundary pattern is in part an extension of the internal pattern.

Now to return to the question of simplicity in the sense of combining rules and reducing the number of rules to the fewest possible. Child phonology is a research area which can offer important evidence of the sameness or difference in function of phonological units and processes, and in the case under discussion this evidence seems more compelling than a misplaced notion of simplicity. [9] In a review of another sound pattern book over a decade ago (Ferguson 1965), I poked fun at the simplicity metric; but I did not poke fun hard enough, since I was still too fond of simplicity in linguistic description myself. Now I hold a position similar to the one expressed by Stephen Anderson in the last chapter of his recent book. I take the liberty of quoting it in full:

There is absolutely no a priori reason to imagine that the descriptively correct analysis of a given set of facts from natural language will also be the simplest formally, if the

primes of the description are imposed for other reasons.
One must start from the description and search for an explanation, rather than attempting to make the explanation
shape the description. (Anderson 1974:293)

3. Conclusion. The child phonology research I have reported on
here was conducted under a general assumption which certainly Sapir
and Jakobson would share, and very likely Jespersen and Chomsky
and Halle as well. The assumption is that phonological theory, at
least in the sense of valid universal tendencies, is manifested not only
in the traditional objects of linguistic description or the phenomena of
diachronic change, but wherever and however language is used.
Appropriate research areas range from the study of slips of the tongue
and errors in second language acquisition to cross-language comparisons of inventories and processes. In particular, however, this report
is a case of special pleading. I have tried to argue convincingly that
the study of phonological development in children is not just one of
many possible areas of research but is one of such importance and
accessibility that it should be recognized as a regular part of the
general study of phonology.

Stephen Anderson's book, which I just cited with approval, is a
step backward in this respect. In the preface the author acknowledges
that language acquisition is a 'valid concept' but dismisses it along
with markedness and naturalness as not necessary in a general book
on phonology. Language acquisition is not a theoretical construct like
markedness or naturalness; it is an active field of empirical research.
I hope that the Anderson book will be the last general work on sound
patterns in language to leave it out, just as I hope material on phonological development will come to be included even in introductory
courses on phonology.

I am at the end of my report, but I cannot resist a final footnote
on applications. The study of sound patterns in language acquisition
has immediate relevance for such fields as speech therapy, reading
research, and bilingual education.

NOTES

1. The research reported here was conducted by the Child
Phonology Project and the Phonology Archiving Project at Stanford
University, with the financial support of the National Science Foundation, under grants GS 41728X and SOC 74 22224 respectively.

2. A much shorter version of the study appeared in German
(Gamkrelidze 1973). The German article differs in a number of
respects and does not contain most of the theoretical discussion and

source references of the Russian study, but it includes the basic claim referred to here and is more accessible to American linguists.

3. The manual search of the 570 phonologies was done by Merritt Ruhlen of the Archive staff, who had prepared the original worksheets, and his assistance is gratefully acknowledged. Don Sherman, also of the Archive staff, has prepared a working paper based on computer searches of various kinds on the 106 language sample (Sherman, forthcoming).

4. The Spanish counts given here were done by Irene Vogel on data furnished by Marcy Macken of the Child Phonology Project.

5. The behavior here is of children's speech during the second and third years. No attempt has been made to integrate our observations with the studies of still earlier development of voicing at Johns Hopkins University and the Haskins Laboratories (cf. Preston 1971; Stark 1972; Kewley-Port and Preston 1974).

6. The independence of the two is suggested by K's having only /g/ instability in initial position, the children's reverse preference medially, and the fact that only five languages in the sample have the double gap /g p/ out of 21 with a double gap. Also, there is a tendency for languages (and, less clearly, children) to have a fricative /f/ to 'compensate' for the lack of /p/ (of 27 without /p/, 17 have /f/), but there is no such tendency for the /g/, in spite of Gamkrelidze's claim (Gamkrelidze 1974:42).

7. The following are items actually produced by the children which illustrate the stages; the clusters are the [ŋκ] of brincar/ brincando and the [nd] of jugando/quemando:

NC
β̥kæno
ĩkar
ĩŋkando
briŋkando

NC
fuæno
keman:o
hũwãnᵈo
huando

8. The evidence from acquisition is, of course, not decisive for the phonological status in the adult language, since it is at least theoretically possible that after acquiring two processes speakers of the language may restructure them into a single process. It is the combined force of the developmental findings and evidence from adult behavior which seems decisive (cf. Hernandez et al. 1974).

9. Simplicity is not to be rejected in toto as a criterion in theory construction, but rather the misplaced simplicity in phonological description which attempts, for example, to reduce the number of features, feature specifications, phonemes, or rules without regard for their linguistic function or 'psychological reality' as reflected in language behavior.

REFERENCES

Alarcos Llorach, E. 1961. La fonología española. Madrid, Gredos.
Anderson, Stephen R. 1974. The organization of phonology. New York, Academic Press.
Chomsky, Noam and Morris Halle. 1968. The sound pattern of English. New York, Harper and Row.
Drachman, G. and A. Malikouti-Drachman. 1973. Studies in the acquisition of Greek as a native language. I. Some preliminary findings in phonology. Working Papers in Linguistics 15:99-114. Columbus, Ohio, Ohio State University.
Ferguson, Charles A. 1962. Review of Morris Halle, Sound pattern of Russian. Language 30:184-98.
_____. 1966. Linguistic theory as behavioral theory. In: Speech, language and communication. Edited by E. C. Carterette. Berkeley and Los Angeles, University of California Press.
_____. 1968. Contrastive analysis and language development. Georgetown University Round Table 1968. 101-112.
_____ and Carol B. Farwell. 1975. Words and sounds in early language acquisition. Language 51. Original version PRCLD 6:1-60.
Gamkrelidze, T. V. 1973. Über die Wechselbeziehung zwischen Verschluss- und Reibelauten im Phonemsystem; zum Problem der Markiertheit in der Phonologie. Phonetica 27:213-8.
_____. 1974. Sootnošenie smyčnyxi frikativnyx v fonologičeskoj sisteme (k probleme markirovannosti v fonologii). [Relation of stops and fricatives in the phonological system (on the problem of markedness in phonology)] Moscow, Institut Russkogo Jazyka AN SSSR.
Garnica, Olga K. 1973. The development of phonemic speech perception. In: Cognitive development and the acquisition of language. New York, Academic Press.
Greenberg, Joseph H. 1965. Some generalizations concerning initial and final consonant sequences. Linguistics 18:5-34.
Harris, James. 1969. Spanish phonology. Cambridge, Mass., MIT Press.
Hernandez-Chavez, E., Irene Vogel, and Harold Clumeck. 1974. Rules, constraints, and the simplicity criterion: An analysis based on the acquisition of nasals in Chicano Spanish. Paper read at the Nasalfest, University of California, Berkeley.
Ingram, David. 1974. Phonological rules in child language. Journal of Child Language 1:49-64.
Jakobson, Roman. 1968. Child language aphasia and phonological universals. The Hague, Mouton.
Jespersen, Otto. 1922. Language, its nature, development and origin. New York, Holt.

Johnson, Carolyn F. and Clara N. Bush. 1972. A note on transcribing the speech of young children. PRCLD 3:95-100.

Kewley-Port, Diane and Malcolm S. Preston. 1974. Early apical stop production: A voice onset time analysis. Journal of Phonetics 2:195-210.

Leopold, Werner F. 1942. The speech development of a bilingual child. Vol. II. Sound-learning. Evanston, Ill., Northwestern University Press.

Moskowitz, Breyne Arlene. 1972. Idiomatic phonology and phonological change. UCLA MS.

Newton, Brian. 1972. The generative interpretation of dialect: A study of Modern Greek phonology. Cambridge, University Press.

Olmsted, David. 1971. Out of the mouth of babes. The Hague, Mouton.

Pertz, Doris L. and Thomas R. Bever. 1973. Sensitivity to phonological universals in children and adolescents. WPLU 13:69-90.

Preston, Malcolm S. 1971. Some comments on the developmental aspects of voicing in stop consonants. In: Perceptions of language. Edited by D. L. Horton and J. J. Jenkins. Ohio, Merrill.

Sapir, Edward. 1925. Sound patterns in language. Language 1:37-51.

Sherman, Donald. Forthcoming. Patterns in stop systems. To appear in WPLU.

Smith, W. V. 1973. The acquisition of phonology. Cambridge, The University Press.

Stanley, Richard. 1967. Redundancy rules in phonology. Language 43:393-436.

Stark, Rachel E. 1972. Some features of the vocalizations of young deaf children. In: The mouth of the infant (= Third symposium on oral sensation and perception). Edited by J. F. Bosma. Springfield, Ill., Charles C. Thomas.

Trager, George L. 1939. The phonemes of Castilian Spanish. TCLP 8:217-22.

Shvachkin, N. KH. 1973. The development of phonemic speech perception in early childhood. In: Studies of child language development. Edited by C. A. Ferguson and D. I. Slobin. New York, Holt, Rinehart and Winston.

Velten, H. V. 1943. The growth of phonemic and lexical patterns in infant language. Language 19:281-92.

THE SPECIES-SPECIFICITY OF SPEECH

WILLIAM ORR DINGWALL

University of Maryland

Abstract. This paper consists of four main sections. In the first, the concepts of innateness, species-specificity and task-specificity are clarified. In addition, E. Mayr's useful distinction between closed and open genetic programs is introduced and discussed using examples of language-related phenomena first noted by ethologists. The second section provides abundant evidence--both functional and structural--demonstrating the lack of homology between human and non-human primate vocalization. It is concluded that the ability to produce vocalization which is articulated as opposed to holistic in nature, which is mediated by the neocortex as opposed to the limbic system is unique to the genus: homo sapiens. The question then arises whether other aspects of communication systems are homologous. It will be argued in section three that at present there is insufficient structural evidence to decide this issue but that evolutionary, ontogenetic and neurological evidence currently available tends to support homology rather than homoplasy. The final section of the paper deals with the ontogenesis of speech. It will be demonstrated that the behaviorist claim that babbling constitutes the keystone of speech is totally without foundation. The role of neurological feature detectors, early feedback and learning in the acquisition of speech will be considered. Evidence will be adduced in support of Ladefoged's auditory-motor theory of speech production. Finally, the automatization of the auditory-speech gesture tie will be briefly considered.

1. Innateness and specificity. One of the basic tenets of linguistics today, argued for ardently in almost every introductory textbook, is that Language (i. e. the universal aspects of languages essentially) is

innate, that it is unique to man, and that the mechanisms that subserve it are task-specific. Three things should be pointed out about
this hypothesis at the outset. (1) Language is defined as a global concept. Either the attributes of innateness and specificity apply to it as
a whole or not at all. (2) Species-specificity and task-specificity are
logically independent. The fact that we are able to characterize some
behavior appropriately as species-specific has no bearing on the issue
of task-specificity and vice versa. (3) Finally, innateness is a relative rather than polar concept.

   A useful framework within which to consider this latter point has
been provided by Ernst Mayr (1974). Mayr notes that 'innate' refers
to the genotype (i. e. the genetic material that an organism receives
from its parents) while 'acquired' refers to the phenotype (i. e. behavioral and morphological characteristics of the organism). Neither
term is the exact opposite of the other. A more reasonable way of
approaching the innateness question, in Mayr's view, is in terms of
genetic programs. Such programs are of two types:

(1) 'closed genetic programs' which do not allow "appreciable
modification" during their translation into the phenotype

(2) 'open genetic programs' which allow for varying degrees
of input during the lifespan of their owners. This input is
represented in the translated program in the nervous system
not in the genetic program, i. e. it is not passed on to succeeding generations.

Note that all behavior is a property of the phenotype and thus there is
no purely innate behavior in Mayr's framework. Also there is no
purely acquired behavior since all behavior results from the translation of a 'genetic' program.

   Since genetics is properly studied in terms of populations rather
than single individuals, we can construct a mathematical model of
the relations we have been discussing using a measure of dispersion
such as the variance:

$$\sigma_p^2 = \sigma_g^2 + \sigma_e^2 + \sigma_{ge}^2$$

What this model states is that the variances we observe in behavior or
morphology (σ_p^2) involve genetic (σ_g^2) and environmental (σ_e^2) variances as well as their interaction (σ_{ge}^2). An estimate of heritability
can be obtained if σ_g^2 can be determined:

$$h^2 = \sigma_g^2 / \sigma_p^2 .$$

Note that h^2 will never equal 1.00, as σ_e^2 and σ_{ge}^2 can never be reduced to 0.00. This is simply another way of stating that no purely innate behavior exists (cf. Murphey (1973) and Whalen (1971) for full discussions of the variance model).

It should not be thought that it is only in the development of behavior that environmental and genetic components are inextricably bound up with one another. It is quite clear that environment plays an important role in structural development of the brain as well as other parts of the organism (Rose 1972). Even monozygotic twins of a number of species including man (where, for the pair, $\sigma_g^2 = 0$) have been noted to differ markedly in morphology (cf. Murphey 1973).

Thus, the answer to the question: Is Language innate? turns out to be trivially: yes. What has traditionally been of more interest to linguists, psychologists, and ethologists is the question of the degree to which a behavior is dependent on what may be termed: experience as opposed to trial-and-error learning or training. As would be expected, what is observed here is a continuum. At one end of this continuum we have various types of 'reflexive behaviors' such as early grasping, walking, swimming movements in the child (also, as we shall see, perhaps babbling) as well as the so-called 'fixed action patterns' so well documented by ethologists. The vocalizations of some birds constitute examples of such patterns. Thus, white throats (Sylvia communis) raised in soundproof chambers have been reported to develop all 25 of their species-typical songs. The same is true of a number of other species (cf. Eibl-Eibesfeldt 1970:23ff.).

In some cases, it appears clear that a relatively closed genetic program controls a so-called 'releasing mechanism' that responds to a narrow range of 'sign stimuli'. Such a releasing mechanism may be conceptualized as a filter selecting the relevant signal from a variety of stimuli, excluding noise, and alerting a motor coordination center which is capable of triggering fixed action patterns (Schleidt 1973). Both peripheral and central neurological correlates for releasing mechanisms have been identified in a number of species (Konishi 1971). For example, Wollberg and Newman (1972) have recently demonstrated that the auditory cortex of the squirrel monkey may be crucially involved in the analysis of species-typical vocalizations. A number of investigators have speculated that such 'neurological feature detectors' might play an important role in speech processing in humans (Abbs and Sussman 1971; Mattingly 1972). We shall examine this suggestion and evidence for it as they relate to ontogeny in a later portion of this paper.

Open genetic programs appear to be involved in the special type of experiential learning termed: 'imprinting' (Prägung) by ethologists. Here the genetically fixed part of the program is thought to involve some action which is triggered by an object which is introduced in the open part of the program. Surely the best known example of this phenomenon involves greylag geese. Freshly hatched goslings of this species will follow the first moving object making sounds and adopt it as a parent and possible mate. That imprinting differs from trial-and-error learning or training is argued on the following grounds: (1) it takes place during a usually quite short critical period after which the animal can no longer be imprinted, (2) the resulting behavior is retained for life (i. e. forgetting does not occur), (3) massed as opposed to distributed trials are more effective, (4) painful stimuli tend to strengthen imprinting, (5) primacy rather than recency is important. Some have argued that something like imprinting may be involved in the learning of language, once again regarded as a global concept (e. g. Lenneberg often appears to be arguing this). It seems to me that some aspects of language may involve the rapid and largely irreversible learning that characterizes observed cases of imprinting. But most aspects of language, as developmental psycholinguists have become well aware, are not learned as rapidly as we once thought, are not acquired without considerable trial-and-error, and are not irreversible.

This appears to follow quite naturally from the extended period of immaturity that characterizes human offspring. As Mayr points out, the longer the period of immaturity, the greater the time available for learning. Among primates, man evinces the most extended period of sensori-motor immaturity (cf. Figure 1). This is coupled with a much slower maturation of the brain in man as compared to other primates (cf. Lenneberg 1967; Holloway 1968). While precocial animals that are often short-lived and reach maturity rapidly are dependent for survival on closed genetic programs, altricial species such as man can rely on open genetic programs because of the longer period of parental care. As long as maturation takes place within the customary environment of individuals of the species, behavior patterns will be appropriately invariant. As ethologists have known for a long time, the fact that behavior is stereotyped and relatively invariant in various members of a species says nothing about its genetic component. The great selective advantage of the open genetic program is that it allows for the acquisition of a much greater amount of information about the environment than can be transmitted in the DNA of the fertilized zygote. The greater storage capacity required by open genetic programs entails, as Mayr notes, larger central nervous systems.

Having, hopefully, managed to elucidate somewhat the term: 'innate' as applied to Language, we can now turn our attention to the question of 'specificity'. The most reasonable interpretation of the claim that Language is 'species-specific' is that no convincing homology for this trait can be established in closely related species.

FIGURE 1. The trend toward prolonged growth and maturation periods in primates. (From A. H. Schultz. 1969. With permission.)

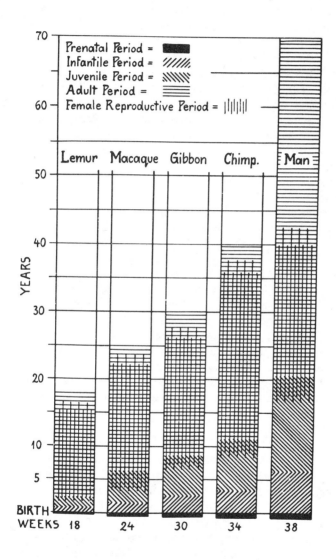

The obvious candidates for comparison are, of course, chimpanzees and gorillas which recent biochemical evidence indicates are much more closely related to man than previously thought (Goodman 1974). Although the term 'homology' was originally applied solely to structural characteristics of organisms, a number of ethologists and comparative psychologists among others have argued that the concept can, in principle, be extended to behavior (cf. Atz (1970) and Hodos (in press) for critical reviews). Behaviors that are similar in closely related species, that can be related to structures which show a high degree of concordance in a number of parameters, and that could together with their structural correlates be traced back to a common ancestor--such behaviors provide the most convincing examples of homology. Thus, as Hodos (in press) points out, vocalizations in marine and terrestrial animals, even though they share many similar acoustic characteristics, cannot be judged homologous as they are subserved by completely different peripheral mechanisms. As I shall argue in the second section of this paper, the same lack of homology can be demonstrated between the vocalizations of human and nonhuman primates.

Besides homologous behaviors that have structural correlates that can be traced back to a common precursor, there are behaviors that while similar cannot be related to such ancestral structures. These are termed 'behavioral homoplasies'. One process that results in behavioral homoplasy which will concern us later is the phenomenon of 'convergence' which involves similarity of behavior in animals without common ancestry. In applying this term it is generally required that one demonstrate that the similarity in behavior arose through adaptation to similar ecological conditions. As we shall see, there is some evidence of convergence between vocalization in man and in various species of altricial song-birds.

The contention that the mechanisms that subserve Language are specific to this task is, of course, built into the general theory of transformational grammar. All of the arguments concerning excessive weak and strong generative power of classes of grammars essentially revolve around this issue. What is being claimed here is that language abilities are in some sense separate from other cognitive or intellectual abilities and further, to use our previous terminology, that the information that can be inserted into the open genetic program underlying language behavior is quite restricted. It is difficult to imagine what kinds of evidence could be adduced in support of this position. Atherton and Schwartz (1974) have suggested three possibilities that might be promising:

(1) we might seek out an organism whose intelligence was demonstratively inferior to our own (such as the turkey)

but which could nevertheless converse with us in fluent English
or, better yet, learn any language during a critical period,

(2) failing this sort of evidence, we might happen upon a visitor
from some other planet whose cognitive abilities were clearly
superior to our own but whose children, while easily picking up
several computer languages as well as perhaps the essentials
of quantum mechanics in the first grade, simply failed to
master English or some other 'natural' language,

(3) or perhaps we might find some animal whose intellectual
abilities approached those of man but that failed to evince
any ability in language learning.

It was to this last case that one could, until recently, point as
evidence of both species-specificity and task-specificity. I think that
what has been demonstrated so far in the on-going research into the
communicative abilities of chimpanzees and gorillas casts serious
doubt on this source of evidence for task-specificity. Note, however,
that if it turns out to be the case that certain aspects of Language are
not species-specific (i. e. constitute an instance of homology), this
does not rule out the possibility that structures subserving these
abilities might be task-specific.

Aside from the possibility just touched on that Language (or some
aspect thereof) might be task-specific but not species-specific, there
are three other logical combinations of these attributes. Each of
these, unlike the one we have discussed, has attracted a large number
of supporters within the fields of linguistics and psychology. In
Table 1 I have identified these differing stands with the names of
their most prominent advocates.

TABLE 1. Stands on the species-specificity and task-specificity
of Language taken by schools within the disciplines of
linguistics and psychology.

	Species-specificity	Task-specificity
Chomsky-Lenneberg	+	+
Piaget	+	-
Skinner	-	-

2. The species-specificity of speech. It is, of course, possible
for homologous behaviors and the structures that underlie them to be
quite dissimilar in different species. Thus, for example, the incus
and maleus in the mammalian middle ear derive from the quadrate
and articular bones of the jaws of ancestral reptiles (Hodos, in press).

The tympanic membrane (ear drum) may be homologous or derived from the first, or spiracular, pouch of the phargox of fishes (cf. van Bergeijk 1966). Nevertheless, in closely related species such as man and his pongid relatives, general resemblance serves as one of the basic heuristics in establishing homologies. The idea here is quite analogous to methods used in the reconstruction of proto-languages. As Bock (1969:73) states it:

> The rationale for using resemblance as a criterion of homology is quite simple. If two organisms are related, they both stem from the same common ancestor, at which time in their evolutionary history, both organisms (both phyletic lines) were identical in their features. During their separate phyletic evolution, each changed somewhat but not completely. Those aspects of the two organisms that are still similar can be assumed to be unchanged from the time of their common ancestry.

Thus, in the case of the Pongidae and Hominidae, we can picture the process as shown in Figure 2. Black dots indicate homologous features; circles and crosses indicate nonhomologous features developed after the time of common ancestry. Such features would, in this instance, be species-specific.

With this basic heuristic in mind, we can now turn our attention to vocalization in human and non-human primates. Since, as has been noted, behaviors can be considered homologous only if they can be related to structures that could, in principle, be traced to a common precursor, I shall first examine the behavior involved and then the structures of the vocal tract and the central nervous system that subserve it.

2.1 Vocalizations. Like their human relatives, nonhuman primates are not limited to vocalization for communication; gestural, chemical, tactile modes are also employed and it is the latter which are the most important. Lawick-Goodall (1971) has pointed out numerous similarities in the gestures and postures used by chimps and man. Bowing, holding hands, kissing, embracing, chucking under the chin have all been observed.

The ontogeny of vocalization has not been studied carefully in many species. Ploog (1969) recorded some of the 26 distinguishable calls of the squirrel monkey during the first week after birth. He notes that at least some of the calls are not observed until the behavior linked with them develops. The infant calls are more irregular and show greater variability than those of adults. Since these monkeys

FIGURE 2. Diagram representing the divergence of two evolutionary sequences--the Pongidae (great apes) and the Hominidae (modern and extinct man). The two sequences inherit a common ancestry--characters of common inheritance (black circles). As the lines diverge, each one acquires its own distinctive features or characters of independent acquisition; those distinctive of the hominid sequence of evolution are represented by crosses and those of the pongid sequence by white circles. (From S. I. Rosen. 1974. With permission.)

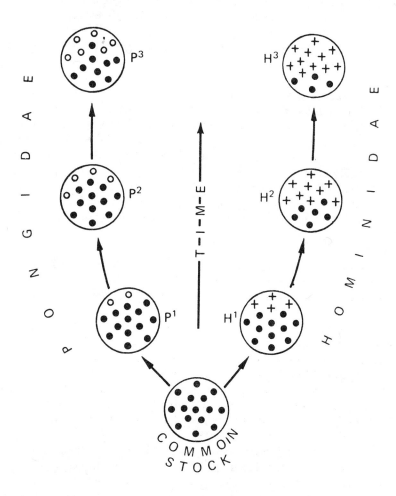

do not appear able to imitate sounds, Ploog does not believe any calls
are learned.

We are fortunate in having relatively detailed descriptions of adult
vocal behavior in gorillas and chimpanzees (Schaller 1963; Lawick-
Goodall 1968, 1971). The vocalizations of the two species are somewhat different; but both employ various grunts, barks, hoots, screams,
and roars. Of the two, the chimpanzee is decidedly the more vocal.
In neither, does the number of distinguishable calls exceed 30. Most
calls allow for some variation in loudness, frequency, etc. which appears to reflect the intensity of the state that elicits them. In both
apes and monkeys, calls are invariably tied to various emotional contexts such as threats, aggression, fear, pain, pleasure, feeding,
separation, etc.

In sum, pongid vocalization differs in a number of respects from
vocalization in humans:

(1) the number of vocalizations is limited,
(2) they are tied to a particular time and place,
(3) they appear to be triggered by only a small set of emotional
    stimuli,
(4) there is some evidence that they are the product of an essen-
    tially closed genetic program,
(5) finally, they do not evince what Hockett (1960) has termed
    'duality of patterning', i. e. they differ from one another as
    total gestalts not composed of recombinable, meaningless
    components.

This latter point underlies what appears to me to be one of the most
essential differences between speech and vocalization in nonhuman
primates. Speech is articulated; vocalization is not.

2. 2 The vocal tract. It is, of course, well known that despite
great efforts and despite the obvious intelligence of the animal, no
chimpanzee has ever been able to acquire articulated speech. It is
sometimes held that the four 'words' which the Hayeses' (Hayes 1951)
chimpanzee, Viki, was able to produce after six years of training is
an exception to this statement. I doubt that anyone who has heard and
observed Viki making these vocalizations, all based on a single,
whispered 'vowel' accompanied by manipulation of the jaw and lips
by the Hayeses, will come away convinced that they have witnessed
the beginnings of articulated speech. In fact, on the basis of his
anatomical investigations, Kelemen (1948) had concluded several
years prior to the Hayes experiment that despite the range of vocalization of which the chimpanzee is capable, the structure of its vocal

apparatus made it impossible to produce the phonetic elements of human speech (but cf. Lieberman 1975 96ff.).

Both in function and in structure the facial musculature of Pan is very similar to man's. This musculature is used in a wide range of facial expressions as well as during vocalization. The lips are capable of extremely fine movements such as the picking up of pins. Although most of the facial muscles are clearly similar to those in man, Duckworth (1910) holds that the risorius muscle which is involved in lip rounding may be unique in man.

The tongue in nonhuman primates is flatter and thinner than in man. It is supplied with muscle spindles which may play an important role in feedback during articulation in humans (Bowman 1971; Smith 1973) and is capable of assuming a large number of positions (cf. Leyton and Sherrington 1917). Nevertheless, according to Bastian (1965), the tongue remains relatively immobile during the production of calls.

In a number of articles (1948, 1969), Kelemen has catalogued the numerous ways in which the structure of the chimpanzee larynx differs from that of man. First of all, as Figure 3a clearly shows, the position of the larynx directly behind the tongue is in marked contrast to that of man. This gives these animals a relatively straight vocal tract without any pharyngeal cavity. In man, the vocal tract is bent in an inverted L-shape: ⌐ with the pharynx forming the posterior leg. Because of this high positioning, the epiglottis and velum are in close proximity. This results in the lack of purely oral vocalization. While the lower position of man's larynx may extend the range of sounds he can make, it is not without its disadvantages. We cannot seal off our oral cavity during inspiration, thus diminishing our acuity of smell when we have food in our mouth; and we also are more prone to asphyxiation through food becoming lodged in our pharyngeal cavities (cf. Lieberman 1973).

Unlike man, the great apes have air sacs which are connected to the laryngeal ventricles via a structure called the appendix. These sacs may be inflated during inhalation or exhalation and provide an air source completely independent of the lungs. Air from the sacs can vibrate an appendage to the true vocal cords (plica vocalis) called the vocal lip (labium vocale) which in conjunction with the ventricular band forms a glottis totally lacking in man (cf. Figure 3b).

Chimpanzees, unlike man, are able to produce double tones, i.e. tones of different pitches sounded simultaneously. This is possible because the vocal folds close at different levels in front and behind the vocal processes. In addition to the above points, there are numerous other smaller details in which the larynges of humans and chimpanzee differ (cf. Negus 1949; Kelemen 1969).

Besides utilization of the air sac mechanism, vocalization in chimpanzees can occur during both exhalation and inhalation. The

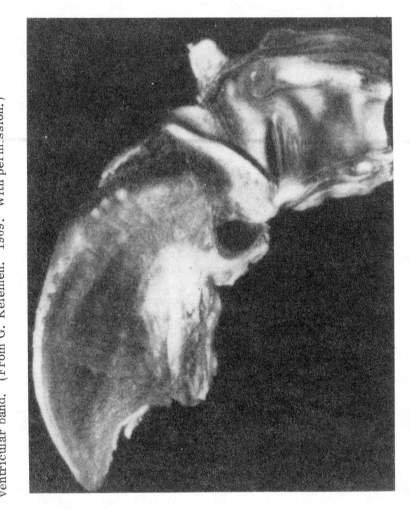

FIGURE 3a. The chimpanzee larynx. Sagittally halved larynx with tongue. Hyoid bulla. Vocal lip with smooth edge along all its length. 'Third glottis' formed between vocal lip and edge of ventricular band. (From G. Kelemen. 1969. With permission.)

FIGURE 3b. The chimpanzee larynx. Frontal section. Upper part: ventricular band, loose tissue with glands; the cartilaginous island belongs to the epiglottis. The appendix leaves, with divided lumen, the wide ventricle at the upper lateral corner. Ventricle covered with papillae except at the edge of the protruding lip of the vocal ligament; medially from the lip the mucous membrane is smooth. The tyreoarytenoid muscle bulges against the laryngeal lumen. It is covered by solid connective tissue which is followed by a glandular layer under the mucous membrane of the conus elasticus. Glands, around the ventricle. (From G. Kelemen. 1969. With permission.)

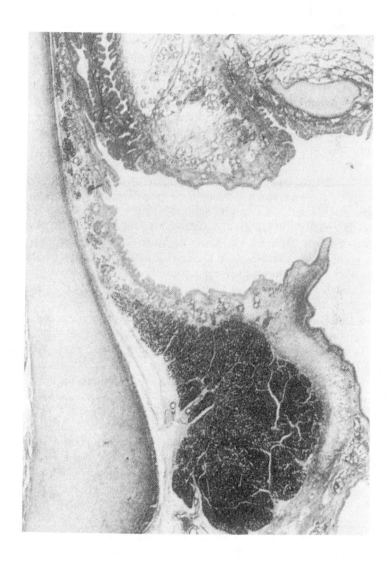

latter pulmonic air-stream mechanism is not employed in normal
speech production in humans (Ladefoged 1971).

Thus we see, as in the case of the behaviors they underlie, there
are numerous differences in the structure of the vocal tract of man
and his closest pongid relatives.

2.3 The brain. Campbell and Hodos (1970) suggest that the following types of information may be among the most important for establishment of homologies in the central nervous system: (1) experimentally determined fiber connections, (2) topology, (3) topography,
(4) the position of reliably occurring sulci, (5) embryology, (6) morphology of individual neurons, (7) histochemistry, (8) electrophysiology,
(9) behavioral changes resulting from stimulation, lesions, etc. In
this section, I shall consider factors such as these in connection with
two basic procedures which have been employed in the comparison of
primate brains: the first, quantitative and the second, experimental
(or what I have termed elsewhere: 'manipulative' (Dingwall and
Whitaker 1974)).

2.31 Quantitative procedures. Almost anything in connection with
the brain that investigators felt could be quantified has been employed
in comparative work. As can be seen in Figure 4, there has been a
massive increase in brain size, whether measured in terms of brain
weight or capacity, in man vis-à-vis the great apes and monkeys.
Even when one takes into regard the lawful relationship that obtains
between body and brain weight, man outstrips all other closely related primates (although not all other mammals--e.g. the porpoise
ranks higher than man) (cf. Holloway 1974). If one constructs a regression line for neocortex on body weight among the primates, the
value assigned to man differs significantly from the predicted value
for his body weight (Passingham 1973). Although there is a close
correlation between relative brain size and 'intelligence' as measured
in various learning tasks across species, this is about the only behavior that one can reliably deduce from this measure. Even this is
in doubt within species such as man where brain capacity may vary
by as much as 1000 cc without any noticeable effect on behavior (cf.
Holloway 1968). Further, we also observe that while chimpanzees
are apparently incapable of articulated speech, human microcephalics
whose brain volumes may fall within the pongid ranges often are capable of speaking. Their intelligence is, of course, subnormal. This
clearly demonstrates that size as well as specific neurological organization must be considered.

If we disregard size and draw the chimpanzee brain to the same
scale as that of man as in Figure 5, we are now struck by the great
similarity that exists in gross topography. Indeed, encephalometric

FIGURE 4. Principal primate horizons, showing the evolutional expansion of the neopallium. The progressive expansion of the psychic area is clearly demonstrated in ascending from tarsius to man. (From F. Tilney. 1928. With permission.)

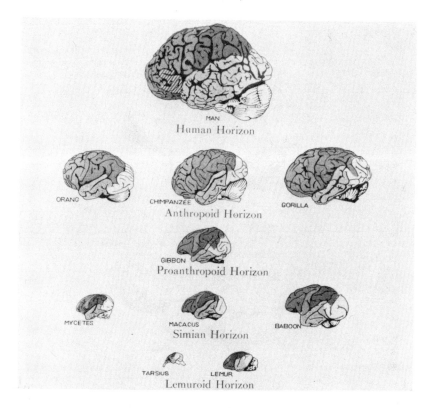

indices show no significant change in the proportions of the major lobes from _Pan_ to _Homo_. It is true that the striate cortex in man is smaller than in other primates, but this must be related to the great expansion of other neocortical areas. There is some evidence that the frontal association cortex in man is significantly larger than in other primates (but cf. Passingham 1973).

As far as cell density or cell size is concerned, there have been no disproportionate changes from nonhuman primates to man. In the case of the number of cells related to proprioceptive control of the jaw muscles, DuBrul (1958) has noted, however, a definite reduction in man. This is presumably tied in with the reduced use of the jaw for prehension.

FIGURE 5. Gross differences in the neurological organization of three primate brains are apparent in the size of the cerebral components of a ceboid monkey (top), a chimpanzee (middle), and modern man (bottom). The small occipital lobe and the large parietal and temporal lobes in man, compared with the other primates, typify the hominid pattern. Lunate sulcus, or furrow, on the chimpanzee's brain bounds its large occipital lobe. (From R. L. Holloway. 1974. The casts of fossil hominid brains. Copyright ©1974 by Scientific American, Inc. All rights reserved.)

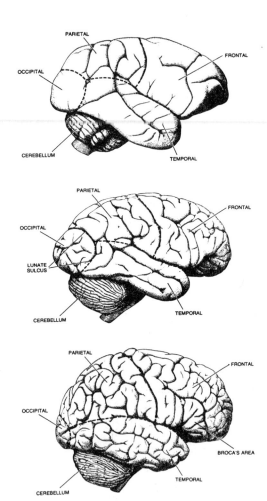

There is now a considerable amount of evidence (cf. Dingwall and Whitaker 1974) from studies of aphasia as well as experimental techniques involving neurosurgery, electrical stimulation, and event related potentials for something like the classical speech areas pictured in Figure 6.

FIGURE 6. Primary language areas of the human brain are thought to be located in the left hemisphere, because only rarely does damage to the right hemisphere cause language disorders. Broca's area, which is adjacent to the region of the motor cortex that controls the movement of the muscles of the lips, the jaw, the tongue, the soft palate, and the vocal cords, apparently incorporates programs for the coordination of these muscles in speech. Damage to Broca's area results in slow and labored speech, but comprehension of language remains intact. Wernicke's area lies between Heschl's gyrus, which is the primary receiver of auditory stimuli, and the angular gyrus, which acts as a way station between the auditory and the visual regions. When Wernicke's area is damaged, speech is fluent but has little content and comprehension is usually lost. Wernicke and Broca areas are joined by a nerve bundle called the arcuate fasciculus. When it is damaged, speech is fluent but abnormal, and patient can comprehend words but cannot repeat them. (From Norman Geschwind. 1972. Language and the brain. Copyright © 1972 by Scientific American, Inc. All rights reserved.)

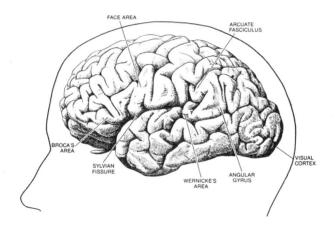

Bonin and Bailey (1961) note that the area in the chimpanzee brain corresponding to that of Broca in man is hard to make out. Further, they note that the large cells in the third and fifth layers of this area in man are to be found only in the third layer of what appears to be the corresponding area in Pan (cf. Sarnat and Netsky 1974:252 as well as Whitaker and Selnes 1974).

Jerzy Konorski (1967:244) claims that the arcuate fasciculus, the bundle of nerve fibers that connects the auditory speech area with Broca's area, is lacking in the chimpanzee and that it is for this reason that imitation of sounds is not observed in this species or other nonhuman primates for that matter. This does indeed appear to be the case from Bailey et al.'s article (Bailey et al. 1943) but

Geschwind (Millikan and Darley 1967:17-18) disputes this stating that the staining technique employed by Bailey et al. is incapable of delimiting the pathway followed by the tract in question.

Geschwind, in a number of publications (Geschwind and Levitsky 1968; Geschwind 1971), has called attention to the fact that there exists a marked asymmetry between the two cerebral hemispheres of man involving the planum temporale. This area which lies behind Heschl's gyrus and thus forms part of Wernicke's auditory speech area is larger in the left (usually dominant) hemisphere of a significant percentage of the brains examined. Recently Witelson and Pallie (1973) have confirmed Geschwind's findings in a second sample of brains and have further demonstrated this asymmetry is also found in neonates, thus lending support to the contention of a number of investigators that dominance may be established at birth (cf. Kinsbourne 1975). A similar asymmetry has been recently documented in nonhuman primates, particularly in the orangutan and chimpanzee (LeMay and Geschwind 1975; Yeni-Komshian and Benson 1975).

Another neocortical speech area that has played a prominent role in the discussion of man's language capacities is the angular gyrus (Geschwind 1965). I shall consider the claims made for this area in another section of this paper. At present, all that need be stated is that this area is well-developed in the chimpanzee and that on cytoarchitectural grounds there is no reason to doubt its homology with the angular and perhaps supramarginal gyri in man (cf. Passingham 1973:352).

One final point that very possibly has a bearing on specificity for speech in man: it has been known for some time that hemispheric dominance exists not only for speech but for fine movements as well (Kimura 1973, 1974). Speech is, of course, the ultimate in fine movement (cf. Sussman 1972). Further, it can be demonstrated that corticalization for this function advances with phylogenetic position (Holloway 1968). In subcortical areas, there is also a clear elaboration of structures dealing with fine movements and coordination as one moves from the great apes to man. Tilney (1928) termed this development 'neokinesis' and presents a number of planimetric indices testifying to its reality. As we shall see, experimental procedures also provide clear evidence of developments in this area.

2.32 Experimental procedures. The use of event related potentials, electrical stimulation of the brain, and ablation have yielded a great deal of insight into which areas of the brain subserve vocalization in human and subhuman primates. It is to these that I now turn.

2.33 The limbic system. A number of studies of squirrel (Jürgens et al. 1967; Ploog 1969; Jürgens and Ploog 1970; Ploog 1970) and rhesus (Robinson 1967a, 1967b, 1972) monkeys clearly show that electrical stimulation of various cortical and subcortical structures can elicit almost the entire repertoire of species-typical calls. These calls sound quite natural and are reacted to appropriately by other monkeys. The sites of stimulation involved are quite diverse; but, in general, they fall within that phylogenetically ancient group of structures termed the limbic system or emotional brain (Curtis et al. 1972:429-36). Some of the structures involved include the hypothalamus, anterior cingulate gyrus, the amygdala, portions of the thalamus, the septum pellucidum, the preoptic areas as well as parts of the brain stem. When we recall the set of emotional contexts with which sub-human primate vocalizations are tied, it seems quite reasonable that this system of structures should be involved. (As W. Hodos has pointed out to me, one can question whether these vocalizations are the direct result of stimulation or rather the concomitants of pain, fear, etc. elicited by the stimulation.)

In man there is also some evidence that parts of the limbic system may, in a limited sense, be involved in vocalization. Brickner (1940) as well as Penfield and Welch (1951) have been able to evoke sounds through stimulation of the mesial cortex just dorsal to the anterior cingulate. Recently, Schaltenbrand (1975) has produced monosyllabic yells and exclamations from stimulation of the ventral oral anterior nucleus of the thalamus and Forel's field. Such speech tends to be automatic and not recalled by patients even though they are conscious during stimulation. More indirect evidence of involvement of the emotional brain in vocalization is the phenomenon of ictal speech automatisms. These are instances of emotionally charged speech which may occur in patients with massive destruction of both Broca's area and the adjacent vocal tract motor cortex who are otherwise totally mute (cf. Whitaker 1971).

While there is thus reason to believe that parts of the emotional brain still subserve speech in man, there is clear evidence of re-organization at this level vis-à-vis what is observed in subhuman primates. First of all, most instances of stimulation in this area in man involve arrest of speech, anomia rather than vocalization. Many investigators believe that parts of this system, particularly the thalamus, may constitute what Penfield and Roberts (1959) termed the centrencephalic system which may be involved with integration of functions of the cortical superstrate (cf. Dingwall and Whitaker 1974: 341-2; Brain and Language 2.1 (1975)). Second, the vocalizations elicited in monkeys cover almost the entire repertoire of their calls; the vocalizations produced in humans are, in contrast, limited to a few yells and exclamations. Finally, all the structures investigated in man appear to be lateralized for function as at the neocortical level. In data from monkeys, sites eliciting vocalization are equally distributed in the left and right brain.

2.34 Neocortical speech areas. As noted in the previous section, there is an increasing body of experimental evidence involving electrical stimulation of the brain (Penfield and Rasmussen 1952; Penfield and Roberts 1959), event related potentials, and neurosurgical techniques (cf. Dingwall and Whitaker 1974; Whitaker and Selnes 1974) supporting the existence of something like the classical, neocortical speech area in man (cf. Figure 6). The data from nonhuman primates unequivocally fails to support neocortical involvement in the production of vocalizations. In an extensive series of studies involving stimulation of the excitable cortex of chimpanzees, orang-utans and gorillas, Leyton and Sherrington (1917) observed elaborate movements of the jaw, lips, larynx, vocal cords, and particularly the tongue; but at no neocortical site could vocalization be elicited. In one particularly interesting case involving a very vociferous young male chimpanzee, stimulation of the lower motor strip produced movements of various parts of the vocal tract (cf. Figure 7). However, stimulation of a field of cortex in front of this area failed to produce any movement of the vocal cords, larynx, lips, or tongue. This area corresponds to Broca's area and in man stimulation of it produces speech arrest. The striped area in Figure 7 was then ablated in this chimpanzee. No facial or other paresis resulted from this surgery and no impairment of vocalization was detected. Kaada (1951) has also resected the lower precentral area bilaterally in a number of species including primates without any modification of vocalization. Such surgery in man would seriously, if not totally, impair speech production (cf. Whitaker and Selnes 1974).

Finally, it might be noted that mapping of the neocortex in human and subhuman primates appears to indicate a considerable increase in the cortical sensorimotor area subserving the vocal tract in man (cf. Miller 1972:76-77 and Passingham 1973:345).

The findings of this section on the brain are summarized in Table 2. It seems reasonable to assume that the limited vocal behavior associated with the limbic system in man is fractionally homologous, as vocalizations, with nonhuman primate calls. Since separating from the common stock, however, it is evident that man has undergone extensive neurological reorganization involving particularly the neocortical speech areas and the emergence of cerebral dominance for speech.

In sum, it is clear that the structures of the central nervous system and the vocal tract as well as the vocal behavior they subserve are nonhomologous in subhuman and human primates. The ability to produce vocalization which is articulated as opposed to holistic in

FIGURE 7. Areas of the motor strip and the field anterior (striped) subjected to electrical stimulation. The striped area was later ablated. (From A. Leyton and C. S. Sherrington. 1917. With permission.)

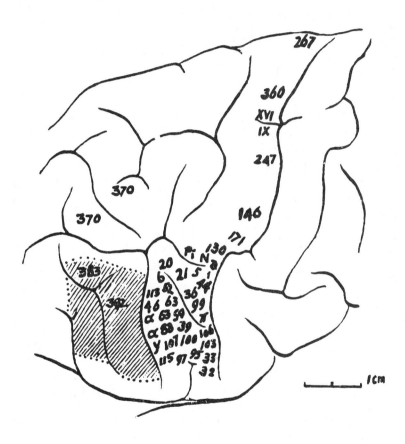

TABLE 2.   Existence of areas or characteristics of the brain in
nonhuman primates (Pan troglodytes unless otherwise
indicated) and homo sapiens.

Area or characteristic	Nonhuman primate	Homo sapiens
Broca's area	No	Yes
Arcuate Fasc.	?	Yes
Hemispheric asymmetry in auditory speech area	Yes	Yes
Angular and supramarginal gyri	Yes	Yes
Limbic involvement in vocalization	Yes (Saimiri sciureus & macacca mulatta)	Yes (limited)
Neocortical involvement in vocalization	No	Yes (extensive)
Cerebral dominance for vocalization	No	Yes

nature, which is mediated by the neocortex as opposed to the limbic
system is unique to the genus: homo sapiens.

3.   The specificity of other aspects of language.   Speech usually
entails language, but language need not entail speech.   Demonstration
that speech is specific to man says nothing about the specificity of
other aspects of language for which it provides but an output mechanism.   In order to ascertain whether behavioral homologies exist
in regard to these aspects, one must provide a model of communication to serve as a suitable framework for such an investigation.

3.1 Aspects of communication systems.   The model that I propose
is schematized in Figure 8.   This view of communication is of great
antiquity stemming at least from the time of the Modistae in whose
theories Aspects I and II would be roughly equivalent to the modes of
understanding and signifying respectively.

In this model, the first symmetric transduction (T_1) involves the
capacity of the brain of an organism to produce and, if they impinge
upon it, comprehend a variety of concepts which may be either simple
or complex.   It seems reasonable to assume that the number of concepts as well as their complexity would increase in higher organisms

FIGURE 8. General aspects of communication systems.

Aspect I.	Brain $\uparrow\ T_1$ Concept (C) $\uparrow\ T_2$
Aspect II.	Neurosign (N_1, N_2) $\uparrow\ T_3$ Input/Output (I, O)

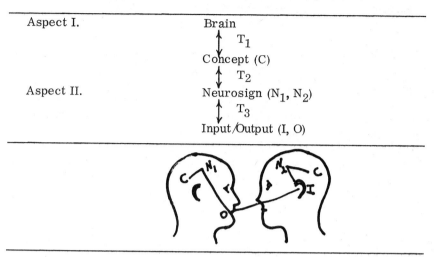

and there would be concomitantly greater reliance on open genetic programs for their specification. Cognitive psychologists such as Piaget have to some extent clarified the nature of this transduction as it develops in humans. Ethologists and comparative psychologists have investigated its nature in other species.

One cannot at present judge whether an animal is in command of a particular concept unless he signals this in some manner. This involves linking the concept with a neurological state that mediates either its production or reception. Theoretical linguistics today, as in the past, regards as its principal concern the nature of the transduction between meaning and sound. This is equivalent to T_2 in this model, as meaning is generally taken to involve an abstract conceptual structure and sound to involve an equally abstract phonetic representation which is only imperfectly reflected in the various stages of its production or reception. Recent work by Sachs (1967), Bransford and Franks (1972) and others has provided the first clear evidence of what conceptual structure might be like, while at the same time neuroscientists have demonstrated in EEG studies that what is being termed the neurosign is more than a theoretical construct (cf. Dingwall and Whitaker 1974). On the other hand, the upshot of a decade of work in experimental psycholinguistics has made it abundantly clear that current linguistic theory fails to provide a viable model of either T_2 or its endpoints (cf. Watt 1972; Dingwall and Shields 1973).

The third transduction (T_3) involves the processes of signal production and detection. It is this transduction, because of its relative accessibility to study, about which most is known thanks to the efforts of physiologists, hearing and speech scientists, experimental phoneticians, and others interested in this aspect of language.

It should now be clear that what has been demonstrated in the previous section is simply that one of the output modalities, one aspect of T_3, is unique to human beings. Can one proceed, as in the second section, to demonstrate that the remaining aspects of communication systems constitute examples of homologous or non-homologous behaviors in our closest pongid relatives? The answer is obviously: no. Remember that in order to investigate possible homologies we must not only compare behaviors but also the structures that underlie them. Excluding the problem of signal detection which will be taken up in the last section of this paper, we have no idea at present what structures are involved in Aspect I of this model. It would seem that they are at least partially biochemical in nature.

Even though structural evidence is, for the time being, lacking, there seem to me to be three considerations that tend to indicate that Aspect I is not specific to human beings.

3.11 Evolution. As Stephen Toulmin (1971) has pointed out, there are at least three processes by which language might have evolved. Language, regarded as a totality, might have developed abruptly via a one-shot genetic saltation in our hominid ancestors. Alternatively, the capacity for language might have existed for some time before it was discovered and subsequently spread by cultural radiation. Toulmin finds the first hypothesis implausible, as the one-shot saltation is simply far too drastic in light of what is known of genetic mutation and recombination. The second possibility is also unattractive when one considers that it would, at the very least, require that all the anatomical and physiological changes we have discussed in connection with speech arise from adaptive pressures totally independent of language. It is much more likely, in Toulmin's view, that language evolved bit by bit over a long period of time. The changes we have observed in the vocal tract and in the central nervous system would have taken place gradually and language as we know it would have slowly and progressively emerged.

This view seems plausible not only when applied to our hominid ancestors but also to the possibility of language-like behavior in our closest pongid relatives. As mentioned previously, recent biochemical evidence (Goodman 1974) involving interspecies comparisons of amino acid sequences of homologous polypeptide chains clearly shows that chimpanzees and gorillas share a closer kinship with homo sapiens than with the other great apes. Furthermore, the genetic divergence from us is so small that it seems most likely that chimpanzees and gorillas shared a common ancestry with man through the entire Miocene and perhaps during the early Pliocene as well. If this is the case and given the fact noted by Whitaker (1973: 107) that the lengthened period between generations characteristic of primates will tend to slow down the rate of genetic change, it appears most unlikely that chimpanzees and gorillas would evince no language-like behavior whatsoever. The recent studies involving the teaching of language-like systems to chimpanzees (Gardner and Gardner 1969, 1971; Premack 1971; Rumbaugh 1974) demonstrate to my satisfaction the types of nascent language abilities I would expect them to possess. It is to one aspect of these studies that I now turn for further evidence in favor of a behavioral homology for language minus speech.

3.12   Ontogensis.   As Campbell and Hodos (1970:361) point out, one of the criteria for the recognition of homologies is ontogenetic similarity. This is the case, as developmental patterns are inherited. If one examines the development of language particularly in Washoe and in the other chimps under Roger Fouts' care (cf. Fleming 1974a and b), one cannot help noticing a number of similarities to ontogenesis of language in humans. The ability to generalize signs learned in one context to other appropriate contexts has been demonstrated repeatedly. Thus, having learned the sign for 'hurt' in a context involving herself, one of Roger Fouts' chimps, Lucy, correctly applied it to her pet cat when its paw was cut. Lucy has also been observed trying to teach signs to the cat as well as other chimps which is not an unknown behavior vis-à-vis pets, dolls, and playmates in human children either. Over-extensions within the same semantic field that bear a striking resemblance to the types of over-extension in children reported on by Eve Clark (1972) have been observed in chimps. To give one example out of many, Washoe applies the sign for 'baby' appropriately to human infants but also to pictures of animals and objects (cf. Clark 1972:81). Practice of language as observed by Ruth Weir (1962) in her child also occurs in chimps who like to make their favorite signs in a mirror which they hold with their feet. In this practice, like human children, they have also been observed to correct themselves when they make errors. Creativity in the use of language has been observed on numerous occasions. The invention of such terms as 'cry hurt food' to refer to a radish, 'candy drink' to refer to a watermelon, 'water bird' to refer to a duck (even when on land) are but a few instances. As Chukovsky (1968) has made us aware, such creativity is one of the great gifts of children learning language. The development of syntax has been studied in detail in a recent article by the Gardners (1971). Roger Brown (1973) who was originally skeptical of the chimp studies now admits that Washoe appears to have acquired the set of relations that characterize Stage I in child speech. In some facets of syntax, Washoe demonstrates greater ability than her human counterparts. The Gardners report that Washoe makes fewer reversals of word order and that she performs at a much higher level of accuracy (90% versus 50% correct) in matching reversible strings such as 'cat bit dog' versus 'dog bit cat' to pictures (cf. Linden 1974:247-8).

As in the case of the evolutionary argument, these striking similarities in ontogenesis of language, while not constituting proof of behavioral homology, clearly point in that direction.

3.13 Brain structure. One argument as to why nonhuman primates might be incapable of language was advanced at this conference a little over 10 years ago by Norman Geschwind (1964, 1965, 1969) and has enjoyed considerable vogue among some anthropologists (cf. Lancaster 1968). Geschwind began by pointing out that there are four zones in the brain that mature early in terms of myelination. These so-called primordial zones which man shares with subhuman primates include the limbic system, the auditory and visual cortexes, and the motor-sensory strip. Adjacent to each of these zones, separating them from each other, are association cortexes. It is known that there are no direct interconnections between the primordial zones; rather, there are connections to the neighboring association areas and long fiber tracts from these areas link up the primary zones.

Basic to Geschwind's theory is that in subhuman primates the only associations that can be formed in learning be between each of the primary, neocortical areas and the limbic system as shown in part (2) of Figure 9. Thus, for example, if a monkey were taught to visually choose between a cross and a circle via some reinforcement presumably activating the limbic system, a visual-limbic association would result. There would be no transfer of this learning to a task involving palpation of a cross and a circle concealed from vision, as this would require that a new sensory-limbic association be formed (cf. Ettlinger and Blakemore 1960). This would be the case because, unlike man, subhuman primates were supposedly incapable of making direct associations between non-limbic modalities as shown in part (1) of Figure 9.

FIGURE 9. Putative associations among primordial zones in man (1) and subhuman primates (2).

(1)   (2)

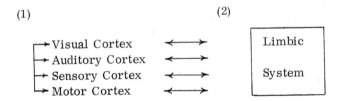

Geschwind appears to believe that the emergence of language in man depends on naming and that naming is the outgrowth of a unique ability to form nonlimbic associations. This ties in with Wernicke's model of the brain according to which production of a name involves indirect linkage of the visual cortex and Broca's area, while understanding a name involves an indirect link between Heschl's gyrus and the visual cortex (cf. Figure 10a and b). It will be noted that in each instance part of this link involves the angular gyrus which Geschwind felt formed a relay station among all association areas.

This theory, while ingenious, is most assuredly incorrect. Davenport and Rogers (1970) have recently demonstrated that both orangutans and chimpanzees are able to match visually presented to tactilely presented stimuli and that learning is not restricted to specific objects. Even more interestingly, Roger Fouts (cf. Fleming 1974:44; Linden 1974:121-2) has been able to show that chimpanzees can transfer from auditory to Ameslan signs in the absence of referents. The chimp, Ally, was taught the Ameslan signs for ten objects for which he already knew the English words. A separate investigator who was unaware of the signs taught tested Ally with a number of referents including those for the signs involved. Ally's performance was errorless. Thus, the inability to produce cross-modal associations is not a barrier to the acquisition of language in chimpanzees (cf. Geschwind 1970). The only difference, as we might expect, is in the nature of the motor activity involving hand versus tongue gestures. Not only is there evidence of similarity in cross-modal association behavior in chimpanzees and man but also, as pointed out in the previous section (p. 34), there is no marked difference in these two species in the angular gyrus which Geschwind holds to be important in mediating this behavior.

In the previous section, we have seen that what is unique to the organization of the brain in man is the existence of lateralized, specialized areas subserving articulated speech. Are only these output and possibly input modalities of language (Aspect II) lateralized or is there lateralization for all aspects of language? A definitive answer to this question cannot be given at this time, but there is a great deal of evidence that not all aspects of language are lateralized. Studies of split brain patients with dominant left hemispheres clearly indicate that the minor hemisphere has considerable ability to process auditory or visually presented words, definitions as well as various syntactic constructions. The same is true in patients in whom the dominant hemisphere has been pharmacologically deactivated. Recent work of Gazzaniga (1972) and others with global aphasics indicates as Kimura and Archibald (1974) put it that 'it is not specifically a symbolic or language system which is affected in aphasia, but the speech system.' Studies utilizing the dichotic listening technique show no

FIGURE 10a. Saying the name of a seen object, according to Wernicke's model, involves the transfer of the visual pattern to the angular gyrus, which contains the 'rules' for arousing the auditory form of the pattern in Wernicke's area. From here the auditory form is transmitted by way of the arcuate fasciculus to Broca's area. There the articulatory form is aroused, is passed on to the face area of the motor cortex, and the word then is spoken. (From Norman Geschwind. 1972. Language and the brain. Copyright © 1972 by Scientific American, Inc. All rights reserved.)

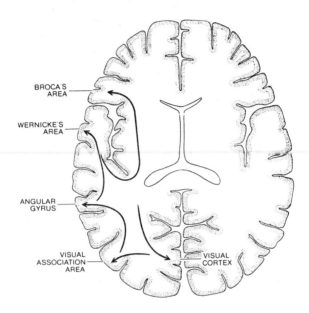

FIGURE 10b. Understanding the spoken name of an object involves the transfer of the auditory stimuli from Heschl's gyrus (the primary auditory cortex) to Wernicke's area and then to the angular gyrus, which arouses the comparable visual pattern in the visual association cortex. Here the Sylvian fissure has been spread apart to show the pathway more clearly. (From Norman Geschwind. 1972. Language and the brain. Copyright © 1972 by Scientific American, Inc. All rights reserved.)

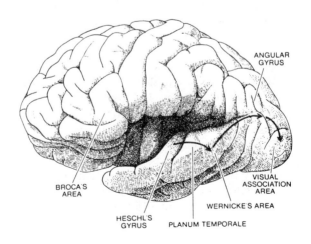

interaction of semantic constraints, abstractness, or surface structure with right ear advantage (Borkowski et al. 1965; Frankfurter and Honeck 1973; Kimura 1973; Herman 1974). Using the same technique, investigators at Haskins have uncovered degrees of encodedness in the processing of the speech signal itself with stops being generally the most encoded speech sounds and vowels the least (Cutting 1972). In cases of hemispherectomy involving the dominant hemisphere, patients have demonstrated surprisingly good language comprehension and even some productive speech ability albeit quite poor (cf. Moscovitch 1973). Taken together, these findings make it difficult to maintain that language as a whole (particularly Aspect I) is lateralized in man. Once again we see a lack of structural evidence for language functions apart from speech.

One final bit of evidence for the special nature of speech and the areas of the brain that subserve it has to do with the phenomenon of plasticity. Milner (1974) has gathered together cases showing that whether language function as assessed by the Wada procedure is transferred to the contralateral hemisphere in instances of early brain damage depends crucially on the site of lesion. If the lesion impinges on either of the classical motor or auditory speech areas (i.e. Broca's or Wernicke's areas), then transfer of function occurs. Lesions outside of these areas evince no effect upon lateralization whatsoever. This casts considerable doubt on the special nature of other areas of the dominant hemisphere particularly the angular and supramarginal gyri in the mediation of language. It is interesting to note that it is these areas that have been claimed to be important in such nonspeech behaviors as naming (Geschwind 1964, 1965) syntax and semantics (Whitaker 1971).

In sum, as we have seen in the second section, there can be no doubt of man's unique ability to produce articulated speech--numerous behavioral and structural differences attest to this. However, if one subtracts this output modality from other aspects of the communication system we call language, we can find no strong support for the thesis that these residual aspects are unique to homo sapiens. In part this is due to the fact that the structural underpinnings of these aspects of communicative behavior simply are not known. In instances where structural differences have been suggested as in the case of the angular gyrus or lateralization for supra-speech functions, there is scant evidence that such differences between us and our pongid relatives exist. On the other hand, the great similarity in ontogenesis of language in man and chimp coupled with the implausibility of a one-shot genetic saltation for all aspects of language strongly suggests that what we see developing in chimpanzees is a behavior forming a continuum with human language.

4. Early stages in the development of speech. Having demonstrated in the previous sections the very special role that speech plays in the communicative behavior of human beings, I wish to turn in this last section to a consideration of its early stages in ontogenesis. Specifically, I shall focus on the role of babbling and neurological feature detectors in the development of speech sketching the relative contribution that the open and closed parts of the genetic program underlying this behavior might play within the framework of Ladefoged's auditory-motor theory of speech production.

4.1 The role of babbling. I initially became interested in the topic of babbling because of the crucial part it plays in behaviorist theories of language acquisition. Thus, e.g. Staats and Staats (1963) cite with favor Osgood's (1953) claim that infants '. . . make all of the speech sounds that the human vocal system can produce . . .' and proceed to build on this the conclusion that: 'The early development of speech consists of the differential reinforcement of certain members of this class . . .' (1963:118). The problem with this theory of the role of babbling is that the data upon which it is based appear to be fallacious, that the predictions that can be deduced from it are not borne out, and that the tests cited as supportive of the theory are irrelevant. At the time Staats and Staats proposed this theory, both Jakobson (1941) and Leopold (1947) had produced evidence which cast doubt on its major premises. For example, Leopold lists a number of sounds of English and German, Hildegard's target languages, that are totally absent in her babbling. Jakobson calls attention to the fact that many sounds that are common to the child's babbling and the language of his environment are lost only to be acquired later after much effort. Recent studies by Cruttenden (1970) and Pierce (1974) clearly show the limited range of the vocalizations produced during the babbling stage.

Of course, our behaviorist might claim it is not really necessary for all human speech sounds to be available from the outset. Rather it might be claimed that those sounds that are available might be gradually shaped to approximate the phonetic inventory of the target language. In fact there appeared to be some impressionistic evidence for this assertion in a study by Weir (1966) where it was held that the babbling of a Chinese infant could be differentiated from that of American and Russian infants by its tonal quality and syllable structure. A later experimental study by Atkinson, MacWhinney, and Stoel (1968) using the same tapes Weir was commenting on yielded the following results for tasks involving identification of taped samples as English or non-English and decisions as to whether paired taped samples were from the same or different language communities:

(1) scores on neither task were significantly different from chance;

(2) there was an increase in errors on the first task as the age of the child increased;

(3) on the second task, there was a tendency to judge younger children (incorrectly) as coming from the same linguistic background and to judge older children (again incorrectly) as coming from different linguistic environments;

(4) finally, prior knowledge of the languages involved had no significant effect on the results.

Essentially the same findings were obtained in a carefully designed study by Rachel Olney (1974) at the University of Maryland utilizing samples of Chinese and American babbling from the same age periods, viz., 6 months, 1 year, and 1 year 6 months. Such results clearly fail to support the theory that differential reinforcement of babbling results in gradual approximation of the sound structure of the native language. Such an outcome should not be startling in that it is surely obvious that the vast majority of parents, not being trained phoneticians, would not know which sounds to reinforce and even if they did, they would not have sufficient time to apply suitable schedules of reinforcement.

A number of investigators have suggested that babbling is initially an example of reflex behavior, analogous to suspension gripping in infants, which only in its later stages comes under cortical control (Bever 1961; Drachman 1970; Whitaker 1973). Whitaker holds that before one year of age there are few if any mature functional connections between the auditory and vocal tract centers. Thus, presumably, before this age babbling could not come under auditory control. There is some behavioral support for this view in the fact that deaf children appear to engage in normal babbling behavior at first which, at a later stage, gradually ceases perhaps because of lack of appropriate auditory feedback (Fry 1966).

Why do children go through a babbling stage at all? The best guess at present is that what is involved is some sort of practice in the complex coordination of muscles required to produce speech (Fry 1966). Mattingly (1973) has suggested that the child may be engaging in a kind of mapping of the vocal tract perhaps providing via various feedback mechanisms the ability to approximate sounds produced by more mature vocal tracts having very different characteristics from his own. These views are in accord with evidence (cf. Hardy 1970) that feedback plays a much more important role during the acquisition of speech than it appears to thereafter.

4.2 The role of neurological feature detectors. Neurological feature detectors may be defined as 'organizational configurations of the sensory nervous system that are highly sensitive to certain parameters of complex stimuli' (Abbs and Sussman 1971). Evidence for such detectors in the auditory and visual systems of a wide range of animals has been collected. Thus, as noted earlier, the squirrel monkey appears to have cells in its auditory cortex that react specifically to vocalizations of this species.

There is now a considerable body of evidence that such feature detectors may exist in human infants for various speech parameters. Thus, for example, it has been demonstrated that one of the most important cues for place of articulation is second formant transition and, furthermore, that perception of this cue is categorical in nature. Thus, in Figure 11, transitions 1-4 in conjunction with the steady state vowel shown at the right will be heard by adult English speakers as [bæ] while 5-6 will be heard as [dæ]. In an experiment reported on in Cutting and Eimas (1974), one group of infant Ss heard within-category stimuli (S), two groups heard different across-category stimuli (D_1, D_2), while a control group heard the same stimulus throughout. Both cardiac rate and sucking rate have been utilized as dependent variables in such experiments. In this experiment, as in others, infants in the S and control groups show habituation to the

FIGURE 11. A schematic spectrogram of the two-formant [bæ] and the acoustic variation in the second formant transition requisite for a [bæ]-to-[dæ] continuum. (From J. Cutting and P. Eimas. 1974. With permission.)

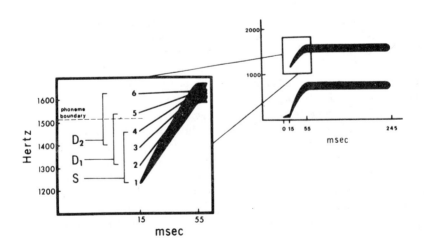

stimuli, while those in the D_1 and D_2 groups do not. The same result has been obtained for perception of voice onset time, the major cue for voicing. That discrimination of place of articulation is linguistic rather than purely auditory in nature was demonstrated by Eimas and his colleagues using formant transitions alone without following vowels. Such stimuli are heard as bird-like chirps by adults. In this non-linguistic context, neither S nor D pairs (cf. Figure 11 insert) produced habituation. Results of this type have been obtained with infants as young as 4 weeks of age (cf. Cutting and Eimas (1974) for a survey of these studies). This remarkably precocious linguistic processing ability has also been attested in studies by Molfese (1972, n.d.). Utilizing the event related potential technique, this researcher demonstrated that infants ranging in age from 1 week to 10 months already evince strong lateralization for speech versus nonspeech sounds. These findings are in accord with others cited earlier in this paper (p. 34) indicating that lateralization for speech may be established at birth.

It has been pointed out in a number of publications (Schiefelbusch 1974; Cutting and Eimas 1974; Doty 1974) that the experiments we have been discussing are far from unproblematical. The nature of the stimuli, the loss of subjects, conflicting outcomes with different response measures, various problems of statistical analysis must all be considered in evaluating the results. Further, as we have noted in the case of chimpanzees, other animals are capable of processing human speech. (In fact, there is evidence for such processing at sub-cortical levels in cats (cf. Walker and Halas 1972).) Evidence for the processing of features as opposed to gestalts, however, is simply not available for other animals. Finally, we must recall Whitaker's views on the maturation of the brain. In his view, there could be no neocortical processing at four weeks. Not everyone, however, shares this view of cortical nonfunction at birth (cf. Robinson 1969).

Despite these problems which clearly must be resolved, I find the concept of neurological feature detectors an extremely attractive one. This is true in part because we are dealing here with a phenomenon widely attested in other species. Further, it appears to make sense that in precocial animals, feature detectors are typically holistic in nature, tuned to the perception of gestalts, while in humans, whose genetic programs allow for massive insertion of material only the bare necessities are spelled out. What are these bare necessities? Once again following Mattingly (1972), I would suggest that they might consist in solutions to what he has termed the 'Speech Detection Problem' and the 'Representation Problem'. On the one hand, neurological feature detectors appear to allow the infant to sort out speech from nonspeech (this may constitute the answer to Lakoff's (1965) interesting question of why the child comes up with a theory of language (he should have said speech!) as opposed to a theory of acoustics); and, on the other, they aid him in the establishment of phonetic categories--to adopt the opposite computer analogy of Dorman (1972), they allow the child to digitize what is in effect an analog input.

4.3 The auditory-motor theory of speech perception. Neurological feature detectors may aid the child in the acquisition of speech by providing a solution to the 'Speech Detection Problem' and, at least, a partial solution to the 'Representation Problem'; but even if such filtering processes are available at birth, they provide minimal assistance in the recognition of speech sounds involving complexes of features to say nothing of the production of such sounds. Thus, e.g. even though Eimas' studies indicate that categorical perception of VOT distinctions occurs at 4 weeks of age, a study by Garnica (1973) in phonemic speech perception in children ranging in age from 1;5 to 1;10 shows that by the end of the study only 63% have acquired this distinction in consonants. The acquisition of the production of this distinction, as careful studies by Port and Preston (1972) demonstrate, is even more prolonged perhaps requiring as long as five years. Thus, to a large extent, the acquisition of speech is dependent on an open genetic program. We even have evidence of this at the cortical level. Thus, Van Lackner and Fromkin (1973) utilizing the dichotic listening paradigm demonstrated lateralization for pitch distinctions in speakers of Thai where such distinctions play a linguistic role, while they find no evidence of a right ear effect for such distinctions in speakers of English where they do not play a linguistic role (cf. also Wood et al. 1971). There is a clear parallel here with recent electrophysiological studies of rhesus monkeys. These studies indicate that single cells in the auditory cortex respond differentially in animals trained in an auditory discrimination task as opposed to animals not trained in this task. Further, although the pattern of activity is the same, the firing frequency of the cell is far greater when the trained animal is performing this task as opposed to when he is not. In a word, the results of practice are clearly reflected in changes at the cortical level.

At this point comparison with what appear to be convergent phenomena (v. p. 22 for a definition of convergence) in the development of species-typical vocalizations in birds is instructive (cf. Nottebohm 1970, n. d.). Some birds such as ring doves show a pattern of development very divergent from that which we have seen in humans. They evince no early subsong stage parallel to babbling; their vocalization develops normally despite isolation or early deafening. Other, more altricial, song-birds such as the chaffinch not only display a period of subsong but show the same need as humans for experience of species-specific vocalization and for early auditory feedback. As in these birds, early deafness in humans prevents the development of vocalization while acquired deafness in adults has no <u>immediate</u> effect (cf. Fry 1966).

While the role of feedback mechanisms in speech is far from clear, it does seem to be the case that all forms of feedback play their most crucial role during the acquisition stage. After the speech production process is learned, interference with auditory or tactile feedback affects mainly fine positioning of articulators, but speech remains intelligible (cf. Fry 1966; Hardy 1970). As Hardy points out, both the auditory and tactile-proprioceptive error-detecting systems initially allow for relatively wide limits of acceptable performance that only gradually become narrowed during the learning process. Exchanges such as the following:

Adult: (pointing to a picture) 'What's that?'
Child: 'That's a [wæbɪt].'
Adult: 'No, say [ræbɪt], not [wæbɪt].'
Child: 'But I didn't say [wæbɪt]; I said [wæbɪt]!'
(From Kornfelt and Goehl 1974)

indicate that children can distinguish sounds that fall within a non-distinctive range for adults (cf. Kornfeld 1971). Learning in recognition and production may thus involve a considerable amount of fine tuning, as Hardy implies.

The view of the processes underlying the early stages of speech production which emerges from the preceding considerations fits nicely within the framework of Ladefoged's auditory-motor theory of speech production (1972). This theory developed from cineradiographic observation by Ladefoged of the articulatory gestures used by different speakers to produce what were judged to be identical vowel sounds. What Ladefoged found was that these gestures were very diverse. To account for this Ladefoged suggests that 'acoustic properties and their sensory counterparts (or, more likely, the corresponding neurological processes) become part of the producing process, mediating between the possible articulatory gestures and their ultimate production.' This position is in general agreement with the neurological formulation of Geschwind mentioned earlier (cf. Figure 10) where production is held to involve transfer of the auditory image via the arcuate fasciculus to Broca's area where the articulatory form is aroused (cf. Luria (1970) for a somewhat more elaborate view which is probably closer to the truth; also cf. Brain (1961)). It is interesting to note in connection with such a model that event related potential studies of both speech production and recognition indicate maximal negativity in the temporo-parietal region with progressive attenuation of amplitude in more anterior sites (cf. Dingwall and Whitaker 1974 for discussion). It seems clear that the neocortical auditory centers are crucially involved in both speech production and recognition. While the motor theory of speech recognition may account for some aspects of recognition in adults, it is difficult to see what role it might play in the acquisition of speech (cf. Fry 1974).

One final point needs to be touched on, viz., the automatization of speech production. As every pianist knows, learning a difficult passage is a slow, painful process but once this process is over the passage flows along flawlessly allowing one to turn one's attention to elements of phrasing and accentuation. Although the motor activity involved is much more complex, the same is true in speech production. The learner of a second language when not attending to his production may lapse into gross errors; no such attention is acquired for one's native language(s). Once again nonhuman primate studies are suggestive of what processes might be involved in automatization. Evarts (1973) has shown that learned movements may involve the establishment of some form of servo-loop perhaps along the lines of (c) in Figure 12 resulting in latencies of the length usually associated with reflex behavior (cf. Lieberman 1975:14ff. for further discussion).

By discussing in this section the early stages of the development of speech, we have been able to arrive at a somewhat clearer understanding of the nature of this immensely complex, species-specific behavior. Speech has been seen to involve an open genetic program. Pre-linguistic vocalization as well as some form of feature detection appear to be pre-wired. These closed portions of the program may provide the child with at least partial solutions to the problems of vocal tract mapping, speech detection, and speech representation. The open portion of the program allows for the gradual acquisition of language-specific sound systems. This involves the grouping of features into complex auditory representations which gradually approximate the speech sounds of the environment. It is this auditory representation which guides production. Both production and recognition are linked by a complex feedback system involving at least tactile, proprioceptive, and acoustic feedback loops. This feedback system appears to play a particularly important role in the early stages of speech acquisition during which what we have termed the automatization of speech production is taking place. It is this ability to automatize the auditory-gesture tie, to encode and decode vocalization which is articulated rather than holistic in nature that constitutes the unique characteristic of human communication systems.

FIGURE 12. Three methods for testing to determine if there are
longtime effects (lasting days, weeks, or years) on
the sensitivity or response of neurons, which might
be the equivalent of 'learning'. (From V. L. Parsegian. 1973. With permission.)

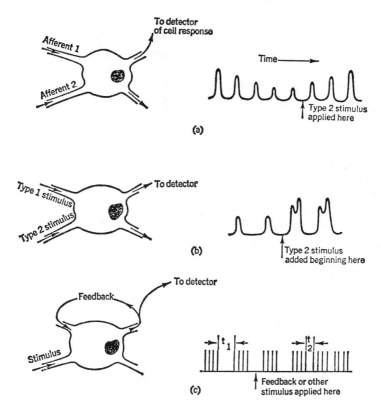

ACKNOWLEDGMENTS

Many colleagues from various disciplines have given freely of their
time in commenting on this paper and discussing with me the issues it
raises. I wish to thank particularly William Hodos (Psychology, U.
of Maryland), Wolfgang Schleidt (Zoology, U. of Maryland), Harry
Whitaker (Psychology, U. of Rochester), and William Wang (Linguistics, U. of California, Berkeley).

Permission to reproduce figures included in this paper is acknowledged as follows: Figure 1: From A. H. Schultz. 1969. The
life of primates. New York, Universe Books. Figure 2: From S. I.
Rosen. 1974. Introduction to the primates, living and fossil.

Englewood Cliffs, Prentice-Hall, Inc. (after LeGros Clark, 1959).
Figures 3a and 3b: From G. Kelemen. 1969. Anatomy of the larynx
and the anatomical basis of vocal performance. In: The chimpanzee.
Ed. by G. H. Bourne, 165-186. Baltimore, University Park Press.
Copyright S. Karger AG, Basel, Switzerland. Figure 4: From F.
Tilney. 1928. The brain from ape to man. New York, Paul B.
Hoeber. Copyright Harper and Row, Publishers, Inc., Medical
Department, Hagerstown, Maryland. Figure 5: From Ralph L.
Holloway. 1974. The casts of fossil hominid brains. Scientific
American 231.1.106-115. Figure 6: From Norman Geschwind.
1972. Language and the brain. Scientific American 226.4.76-83.
Figure 7: From A. Leyton and C. S. Sherrington. 1917. Obser-
vations on the excitable cortex of the chimpanzee, orang-utan and
gorilla. Quarterly Journal of Experimental Physiology. 11.135-222.
Figures 10a and 10b: From Norman Geschwind. op. cit. (cf.
Figure 6). Figure 11: From J. Cutting and P. Eimas. 1974.
Phonetic feature analyzers and the processing of speech in infants.
SR-37/38.45-63. Haskins Laboratory. Figure 12: From V. L.
Parsegian. 1973. This cybernetic world of men, machines, and
earth systems. New York, Doubleday (reprinted from Introduction
to natural science. New York, Academic Press).

REFERENCES

Abbs, J. and H. Sussman. 1971. Neurophysiological feature detectors and speech perception: A discussion of theoretical implications. JSHR 14.23-36.
Atherton, M. and R. Schwartz. 1974. Linguistic innateness and its
evidence. Journal of Philosophy 71.155-168.
Atkinson, K., B. MacWhinney, and C. Stoel. 1968. An experiment
on the recognition of babbling. Working Paper 15. Language-
Behavior Research Laboratory. Berkeley, University of California.
Atz, James W. 1970. The application of the idea of homology to
behavior. In: Development and evolution of behavior. Edited
by Lester R. Aronson et al., 53-74. San Francisco, W. H.
Freeman and Co.
Bailey, P. et al. 1943. Long association fibers in cerebral hemi-
sphere of monkey and chimpanzee. Journal of Neurophysiology
6.129-34.
Bastian, J. 1965. Primate signaling systems and human languages.
In: Primate behavior: Field studies of monkeys and apes.
Edited by I. Devore. New York, Holt, Rinehart and Winston.
Bever, T. G. 1961. Prelinguistic behavior. Unpublished honors
thesis. Dept. of Linguistics. Cambridge, Harvard University.

Bock, Walter J. 1969. Discussion: The concept of homology. Annals of New York Academy of Science 167. 71-73.

Bonin, G. and P. Bailey. 1961. Pattern of the cerebral isocortex. In: Primatologia 2(10). Edited by H. Hofer et al. Basel, Karger.

Borkowski, J. et al. 1965. Ear preference and abstractness in dichotic listening. Psychonomic Science 3. 547-548.

Bowman, James P. 1971. The muscle spindle and neural control of the tongue. Springfield, Charles C. Thomas.

Brain, R. 1961. The neurology of language. Brain 84. 145-66.

Bransford, J. and J. Franks. 1972. The abstraction of linguistic ideas: A review. Cognition 1. 211-49.

Brickner, R. 1940. A human cortical area producing repetitive phenomena when stimulated. Journal of Neurophysiology 3. 128-130.

Brown, R. 1973. A first language: The early stages. Cambridge, Harvard University Press.

Campbell, Bernard G. 1974. The physical basis of language in primates. In: Frontiers of anthropology. Edited by M. Leaf, 290-307. New York, Van Nostrand Co.

Campbell, C. G. B. and W. Hodos. 1970. The concept of homology and the evolution of the nervous system. Brain, behavior and evolution 3. 353-367.

Chukovsky, Kornei. 1968. From two to five. Berkeley, University of California Press.

Clark, Eve. 1972. What's in a word? On the child's acquisition of semantics in his first language. In: Cognitive development and the acquisition of language. Edited by T. Moore, 65-110. New York, Academic Press.

Cruttenden, A. 1970. A phonetic study of babbling. British Journal of Disorders of Communication 5. 110-118.

Curtis, Brian et al. 1972. An introduction to the neurosciences. Philadelphia, W. B. Saunders Co.

Cutting, James E. 1972. A parallel between encodedness and the magnitude of the right ear effect. SR-29/30. 61-68. Haskins Laboratory.

_____ and Peter Eimas. 1974. Phonetic feature analyzers and the processing of speech in infants. SR-37/38. 45-63. Haskins Laboratory.

Davenport, R. and C. Rogers. 1970. Intermodal equivalence of stimuli in apes. Science 168. 279-281.

Dingwall, W. and J. Shields. 1973. From utterance to gist: Four experimental studies of what's in between. Unpublished ms.

_____ and H. Whitaker. 1974. Neurolinguistics. Annual Review of Anthropology 3. 323-356.

Dorman, M. 1972. Auditory evoked potential correlates of speech sound discrimination. SR-29/30.111-120. Haskins Laboratory.

Doty, Dennis. 1974. Infant speech perception. Human Development 17.74-80.

Drachman, Gaberell. 1970. Assumptions about acquisition. Unpublished ms.

DuBrul, E. Lloyd. 1958. Evolution of the speech apparatus. Springfield, Charles C. Thomas.

Duckworth, W. L. 1910. A note on sections of the lips of the primates. Journal of Anatomy and Physiology 44.348-353.

Eibl-Eibesfeldt, I. 1970. Ethology. New York, Holt, Rinehart and Winston.

Ettlinger, G. and C. B. Blakemore. 1960. Cross-modal transfer set in the monkey. Neuropsychologia 7.41-47.

Evarts, E. V. 1973. Motor cortex reflexes associated with learned movement. Science 170.501 3.

Fleming, J. 1974a. The state of the apes. Psychology Today 7.8.31ff.

_____. 1974b. The ABC's of chimp language. Psychology Today Interview Cassettes. Del Mar, California, Psychology Today.

Fodor, J. et al. 1974. The psychology of language. New York, McGraw-Hill Book Co.

Fouts, R. S. 1973. Acquisition and testing of gestural signs in four young chimpanzees. Science 180.978-980.

Frankfurter, A. and R. Honeck. 1973. Ear differences in the recall of monaurally presented sentences. Quarterly Journal of Experimental Psychology 25.138-146.

Fry, D. B. 1966. The development of the phonological system in the normal and the deaf child. In: The genesis of language. Edited by F. Smith and G. Miller, 187-206. Cambridge, The MIT Press.

_____. 1974. An auditory theory of speech production. World papers in phonetics, Festschrift for Dr. Onishi's Kiju. 21-36. Tokyo, The Phonetic Society of Japan.

Gardner, R. and B. Gardner. 1969. Teaching sign language to a chimpanzee. Science 165.664-672.

_____. 1971. Two-way communication with an infant chimpanzee. In: Behavior of nonhuman primates. Edited by A. Schrier and F. Stollnitz, 117-184. New York, Academic Press.

Garnica, Olga K. 1973. The development of phonemic speech perception. In: Cognitive development and the acquisition of language. Edited by T. Moore, 215-222. New York, Academic Press.

Gazzaniga, M. 1972. One brain--two minds? American Scientist 60.311-317.

Geschwind, N. 1964. The development of the brain and the evolution of language. MSLL 17.155-169.

Geschwind, N. 1965. Disconnection syndromes in animals and man. Brain 88. 237-94; 585-644.

_____. 1969. Anatomy and the higher functions of the brain. In: Boston studies in the philosophy of science, vol. IV. Edited by R. Cohen and M. Wartofsky, 98-136. Dordrecht-Holland, D. Reidel Publishing Co.

_____. 1970. Intermodal equivalence of stimuli in apes. Science 168. 1249.

_____. 1971. Some differences between human and other primate brains. In: Cognitive processes of nonhuman primates. Edited by L. Jarrard, 149-154. New York, Academic Press.

_____. 1972. Language and the brain. Scientific American 226. 4. 76-83.

_____ and W. Levitsky. 1968. Human brain: Left-right asymmetries in temporal speech area. Science 161. 186-7.

Goodman, Morris. 1974. Biochemical evidence on hominid phylogeny. Annual Review of Anthropology 3. 203-228.

Hardy, James C. 1970. Development of neuromuscular systems underlying speech production. American Speech and Hearing Association Reports 5. 49-68.

Hayes, C. 1951. The ape in our house. New York, Harper.

Herman, S. 1974. The right ear advantage for the processing of linguistic stimuli. Natural Language Studies No. 14. Ann Arbor, Phonetics Laboratory, The University of Michigan.

Hewes, Gordon W. 1973. Primate communication and the gestural origin of language. Current Anthropology 14. 5-24.

Hill, Jane. 1972. On the evolutionary foundations of language. American Anthropologist 74. 308-17.

_____. 1974. Possible continuity theories of language. Language 50. 134-150.

Hockett, C. F. 1960. The origin of speech. Scientific American 203. 89-96.

Hodos, W. In press. The concept of homology and the evolution of behavior. In: Evolution, brain and behavior: Persistent problems. Edited by R. B. Masterton et al. Potomac, Erlbaum Press.

Holloway, Ralph L. 1968. The evolution of the primate brain: Some aspects of quantitative relations. Brain Research 7. 121-172.

_____. 1974. The casts of fossil hominid brains. Scientific American 231. 1. 106-115.

Jakobson, Roman. 1968. Child language, aphasia and phonological universals. The Hague, Mouton.

Jürgens, U. et al. 1967. Vocalization in the squirrel monkey (Saimiri sciureus) elicited by brain stimulation. Experimental brain research 10. 532-554.

Jürgens, U. and D. Ploog. 1970. Cerebral representation of vocalization in the squirrel monkey. Experimental brain research 10.532-554.

Kaada, B. R. 1951. Somato-motor, autonomic and electrocortical responses to electrical stimulation of 'rhinencephalic' and other structures in primates, cat and dog. Acta Physiologica Scandinavica 24: Suppl. 83.

Kappers, C. et al. 1936. The comparative anatomy of the nervous system of vertebrates including man. New York, Hafner Publishing Co.

Kelemen, G. 1948. The anatomical basis of phonation in the chimpanzee. Journal of Morphology 82.229-59.

_____. 1958. Physiology of phonation in primates. Logos 1.32-35.

_____. 1969. Anatomy of the larynx and the anatomical basis of vocal performance. In: The chimpanzee. Edited by G. H. Bourne, 165-186. Baltimore, University Park Press.

Kimura, Doreen. 1973. The asymmetry of the human brain. Scientific American 228.3.70-78.

_____ and Y. Archibald. 1974. Motor functions of the left hemisphere. Brain 97.337-350.

Kinsbourne, Marcel. n.d. Minor hemisphere language and cerebral maturation. Unpublished ms.

_____. 1975. The ontogeny of cerebral dominance. Conference on developmental psycholinguistics and communication disorders. The New York Academy of Sciences.

Konishi, M. 1971. Ethology and neurobiology. American Scientist 59.56-63.

Konorski, Jerzy. 1967. Integrative activity of the brain. Chicago, University of Chicago Press.

Kornfeld, J. R. 1971. Theoretical issues in child phonology. Papers from the 7th Regional Meeting. Chicago Linguistic Society. Chicago, Illinois.

_____ and H. Goehl. 1974. A new twist to an old twist to an old observation: Kids know more than they say. In: Papers from the Parasession on Natural Phonology. Edited by A. Bruck et al., 210-219. Chicago, Chicago Linguistic Society.

Ladefoged, Peter. 1971. Preliminaries to linguistic phonetics. Chicago, University of Chicago Press.

_____ et al. 1972. An auditory-motor theory of speech production. UCLA Working Papers in Phonetics 22.48-75.

Lakoff, G. 1965. On the nature of syntactic irregularity. Published doctoral dissertation. Bloomington, Indiana University.

Lancaster, Jane. 1968. Primate communication systems and the emergence of human language. In: Primates. Edited by Phyllis C. Jay, 439-457. New York, Holt, Rinehart and Winston.

Lawick-Goodall, Jane van. 1968. A preliminary report on expressive movements and communication in the Gombe Stream chimpanzees. In: Primates. Edited by Phyllis C. Jay, 313-374. New York, Holt, Rinehart and Winston.

_____. 1971. In the shadow of man. Boston, Houghton Miflin Co.

LeMay, M. and N. Geschwind. 1975. Hemispheric differences in the brains of great apes. Brain Behav. Evol. 11.48-52.

Lenneberg, Eric. 1967. Biological foundations of language. New York, Wiley and Sons.

_____. 1969. On explaining language. Science 164.635-643.

_____. 1971. Of language knowledge, apes and brains. Journal of Psycholinguistic Research 1.1-29.

Leopold, Werner F. 1947. Speech development of a bilingual child. New York, AMS Press.

Leyton, A. and C. S. Sherrington. 1917. Observations on the excitable cortex of the chimpanzee, orang-utan and gorilla. Quarterly Journal of Experimental Physiology 11.135-222.

Lieberman, P. 1968. Primate vocalizations and human linguistic ability. JASA 44.1574-84.

_____. 1973. On the evolution of language: A unified view. Cognition 2.59-94.

_____. 1975. On the origins of language. New York, MacMillan Publishing Co.

Linden, E. 1974. Apes, men, and language. New York, Saturday Review Press/E. P. Dutton Co.

Luria, A. R. 1970. The functional organization of the brain. Scientific American 222.66-78.

Magoun, H. et al. 1960. The evolution of man's brain. In: The central nervous system behavior. Edited by M. Brazier. The Josiah Macy, Jr. Foundation.

Mattingly, Ignatius G. 1972a. Phonetic prerequisites for first-language acquisition. SR-34.65-69. Haskins Laboratory.

_____. 1972b. Speech cues and sign stimuli. American Scientist 60.327-337.

Mayr, Ernst. 1974. Behavior programs and evolutionary strategies. American Scientist 62.650-59.

Miller, G. 1972. Linguistic communication as a biological process. In: Biology and the human sciences. Edited by J. W. S. Pringle, 70-94. London, Oxford University Press.

Miller, J. M. et al. 1972. Single cell activity in the auditory cortex of rhesus monkeys. Science 177.449-451.

Millikan, C. and F. Darley, eds. 1967. Brain mechanisms underlying speech and language. New York, Grune and Stratton.

Milner, Brenda. 1974. Hemispheric specialization: Scope and limits. The neurosciences, Third study program. Edited by F. Schmitt and F. Worden, 75-89. Cambridge, The MIT Press.

Molfese, Dennis L. 1972. Cerebral asymmetry in infants, children, and adults: Auditory evoked responses to speech and music stimuli. 84th Meeting, Acoustical Society of America. Miami, Florida.

Moscovitch, Morris. 1973. Language and the cerebral hemispheres: Reactiontime studies and their implications for models of cerebral dominance. In: Communication and affect. Edited by P. Pliner et al., 89-126. New York, Academic Press.

Murphey, R. 1973. Genetic correlates of behavior. In: Perspectives on animal behavior. Edited by G. Bevmont, 72-101. Glenview, Scott, Foresman and Company.

Negus, V. E. 1949. The comparative anatomy and physiology of the larynx. New York, Hafner Publishing Co.

Nottebohm, F. 1970. Ontogeny of bird song. Science 167.950-956.

_____. n. d. A zoologist's view of some language phenomena with particular emphasis on vocal learning. Unpublished ms.

Olney, Rachel L. 1974. Discrimination of babbling: Tests of the prelinguistic, universal content of infant vocalization. Unpublished master's thesis. College Park, University of Maryland.

Osgood, C. 1953. Method and theory in experimental psychology. New York, Oxford University Press.

Parsegian, V. L. 1973. This cybernetic world of men, machines, and earth systems. New York, Doubleday and Co.

Passingham, R. E. 1973. Anatomical differences between the neo-cortex of man and other primates. Brain, behavior, and evolution. 7.337-59.

Penfield, W. and T. Rasmussen. 1952. The cerebral cortex of man. New York, The Macmillan Co.

_____ and L. Roberts. 1959. Speech and brain-mechanisms. Princeton, Princeton University Press.

_____ and K. Welch. 1951. The supplementary motor area of the cerebral cortex. A clinical and experimental study. Archives of Neurology and Psychiatry 66.289-317.

Pierce, Joe. 1974. A study of 750 Portland, Oregon children during the first year. Papers and Reports on Child Language Development 8.19-25. Stanford University.

Ploog, Detlev. 1969. Early communication processes in squirrel monkeys. In: Brain and early behavior. Edited by R. J. Robinson, 269-98. New York, Academic Press.

_____. 1970. Social communication among animals. In: The neurosciences, Second study program. Edited by F. Schmitt, 349-360. New York, The Rockefeller University Press.

_____ and T. Melnechuk. 1969. Primate communication. NRP Bulletin 7(5). 419-510.

Port, D. and M. S. Preston. 1972. Early apical stop production: A voice onset time analysis. SR-29/30. 125-149. Haskins Laboratory.

Premack, D. 1971. Language in chimpanzee? Science 172. 808-822.

Robinson, Bryan W. 1967a. Vocalization evoked from forebrain in Macaca mulatta. Physiology and Behavior 2. 345-54.

_____. 1967b. Neurological aspects of evoked vocalizations. In: Social communication among primates. Edited by S. A. Altmann, 135-147. Chicago, Chicago University Press.

_____. 1972. Anatomical and physiological contrasts between human and other primate vocalizations. In: Perspectives on human evolution 2. Edited by S. L. Washburn and P. Dolhinov, 438-443. New York, Holt, Rinehart and Winston.

Robinson, R. J. 1969. Cerebral hemisphere function in the newborn. In: Brain and early behavior. Edited by R. J. Robinson, 343-349. New York, Academic Press.

Rose, Steven. 1972. Environmental effects on brain and behavior. In: Race and intelligence. Edited by K. Richardson and D. Spears, 128-146. Baltimore, Penguin Books, Inc.

Rosen, S. I. 1974. Introduction to the primates. Englewood Cliffs, Prentice-Hall, Inc.

Rumbaugh, D. et al. 1974. Lana (Chimpanzee) learning language: A progress report. Brain and Language 1. 205-212.

Sachs, J. 1967. Recognition memory for syntactic and semantic aspects of connected discourse. Perception and Psychophysics 2. 437-42.

Sarnat, H. and M. Netsky. 1974. Evolution of the nervous system. New York, Oxford University Press.

Schaller, G. B. 1963. The mountain gorilla. Chicago, University of Chicago Press.

Schaltenbrand, G. 1975. The effects on speech and language of stereotactical stimulation in thalamus and corpus callosum. Brain and Language 2. 70-77.

Schiefelbusch, R. and L. Lloyd, eds. 1974. Language perspectives-- acquisition, retardation, and intervention. Baltimore, University Park Press.

Schleidt, W. 1973. Ethology. In: Handbook of perception. Edited by E. Carterette and M. Friedman, 119-138. New York, Academic Press.

Schultz, Adolph H. 1969. The life of primates. New York, Universe Books.

Shantha, T. and S. Manocha. 1969. The brain of chimpanzee. In: The chimpanzee, vol. I. Edited by G. H. Bourne, 187-368. Baltimore, University Park Press.

Smith, T. S. 1973. Review: The muscle spindle and neural control of the tongue (Bowman). Journal of Phonetics 1.171-9.

Staats, A. W. and C. K. Staats. 1963. Complex human behavior. New York, Holt, Rinehart and Winston.

Sussman, H. 1972. What the tongue tells the brain? Psychology Bulletin 77.262-272.

Tilney, F. 1928. The brain from ape to man. New York, Paul B. Hoeber.

Toulmin, Stephen. 1971. Brain and language: A commentary. Synthèse 22.369-95.

Van Bergeijk, W. A. 1966. Evolution of the sense of hearing in vertebrates. American Zoologist 6.371-377.

Van Lancker, Diana and V. Fromkin. 1973. Hemispheric specialization for pitch and 'tone': Evidence from Thai. Journal of Phonetics 1.101-109.

Walker, J. and E. Halas. 1972. Neuronal coding at the subcortical auditory nuclei. Physiology and Behavior 8.1099-1106.

Washburn, S. and J. Lancaster. 1971. On evolution and the origin of language. Current Anthropology 12.384-6.

Watt, W. C. 1972. Competing economy criteria. Social Sciences Working Papers 5. Irvine, University of California.

_____. 1974. Review: Behavior of nonhuman primates (Schrier and Stollnitz, eds.) Behavioral Science 19.70-75.

Weir, Ruth. 1962. Language in the crib. The Hague, Mouton.

_____. 1966. Some questions of the child's learning of phonology. In: The genesis of language. Edited by F. Smith and G. Miller, 153-168. Cambridge, The MIT Press.

Whalen, R. E. 1971. The concept of instinct. In: Psychobiology. Edited by James L. McGaugh, 53-72. New York, Academic Press.

Whitaker, H. A. 1971. On the representation of language in the human brain. Edmonton, Linguistic Research, Inc.

_____. 1973. Comments on the innateness of language. In: Some new directions in linguistics. Edited by R. Shuy, 95-120. Washington, D.C., Georgetown University Press.

_____ and O. Selnes. 1974. Broca's area: A problem in language-brain relationships. Unpublished ms.

Yeni-Komshian, G. and D. Benson. 1975. Anatomical study of cerebral asymmetry in humans, chimpanzees and rhesus monkeys. Unpublished Ms.

PSYCHOLOGICALLY REAL GRAMMAR EMERGES BECAUSE OF ITS ROLE IN LANGUAGE ACQUISITION

T. G. BEVER

Columbia University

The revolution in linguistics in 1957 appeared to be a revolution about the theoretical form of grammar; the succeeding decade was filled with arguments against the descriptively inadequate taxonomic models and in favor of such distinctions as the one between deep and surface structure. The preoccupation with proselytization of the descriptive virtues of transformational grammar obscured a separate aspect of the revolution: the proposal that a grammar is a potential model of linguistic knowledge and cannot be bound by any specific set of discovery procedures. This represented a decisive break with the empiricist and behaviorist doctrines that had dominated linguistics for 25 years. It was of profound importance since it elevated linguistic description from the statistical statement of regularities in finite texts and corpora, to a theory of a part of human knowledge. Yet, this aspect of generative grammar was attended to primarily by philosophers and psychologists. Linguists immersed themselves in the technical (and comforting) questions concerning specific formal mechanisms, and ignored questions about the purpose of linguistic investigation. In this way, an intellectual generation of linguistic technicians has been spawned and trained: they understand what to argue about in linguistic description, but do not understand why it is important to argue correctly. 1

It is no revelation to an audience of linguists that the field is in great disarray at the moment. There are as many revisions of transformational grammar as there are self-proclaimed theorists.

Some researchers even question whether the domain of grammar is itself a discrete part of language structure. Arguments and theories slip past each other because of the lack of shared conceptual assumptions about what a grammar is for: we are paralyzed by the frenzied virtuosity of our scholastic momentum, which generates a counterargument for every technical proposal.

I think that the philosophical arguments against the despair of fictionalist and encyclopaedic views of grammar are overwhelming, and I am among those who have defended the rationalist and interactionist position. In the present discussion I shall focus on the psychological role that a grammar plays in language learning, remind you of some direct evidence that children and adults represent linguistic knowledge separate from language behavior, and propose a model for the notion of a 'critical' period for second language learning. The essentials of my argument parallel a marxist-structuralist interpretation of the persistence of the state after the conditions that formed it are removed. That interpretation runs like this:

(1) A. The state emerges as the vehicle to regulate conflict between classes as they emerge in economic behavior.
   B. If class conflicts are removed or the classes are separated, the state should wither away.
   C. If it does not, it can be because of the entrenchment of the bureaucracy that has developed--the regulatory functions of the state persist even when they are no longer needed.

I wish to apply this kind of argument of the notion of a 'psychogrammar'. A psychogrammar is (by hypothesis and definition) the psychologically internalized representation of linguistic structure. In this sense a psychogrammar can be distinguished from a grammar. A grammar describes what a language is. The psychogrammar describes an internalized representation of the grammar that is a model of neither speech perception nor production, but a representation, in part, of what those skills imply. It may turn out that the psychogrammar is strongly equivalent with current grammars: I set up the concept for this discussion to avoid claiming 'psychological reality' for any particular linguistic grammar. Rather, I wish to explore the implications of the claim that some psychogrammar exists.

The basic question is: when does the child acquire the psychogrammar? A common view of language learning suggests that the psychogrammar is acquired at a relatively late age--around five years. On this interpretation, the younger child has no 'need' for a grammar. It communicates by using primitive, but effective, habits of comprehension and talking. Since the adult environment is highly tolerant of mistakes and ungrammatical utterances, a grammar is not required. Around age five years, the child cannot refrain from using its abstracting capacities to construct a psychogrammar that represents what is shared between speech production and perception. It is useful in refining our linguistic capacities and simplifying the storage of linguistic knowledge. On this view, psychogrammar is one of the responsibilities of growing up and one of the joys of maturity. [2]

It is the hypothesis of the present discussion that this view is exactly wrong. Rather, the reason that a psychogrammar exists is because of the vital role it plays during language acquisition, much of which occurs during the first five years of life. The psychogrammar is needed during that period to mediate between the systems of speech production and perception. It is the internal translator that regulates conflicting capacities which arise as each of the two systems of speech behavior develop separately: if one system gets ahead of the other, the psychogrammar can equilibrate their capacities. The parallel between this and the description of the evolution and persistence of the state should be clear.

(2) A. The psychogrammar emerges as the vehicle to regulate conflicts between the capacity of language systems as they emerge in speech behavior.

B. If such conflicts are successfully equilibrated (as they are by age 12), then the psychogrammar should wither away.

C. If it does not, it can be because of the entrenchment of the mental system of the psychogrammar that has developed--the regulatory functions of the psychogrammar persist even when they are no longer needed.

Accordingly, the psychogrammar is not a joy of adulthood, but a burden, an adventitious relic left from a dozen years of language learning. Like the state, it does not disappear after its usefulness has passed, because it is so entrenched as a mental system: the psychogrammar is the bureaucracy of linguistic life. In the next few pages I outline the evidence demonstrating this, and attempt to explain why it should be.

Adult speech perception and production

The fundamental mental activity in using speech is to relate inchoate ideas with explicit utterances. The direction of this mapping characterizes the difference between speech production

and perception. The main question is whether the two systems are
the same one, running in opposite directions, or whether they use
different processes and are independently represented in behavior.

(3)

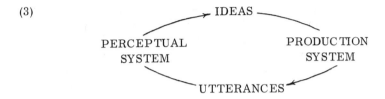

There are three kinds of considerations supporting the view that these
two systems can operate independently of each other: the needs of the
speaker are opposite to those of the listener; preliminary experiments
suggest the systems use different kinds of behavioral processes; there
are empirical examples of sentences that are unusable productively
but not perceptually, and vice versa.

Consider first the conflicting needs of the speaker and listener.
The listener optimally requires that the internal grammatical and
semantic relations be explicitly marked in the surface sequence.
This would make the perception of the sentence homonymous with
the recognition of the surface elements--no further processing would
be necessary. The needs of the speaker are the converse of explicit-
ness: the optimal situation for the speaker would be one in which
each utterance could consist of a single monosyllabic grunt, which
the listener would always interpret correctly.

Actual utterances clearly strike a balance between these two ex-
tremes. It would be a mistake to draw direct conclusions about the
nature of the psychogrammar from the behavioral balance between
speech perception and production. However, the conflicting constraints on optimal utterances do suggest that the behavioral systems
themselves could differ internally. This possibility is supported by
the current empirically based theories of perception and production.
The data on these systems are unfortunately meagre (less than a
hundred published studies). However, the most salient difference
between perception and production is that the major planning unit
differs: for the speaker it is something close to the 'surface structure clause', while for the listener it is something close to the 'deep
structure sentoid'. The reason for this is not obscure: the speaker's
problem is to find a mapping of a given, unconscious idea (relatively
close in form to a deep sentoid) onto a compact but comprehensible
explicit surface sequence. The listener's problem is to discover the
underlying sentoids intrinsic to each utterance. [3]

Thus, the different goals of speaker and listener lead to different
organization of the mapping process. It follows from this difference

that psychological processes of production and perception must differ, at least in part. That is, it is not the case that for every process of speech production there corresponds an isolable process of speech perception that is its inverse. It remains to be seen how much the two systems differ: even our current rudimentary knowledge indicates that there are some differences. That is, the systems are independent, at least in part.

Finally, we can isolate in our everyday speech behavior examples of sentences that we can understand but could not say ourselves, and sentences we can say but could not understand if somebody else said them. This, too, is prima facie empirical evidence supporting the behavioral distinctness of the two systems. Sentences that others say that we do not understand are all too common, and need no examples. But, by the same token, sentences that we utter that others do not understand are equally common. While this in itself does not prove that the systems are independent entities, it does show that running the idea-utterance mapping in one direction is not behaviorally equivalent to running it in the opposite direction.

These three kinds of arguments, general, technical, and anecdotal, support the claim that the systems of speech perception and production are independent entities in the adult mind. We understand utterances using one system, and speak using the other. This raises the question of the motivation to postulate a psychogrammar as part of the mental representation of language. There are already two systems for pairing ideas and utterances which combine to provide bidirectional mappings. Why, then, do we postulate a psychogrammar as a separate mental entity?

The psychogrammar and speech behavioral systems

There are three sorts of considerations supporting the distinction between a psychogrammar and the systems of speech behavior: it renders the distinction between linguistic knowledge and behavior; it combines with other linguistic systems to explain a variety of facts about linguistic intentions; there are critical examples of sequences that are intuitively well-formed but unusable, and vice versa.

Consider first the role of the psychogrammar in defining linguistic knowledge. The distinction between linguistic knowledge and language behavior arises initially out of the logical possibility that there is a distinction between what we 'know' and what we 'do'. At first such a distinction may seem obscurantist, especially to the empiricist. However, the postulation of this distinction is by no means unique to a 'higher' abstract function like language. Rather, some of the most basic areas of psychological research find it necessary to postulate this distinction. For example, consider the T-illusion in which we 'know' that the horizontal and vertical lines are equal in length, but we can 'behave' as though the vertical line were longer (this extends both to the perceptual judgment and to the production of a drawing of the lines). Indeed, it is characteristic of illusions that they involve this kind of contrast, and it is for this very reason that the study of illusions has been central to psychology.

We may take the position, as does Piaget, that the distinction is between two kinds of knowledge ('operative' and 'figurative').[4] Or, like others, one could argue that the two ways of observing illusions are really due to two kinds of behavior (e.g. 'measuring' vs. 'estimating'). Whichever view one holds, the fact remains that the distinction is maintained, and that both ways of dealing with the stimulus are assumed to be psychologically real.

This in itself does not prove that there is such a distinction in the case of language. It does, however, establish a precedent in one of the most fundamental areas of psychological study: the postulated distinction is not unique to research in language. If one turns to this research one finds two kinds of empirical arguments supporting the claim that there are two kinds of representations of language--the behavioral systems governing speech behavior and the psychogrammatical representation of linguistic knowledge.

The first is a technical argument resting on the fact that assuming the existence of a psychogrammar allows us to explain a variety of facts about linguistic intuitions and aspects of language. It allows us to investigate and sometimes to answer which kinds of language universals are due to psychogrammatical constraints and which are due to other systems of speech behavior. Essentially, this argument is the claim that if one assumes a distinction between 'competence' and 'performance' (rendering the distinction between linguistic knowledge and language behavior), one can explain a variety of facts about language.

I think that the achievements of this approach have been prodigous and justify the distinction in themselves. I freely grant, however, that such an argument smacks of methodological sermonizing; the indirectness of the argument lacks full convincing power. A more direct argument for the distinction between a psychogrammar and speech behavior systems is the existence of empirical evidence that the two kinds of mental structures are independent. The crucial data are sequences which are intuitively well-formed but unusable, and sequences which are usable but intuitively ill-formed. These cases illustrate that behavioral usability and intuitive well-formedness do not overlap completely, showing that each is accounted for by (at least partially) independent mental representations.

The significance of sentences that are unusable but intuitively well-formed has long been recognized. A classic example of this is a center-embedded sentence such as (4).

(4)   The dog the cat the cricket chirped at miowed at barked at.

Upon ratiocination one can appreciate the fact that such sentences are a combination of singly embedded ones like (5) and (6).

(5)   The dog the cat miowed at barked at me.
(6)   The cat the cricket chirped at miowed at the dog.

Thus (4) seems intuitively well-formed, but is obviously unusable. Furthermore, the fact that (4) is well-formed is demonstrated by the fact that a structurally identical sentence like (7) is completely usable.

(7)   The reporter everyone I met trusts had predicted Thieu's resignation.

Something about (4) (perhaps the homogeneity of the nounphrases and verbphrases) is impossible for the behavioral systems to manage. Such cases show that the domain of structural well-formedness can exceed that of behavioral usability.
    A separate set of cases shows that the domain of usability can exceed that of well-formedness. Consider the cases below, which are all taken from actual observations.

(8)   That's the first time anybody ever sang to me like that before.
(9)   I really liked flying in an airplane that I understand how it works.
(10) Everyone forgot their coat.
(11) Either you or I is crazy.

Each example is perfectly usable, perfectly utterable, and comprehensible. But each is also intuitively ill-formed. This intuition can be backed up by showing that there are structurally identical sequences, differing only in a critical word, that are completely unusable (or at least would not be used) e.g. (12)-(15). This demonstrates that the original intuition of structural oddness was correct, but that specific properties of (8)-(11) make them usable.

(12) *That's the second time anybody ever sang to me like that before.
(13) *I really liked flying in an airplane which I understand how it works.
(14) *Harry forgot their coat.
(15) *Both you and I is crazy.

These three arguments--general, methodological, and empirical-- support the claim that the psychogrammar and the systems of speech behavior are independent in the adult mind. That is, the schematic outline of the representation of language is like that in (16), not (3).

(16)

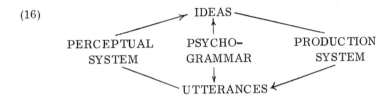

As adults, we have two separate ways of mapping ideas and utterances, through the psychogrammar, or through the conjunct of the systems of speech production and perceptions. Clearly the psychogrammar exists in the adult, and yet clearly it is redundant for language be havior. Why do we have it?

The psychogrammar in language learning

The answer lies in the language-learning child. A child is acquiring two fundamental language abilities, the ability to talk and the ability to understand--that is, the child is acquiring a system of speech production and perception. Since these systems are behaviorally independent in the adult, we might expect them to be learned independently in the child: on this view the role of the psychogrammar is to translate internally between the systems of production and perception, and thereby to build up a representation of what is implied by their conjoint operation. That is, the schema for the language-learning child is like that in (17), rather than (16).

(17)

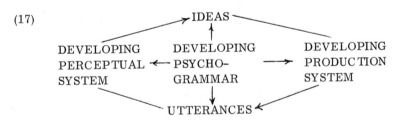

There are three kinds of arguments supporting this view of language acquisition. The psychogrammar provides the behavioral systems with an otherwise unavailable specification of linguistic universals and behavior-free record of what has been learned so far; there is evidence suggesting that the systems of speech perception and production are learned separately, thus requiring the psychogrammar to bring their capacities into alignment; anecdotal data suggest that young children are aware of the disparity between the way they talk and the way they think they ought to.

The first argument is primarily in the form of a formal justification of why the scheme outlined in (17) must be true of the language-learning child. The emerging psychogrammar serves two functions. First, it provides the emerging behavioral systems with an input vocabulary (e.g. 'noun, distinctive feature, tree structure') which gives the behavioral systems a common set of objects to work with. The richness of the initial vocabulary is an open, hopefully empirical, question. Whatever the answer, there must be some initial internal language common to the systems of perception and production. Otherwise, they might never map the same kind of structures for the same kind of idea-utterance pairs.

A second role for the emerging psychogrammar is to record and simplify the amount of memorized material. Very early in language learning each new utterance can be memorized; but as the number increases, the load on memory can be eased by the application of a grammatical organization (given that humans are predisposed to learn grammars at all). Accordingly, the grammar can become a repository for accumulated perceptual and production patterns applying its own organizational reductions to them.

It should be clear from these two proposed functions of the psychogrammar that I am suggesting that it develops in part because of its functional role in equilibrating the independently developing systems of speech perception and production. The heart of the problem is this. If a child learns to understand a new construction (however such 'learning' occurs) how does this become transported to the production system? Conversely, if the child tries out a new speech production process (based on the schemata acquired thus far) and decides it is successful, how does that new knowledge become transported to the perceptual system? It is the role of the psychogrammar to maintain the perceptual and production capacities similar to one another.

Crucial evidence on this point is the fact that the perceptual and production systems develop separately and with different capacities: thus we have initial evidence that what the child says and understands can differ during language acquisition. For example, at around age three the (English-speaking) child shifts its perceptual strategies so that the first noun in a clause is regularly interpreted as the actor. (Earlier in life it was any noun immediately before the first verb.) This shift in a perceptual process is not accompanied by any marked change in what the child utters--indeed, that particular strategy characterizes the speech production pattern of the much younger child. [5]

Considerably further study is needed to demonstrate that the perceptual and production capacities leap-frog one another during development. In particular, there are very few children who have been longitudinally followed with systematic investigation of both speech production and perception. Nevertheless, the preliminary evidence suggests that these systems do develop separately, thus requiring some internal mechanism to equilibrate them; by hypothesis that mechanism is the emerging psychogrammar.

The final argument supporting the schema in (17) is anecdotal evidence that children themselves are aware of the distinction between their own language behavior and what they 'ought' to say. Consider the following true anecdote. It shows that the child says an incorrect form (goed) that it recognizes to be 'wrong'.

(18)   Child: Mommy goed to the store.
       Father: Mommy goed to the store?
       Child: No, Daddy; I say it that way, not you!
       Father: Mommy wented to the store?
       Child: No!
       Father: Mommy went to the store.
       Child: That's right, Mommy wen . . . Mommy goed
              to the store.

Since it cannot produce the right form (at this stage) and understands both correct and incorrect forms, where does the child 'represent' the distinction between the 'right' and the 'wrong' way to say it? A psychogrammar would be the repository of such knowledge. Such anecdotes are common enough to lend initial plausibility to this interpretation (the same child was involved in a similar discussion of the utterance 'mazagine'), but obviously require further study.

These three arguments support the claim that the psychogrammar exists as a mediator between the emerging systems of language behavior: it provides linguistic universals and records accumulated linguistic knowledge; it equilibrates the systems of speech perception and production as they leapfrog one another; and it accounts for the anecdotal evidence that even the young child is aware of the distinction between linguistic knowledge and behavior.

In brief, the psychogrammar serves the function of being the mental 'language' in which the speech perception system and the speech production system communicate: it provides a mental vehicle for translating a perceptual schema into a production capacity with the net inverse effect, and vice versa; when a new perceptual schema is learned, the psychogrammar essentially is a transducer which can translate from one domain of the child's capacity to another. In that sense, it regulates the conflicts between those two separable emerging capacities. The psychogrammar is the bureaucratic manager of the child's acquisition of language abilities. By the time we are adults the systems of perception and production are in almost complete register: we no longer need the psychogrammar to serve the function of an internal mental language. But by that time it has become thoroughly entrenched as an independent representation of the mapping between ideas and utterances. Like the systems of perception and production, its internal structure leads to slightly differing mappings, although they are without consequences for adult behavior.

Decoupling of systems and the critical period for second language learning

Before closing, I wish to point out the implication of this view of first-language learning for a 'critical period' in second language learning. Suppose that the developed systems of speech perception and production become functionally autonomous in the adult. That is, suppose the schema appropriate to the adult representation of language is that outlined in (16); on this view the psychogrammar and the behavioral systems have decoupled (by age 15 years). Learning a language after this point may well be possible, but it now will proceed in a manner fundamentally different from that at a younger age. The problem now is to map each of the distinct first-language behavioral systems onto the corresponding systems in the second language in partial independence of each other. This is not only likely to make the job of learning a language more difficult; it will certainly make it more disjointed.

There is little research on second language learning that would bear on this interpretation of second-language learning after age 15. We have found some evidence suggesting that the acquisition pattern of perceptual capacities is the same in 7-year-old children learning English as a second language as it is in 2- to 4-year-old children learning English as a first language. But the pattern differs dramatically in 15-20-year-old people learning English as a second language. It is not a disorderly development pattern at this age, but it is different. [6]

Conclusion

I have sketched an argument about the role of a psychogrammar which draws on a rationalist view about the nature of knowledge and behavior. The general view is that the mind is composed of partially distinct systems which interact with each other, relying in part on internal languages to translate from one capacity to another and to regulate differences in internal capacities that bear on the same class of external behaviors.[7] A psychogrammar is an example of such an internal communication and regulating system. It regulates the relations between the emerging system of speech perception and the emerging system of speech production. Children need the psychogrammar for this purpose and they need to elaborate it as the other systems become more complex. Adults do not need it anymore, but we are stuck with it. It simply refuses to wither away.

NOTES

1. A discussion of these issues is found in J. Katz and T. Bever, 'The Fall and Rise of Empiricism.' This is to appear in: T. Bever, J. Katz, and D. T. Langendoen, An Integrated Theory of Linguistic Ability, T. Y. Croll Press (in press).

2. This point of view is implicit and explicit in a number of writers. To avoid blaming others I cite only myself: T. Bever, 'Associations to Stimulus-Response Theories of Language.' Verbal Behavior and General Behavior Theory, T. R. Dixon and D. L. Horton, eds., Prentice-Hall, Inc., 1968.

3. For reviews of the literature on speech perception and production see J. Fodor, T. Bever, and M. Garrett, The Psychology of Language, McGraw Hill, 1974, Chapters 6 and 7. See also T. Bever, J. Carroll, and R. Hurtig, 'Speech Production, Perception, and the Formalization of Linguistic Analogy.' This is to appear in T. Bever, J. Katz, and D. T. Langendoen, An Integrated Theory of Linguistic Ability, T. Y. Croll Press (in press).

4. See his The Mechanisms of Perception. London, Routledge and Kegan Paul, 1969.

5. See T. Bever, 'The Integrated Study of Language.' In: J. Morton, ed., Biological and Social Perspectives in Language, Logos Press, 1970, 158-206. These findings have been replicated by M. P. Maratsos, 'Children Who Get Worse at Understanding the Passive: A Replication of Bever.' Journal of Psycholinguistic Research, in press, and S. G. DeVillieurs and P. A. DeVillieurs, 'Development of the Use of Word Order in Comprehension.' Journal of Psycholinguistic Research, in press.

6. See T. Bever, P. Denton, E. Nam, and J. Shallo, 'Second Language Learning and Perception' (in preparation), for a discussion of this.

7. For discussions of this point of view see T. Bever, J. Katz, and D. T. Langendoen, An Integrated Theory of Linguistic Ability, T. Y. Croll Press (in press); T. Bever, 'The Psychology of Language and Structuralist Investigations of Nativism.' In: Gilbert Harman, ed., On Noam Chomsky: Critical Essays, Anchor Press, 1974, 146-164; and T. Bever, 'Some Theoretical and Empirical Issues that

Arise if We Insist on Distinguishing Language and Thought.' This is to appear in D. Aaronson and R. Rieber, eds., <u>Proceedings of the New York Academy of Science Conference on Psycholinguistics, January, 1975.</u>

KNOWLEDGE, CONTEXT, AND STRATEGY IN THE ACQUISITION OF MEANING

EVE CLARK

Stanford University

0. Imagine the following scene: you are a walker crossing a moor up on the West Coast of Scotland, and suddenly you come upon two men talking to each other in a completely strange language. As you come up to them, one of them points towards the north and says to the other: 'Tha ceithir coin aig a'chìobair'. You look to see what he might have been pointing at although you have no idea what he said, and you can see heather, a clump of birches, a cairn, a man with dogs, and a distant glimpse of a road across the moor. Because you are on the West Coast, you might guess the men were speaking Gaelic, but without further clues you have no way of working out what the man actually said. Was he talking about the heather, about the birch trees, about the cairn, the man with some dogs, or none of these?[1]

This situation is, in many respects, analogous to what the young child faces when he begins to learn his first language. He has to work on the mapping problem--the problem of what relation the stream of sound bears to the world around him. Unlike the walker who already speaks a language, the child starts from scratch. He has to segment sound sequences, identify some as the same, and then work out how they are related to the situation around him and to each other. This, of course, sounds much simpler than it is. But the child does not really begin from nothing at all. When he starts on the mapping problem, he already 'knows' a good deal.

What does the child know? He does not begin to use recognizable words until he is a year or a year-and-a-half old. The time before this, though, is not spent idly. He has been gathering a large amount of nonlinguistic knowledge about his environment. He can identify

77

different objects, their properties (e.g. shape, size, texture), their
usual orientation, their customary or possible relations to each other
in space, and so on. He is also setting up primitive notions of causal-
ity and learning to relate events in time, e.g. the customary sequence
in his everyday routines. In general, the young child's knowledge is
rather limited but then his environment is much more restricted than
the adult's. He gathers his information through his perceptual system,
taking in what he can see, hear, smell, taste, touch, and manipulate
as he matures during his first year (e.g. E. Clark 1974a). It is his
organization of this nonlinguistic knowledge that seems to provide the
child with his first hypotheses about what words might mean.

When the child learns what words mean in his first language, he
has to work out the mapping between language and his nonlinguistic
knowledge. More specifically, the child has to find out when a word
can be used to pick out a particular object or property or relationship. The use of words to pick out objects or relations is agreed
upon by convention among the speakers of a particular language. The
convention of using a particular word, though, can be further analyzed
into a set of conditions for application.[2] For example, one could list
the conditions that would have to be met in the extralinguistic setting
or in the speaker's mind in order to use the word crocus appropriately. The conditions for application might involve meeting specified
conditions on shape, relative size, texture, and so on; these properties would probably be interdependent to some degree, although some
may be more important (more salient) than others in different contexts. As long as a sufficient number of the conditions for application
was met, the speaker could use the word crocus and be reasonably
sure that his addressee would pick out the same object.

The conditions of application for a word are at the heart of the
mapping problem for the young child. He has to work out precisely
what the conditions are for each word he acquires and this process
may take quite a long time. To begin with, he may only identify a
few of the necessary conditions (E. Clark 1973a). To take a very
simple example, let's suppose the child has started to use the word
chair. He uses it, appropriately enough, for pieces of furniture that
have a flat, horizontal supporting surface and a back. But then the
child might also apply the word chair to tables and desks. This would
suggest that the only condition the child has worked out at this stage is
that there has to be a flat supporting surface. A further condition of
application for the word chair is that the object designated have a back.
Once the child realizes that this condition must also be met for the
word chair to be applied, then he will stop using chair for tables and
desks. The acquisition of meaning consists of learning which conditions have to be met and what they are (E. Clark 1973a).

Finally, the child probably uses only part of what he knows a priori about objects and relations in working out the conditions of application for different words. As adults, we are all aware that we know much more about chairs, say, than the word <u>chair</u> alone conveys. (From the communicative point of view, the word <u>chair</u> helps the addressee to come to some understanding of what the speaker intended by his use of <u>chair</u> in a particular utterance.) For the child, one aspect of the mapping problem is learning which knowledge is relevant to the meanings of words, in that it is used in the conditions of application.

This preamble is simply intended to set out a general point of view on the acquisition of meaning. I am assuming throughout that meaning inheres in our knowledge about the conventions for the use of language rather than in the words themselves. At the same time, conditions of application can often be presented in a shorthand form as the components of meaning that make up lexical entries for words. When I use terms like features or components of meaning, they should be interpreted as conditions of application.

In 1971, I presented a preliminary proposal about the child's acquisition of semantics in his first language (E. Clark 1973a). Since then, we have found out some more about the acquisition process and have also seen new questions raised. In this paper, I want to take up five issues connected with children's knowledge about meaning. For each one, I shall examine some of the consequences for a general theory about the acquisition of meaning. The issues are: (1) what the child's first words mean, especially his overextensions; (2) what kind of nonlinguistic knowledge the child uses as the basis for his first word meanings; (3) how one decides whether the child has acquired the full meaning of a word or still has only a partial meaning for it; (4) whether all children go through the same sequence of stages, using the same strategies in the course of acquisition, or whether there are alternative routes to adult-like knowledge about meanings; and lastly, (5) what happens to the child's nonlinguistic strategies when they are 'replaced' by semantic knowledge.

1. The child's first meanings: Overextensions revisited. Many observational studies have reported that young children commonly 'overextend' some of the words they use when they begin to talk. For example, many children have been observed overextending a word like <u>doggie</u> to include not only dogs but also horses, cows, sheep, and a variety of other animals. Or they might overextend the word <u>ball</u> to include oranges and doorknobs as well as balls. These are typical examples of the overextensions described in the diary literature for children between 1;0 and 2;6 years (E. Clark 1973a, 1974a).

What do balls, oranges, and doorknobs have in common? Well, they are all round and relatively small. In fact, when one looks closely at the objects the child of this age groups under the same name, one can pick out the properties they have in common. This makes it possible to divide overextensions into several classes depending on what the primary basis for the overextension seemed to be. The largest class involves reliance on some property of shape; other overextensions seem to be based primarily on properties of movement, size, sound, texture, taste, and function (E. Clark 1973a).

When the child uses a word and overextends it, he appears to do so because he has identified only some of the adult conditions of application for that word. Returning to the examples given before, one could say that for the young child, the meaning of doggie is only something like 'four-legged', possibly in combination with certain properties of movement and texture. In other words, the child has picked out only a few of the properties normally required by the adult conditions of application for the word doggie. One can infer that this is the meaning for the child by looking at the properties held in common by all the objects included by the child in the domain of doggie.

This was the view of overextensions that I originally presented in 1971 (E. Clark 1973a). It assumed that the child's overextensions are full 'overextensions'. That is, the child is using whatever criterial properties he has picked out, and only those, whenever he 'overextends' a word. Moreover, those properties form the only conditions of application attached to that word: they constitute its meaning for the child. This approach should probably be modified, however, to include the possibility that some or even most of the child's overextensions may be 'partial overextensions'. In such instances, the child might pick out only some of the criterial properties he has identified with the meaning of a word when he overextends it.[3] Furthermore, the particular properties picked out might vary with context. Whether the child is using full or partial overextensions, one could infer that the meaning of the word, for the child, includes at least those properties--as conditions of application--that are held in common by all the objects to which the child overextends a particular word (E. Clark 1973a, 1974a; Labov and Labov 1974).

The inferences about the child's meanings for the words he overextends are all based on the child's spontaneous production of those words. Does the child also overextend in comprehension? Comprehension, and not production, after all, is usually taken to be a better guide to what the child thinks a word means. It is possible that the child might overextend in production, but not in comprehension, simply because of the limited nature of his vocabulary. He wants to pick out some object for his addressee and uses the best word available in his small repertoire. Most of his overextensions, then, could well be partial overextensions. In comprehension, the child does not have to come up with the word necessary: it is provided by the (adult) speaker. The distinction between production and comprehension here is analogous to the distinction between production and perception in phonological development. Many children can perceive the difference between [s] and [š], say, even when they cannot produce this difference themselves (see Smith 1973). With overextensions, it seems reasonable to expect more of them in production than in comprehension. In addition, given the child's small vocabulary, most overextensions may turn out to be partial overextensions.

Huttenlocher (1974) suggested that one could look at how the child understands words he overextends by giving him pictures of the adult referent of a word (a dog, say) together with something to which he overextends (e.g. a horse) with the request 'Show me the dog'. The child's pattern of choices should then show whether he realizes that dog really refers to dogs rather than to horses. This technique should produce different patterns of choice, depending on whether the child is using full or partial overextensions in his spontaneous speech, or whether he even uses a mixture of the two. For example, if when presented with pictures of a horse and a dog and asked for the dog, the child's choices are distributed 50-50, it would be evident that the child just might be using a full overextension in the case of dog. The only meaning attached to the word involves those conditions of application held in common by the set of dogs and horses. However, if the child's choices showed a greater, or even exclusive, preference for the adult referent, one would have evidence for a partial overextension on the child's part.

A few data bearing indirectly on this issue are available from a study by Labov and Labov (1974). They examined one child's overextensions of the word cat (one of only two words in her repertoire) and identified a core set of features. Animals that fitted any or all these core features were called cat, but the child seemed more confident in her use of the word, the more of the core features there were. Other animals that met only one or two of the criterial conditions were named with some hesitation. Animals that met none of the criteria were never named cat. Although Labov and Labov did no comprehension tests, their meticulous observations suggest that this child's overextensions of cat are partial overextensions. There is similar evidence for partial overextension in some of the diary-study observations where the child appeared to switch from an overextension based on motion, say, to one based on texture (E. Clark 1973a). In this example, both motion and texture must have been core features.

More recently, Thomson and Chapman (1975) have begun to investigate five children's comprehension of those words they overextend in production. Using a technique similar to that suggested by Huttenlocher (1974), they have found that there seems to be a continuum in comprehension. One child never overextended the words in comprehension; three overextended some words and not others; and one overextended all the words overextended in production. These preliminary data provide support for the notion that many overextensions in production are partial overextensions (witness those words not overextended in comprehension). However, it is still not known exactly what the relationship is between the child's production of overextensions and his comprehension of them. The precise patterns of usage during acquisition need much more research before one can come to any firm conclusions.

Whatever the nature of the eventual findings for comprehension versus production, it is still the case that with the entry of new words into the child's repertoire, other words become displaced. For example, the child might start off by applying doggie to a variety of different animals. But once he acquires the words horse and sheep, the word dog is displaced; its domain of application is narrowed by the presence of the other animal words. This displacement is most visible for words formerly overextended. Secondly, the words in the child's vocabulary at this stage tend to have fewer conditions of application attached to their use than the adult equivalents. This is because the mapping between words and nonlinguistic knowledge is still incomplete, and the child's knowledge about the conditions of application for many words is still very limited.

2. Form and function in early word meanings.[4] I have already pointed out that most of the overextensions reported in the speech of young children can be classified according to the type of property that seems to provide the primary basis for overextension. Children seem to rely most heavily on properties of shape (E. Clark 1973a, 1974a, b), as shown in the typical examples given in Table 1. Their other overextensions seem to be based primarily on movement, size, sound, and texture, with a few based on taste. Some examples are listed in Table 2. Lastly, there were a few overextensions that seemed to be based on the action involved in achieving a change of state. For example, one child used our [=open] when at his father's door, of a piece of fruit, of a box, of a pea-pod, and also when asking for his shoes to be undone. Another child used atta [=allgone] first for all departures, then when opening or closing doors, raising a box-lid, and finally, for any disappearance of an object from sight. These action-based overextensions appear to be functional in nature.

The dictionary definition of function is 'The natural or proper action for which a person, office, mechanism or organ is fitted or employed' (American Heritage Dictionary, 1970). If knowledge of

TABLE 1. Some overextensions based primarily on shape.

Lexical item	First referent	Domain of application*
mooi	moon	cakes, round marks on windows, writing on windows and in books, round shapes in books, tooling on leather book covers, round postmarks, letter 'O'
nénin	breast, food	button on garment, point of bare elbow, eye in portrait, face of person in portrait, face of person in photo
buti	ball	toy, radish, stone spheres at park entrance
ticktock	watch	clocks, all clocks and watches, gasmeter, firehose wound on spool, bathscale with round dial
gumene	coat button	collar stud, door-handle, lightswitch, anything small and round
baw	ball	apples, grapes, eggs, squash, bellclapper, anything round
kotibaiz	bars of cot	large toy abacus, toast rack with parallel bars, picture of building with columned façade
tee	stick	cane, umbrella, ruler, (old-fashioned) razor, board of wood, all stick-like objects
kutija	cardboard box	matchbox, drawer, bedside table
mum	horse	cow, calf, pig, moose, all four-legged animals

*Words were overextended to other objects in the order listed.
[Based in part on Clark 1973a]

TABLE 2. Some overextensions based primarily on movement, size, sound, and texture.

Lexical item	First referent	Domain of application*
sch	sound of train	all moving machines
ass	toy goat with rough hide, on wheels	things that move [e.g. animals, sister, wagon], all things that move, all things with a rough surface
fly	fly	specks of dirt, dust, all small insects, child's own toes, crumbs of bread, a toad
em	worm	flies, ants, all small insects, heads of timothy grass
bébé	baby [self]	other babies, all small statues, figures in small pictures and prints
fafer	sound of trains	steaming coffee pot, anything that hissed or made a noise
sizo	scissors	all metal objects
bow wow	dog	toy dog, fur piece with animal head, other fur-pieces without heads
wau-wau	dog	all animals, toy dog, soft house-slippers, picture of old man dressed in furs
va	white plush dog	muffler, cat, father's fur coat

*Words were overextended to other objects in the order listed.
[Based in part on Clark 1973a]

function plays a role in some overextensions (e.g. with open or all-gone), might not it play a more general role in explaining the basis for overextensions in general? Obviously, some of the child's a priori knowledge about objects is functional in nature--he knows what chairs are for, he knows which way up a cup goes, and so on. Dewey (1894), in fact, argued for an extreme functional view to explain overextension. He gave as an example a child who overextended the word ball to the moon, and argued that the child only did so because he knew that if the moon were within reach, he would be able to throw it like a ball. But what if two objects referred to by the same word have different functions, both of which are known to the child? For example, some children are reported to overextend ball to radishes, others overextend it to light-switches. Since one eats radishes, it would seem that that knowledge might well take priority over the possibility of throwing them. Light-switches are clearly fixed to the wall, and the child's knowledge of function seems more likely to be connected with using the switch to turn lights on and off. The functions of balls, radishes, and light-switches, then, are fairly disparate, but all three objects, of course, do have much the same round shape. Dewey's argument raises another more important question: Can all objects be said to have a function for the child at this stage? The child could certainly be using some knowledge of function when using a word like cup for various containers, or chair for certain supporting surfaces. However, it immediately becomes unclear what function is involved when we consider the overextension of a word like dog to horses and sheep. It is very hard to discern what function dogs would have for the two-year-old. To appeal to function as the only or even main explanation for overextensions does not seem to be justified.

But the child could be using some functional knowledge in first assigning meanings to words. The difficulty lies in distinguishing between his use of functional knowledge and his use of perceptual knowledge. Consider the objects a child might call cup: all of them have certain perceptual properties in common, in addition to their common function as containers. The same applies to things called chair. Experimental attempts to discriminate between reliance on form versus function have run into exactly this problem. Nelson (1973), for example, looked at young children's choices of different round and ovoid spheres when asked to give the experimenter the ball. The choices made did not allow a clear separation of form and function, as Nelson herself pointed out. The logic of the experiment did not provide any situations where the child's choices involved a clear distinction between knowledge of function and knowledge of form.

The best way to examine such an argument would be to look at children's choices of objects with the same form but different

functions, versus objects with different forms and the same function.
Then, one might be able to assess the relative contributions made by
knowledge of form and of function to early word meanings. The child
aged one or two clearly knows something about the functions of some
objects, but it remains unclear how much of a role this knowledge
plays in mapping the first meanings for words. The overextension of
words like open and allgone suggests that functional knowledge may
be used in some cases. But the vast majority of overextensions appear to depend on the child's knowledge about form--the perceptual
properties of different objects.

There are three difficulties in dealing with the role of function in
the acquisition of meaning. First, there are many instances where
the function is highly correlated with form. As a result, they are
very hard to separate (e.g. Nelson 1973; E. Clark 1973b). Secondly,
knowledge about function may be acquired fairly late in some instances. For example, the overextension of a word like kotibaiz
(Table 1) from the bars of a crib to an abacus, to a toast-rack, and
to a building with a columned front shows a blatant disregard for
function compared to form. One could presumably argue that the
child assumes all these objects have the same function (that of con-
fining one behind bars), but this seems implausible when we consider
the toast-rack and its everyday use at breakfast (in Britain). A two-
year-old would surely know the difference in function between the
bars of his crib and a toast-rack. There are several other examples
of this type in Tables 1 and 2 (see also Andersen 1975). Thirdly,
there is the issue I have discussed: that many objects would seem
not to have any function for the young child, e.g. horses and dogs.
In cases where overextensions apply to animals, for example, the
child seems to be using perceptual knowledge, not functional knowledge.

In summary, the evidence so far suggests that the child relies
more on form than on function in first assigning some meaning to a
word. But notice that most of the child's early vocabulary and his
overextensions involve the names of objects. The rare overextensions that involve actions (opening doors or lids, undoing shoes,
vanishing from sight, etc.) appear to be more functional in nature.
This suggests that perceptual knowledge may play the most prominent
role in learning to name objects, while functional knowledge might be
more prominent in naming actions or relations of various kinds.
This proposal, of course, would need to be examined in much more
detail, but there does seem to be some evidence for it in children's
acting out of instructions. Their strategies for responding often
take the form of deciding what action to perform (putting something
in a container, for example), and these may well depend on functional knowledge to a greater degree than simply naming objects does.

3. Full meanings and partial meanings: Can we always tell? In 1968, Donaldson and Balfour published an intriguing study of how three- and four-year-olds interpret the words more and less. They found that children this age seemed not to distinguish between the two terms, although more and less, for the adult, are opposites. The children, in fact, seemed to treat less as if it was a synonym of more. For example, when the children were asked to choose from two trees either the one with more apples or the one with less apples, they consistently chose the tree with the greater number. Similar findings have been reported by Palermo (1973), both for individual objects like apples and for liquid volume. These data suggest that the children have already learnt what more means, but have yet to realize that less is its opposite.

Several investigators proposed that children at this stage do know the full (adult) meaning of more, i. e. that it refers to amount and that it refers to a positive quantity. The children studied by Donaldson and Balfour also seemed to know that less referred to amount. It therefore seemed plausible to assume that the children simply inferred that less must mean the same as more (Donaldson and Balfour 1968; Donaldson and Wales 1970; E. Clark 1973a). In other words, the children have already acquired the correct adult meaning for more but they have yet to do this for less. This analysis of the data, which is the one I originally took for granted, embodies what I have called the Full Semantics Hypothesis: children are assumed to have the full meaning for one of the terms.

We could make a much weaker assumption, though, about how much children this age really know about the meanings of more and less. First, suppose both word meanings are actually incomplete at this stage. As a result, children might know only that more and less both refer to amount. The children's spontaneous use of the words tends to support this. For example, when asked to point at which tree had more apples on it, some children replied Both of them, That one does an' that one, Each tree, They two ones, and so on. At the same time, when asked to make the amount less on one tree, another child objected; But it is less on that tree (Donaldson and Wales 1970). Secondly, in addition to this partial meaning for both more and less, one could postulate a nonlinguistic strategy of choosing the greater of two or more amounts, or of choosing objects with greater extension along dimensions like height or length (see H. Clark 1970). Klatzky, Clark and Macker (1973), in fact, found considerable evidence for this assumption. The children's responses, then, would be the outcome of combining their partial semantic knowledge with a nonlinguistic strategy. Because they usually chose the greater amount, they appeared to know what more meant. This analysis is based on what I have called the Partial Semantics Hypothesis (E. Clark 1973b).

The Full Semantics Hypothesis and the Partial Semantics Hypothesis are not true or false in general, but it is important to contrast them when one looks at the acquisition of word meanings. This is because the child may appear to have acquired the full (adult) meaning of a word in some contexts, when in fact he has only acquired part of the meaning. One cannot tell from the data available on more and less whether the children really do know the full meaning of more or whether they are simply relying on the strategy of choosing the greater amount and thus getting more right by accident. If a context could be found in which that particular strategy was neutralized, one might be able to tell what meaning more really had at this stage.

The child's reliance on nonlinguistic organizational strategies for dealing with particular situations shows up very clearly in some studies of the acquisition of locative prepositions like in, on, and under (E. Clark 1973b). In these studies, the child's comprehension was tested by asking him to 'Put X in/on/under Y'. The children (aged 1;6 to 5;0) always appeared to get in right but made a number of errors with on and under. On was treated by the younger children as if it meant 'in' whenever Y was a container, but was otherwise correct. Under was also treated as 'in' whenever Y had a supporting surface (and was not a container). With under, then, we see a classic example of Word-1 being treated as if it means Word-2 in one set of contexts (containers), but as if it means Word-3 in another set (surfaces). Since 'in' and 'on' are incompatible meanings, it is clear that the child has at best only a partial meaning for under, combined with two nonlinguistic strategies. The first strategy, which seems to take priority, is to place objects inside containers; the second is to place objects on top of a supporting surface.

The child's strategies appear to be dependent on properties of the objects and their possible relations in space, e.g. containers versus surfaces. But in addition, the child may also have some specific knowledge about the normal orientation and normal spatial relations between particular objects. For example, some of the youngest children in the first experiment in E. Clark (1973b) consistently turned a box, presented lying on its side, so that its opening was upwards. This orientation is a canonical one for containers (see H. Clark 1973). In the second experiment, several children who were supposed to copy the experimenter always righted a transparent plastic glass placed upside down in front of them, and then put a movable object inside rather than on top as the experimenter had done. (Some of the children also 'corrected' the experimenter's array--righting her glass and putting the other object inside.) The child of 1;6 or 2;0 presumably knows very well that glasses normally are placed opening up. And once the glass is righted, the child can simply apply his 'container strategy' to it. Among the two-and-a-half-year-olds, there was some further evidence of the role played by knowledge of normal spatail relations: several children objected to putting something under the crib because you sleep in it. Nonetheless, they carried out the instructions correctly (E. Clark 1973b).

Some additional data on the prepositions in, on, and under have been collected by Wilcox and Palermo (in press).[5] The pattern of errors they found among the youngest children, namely, a preference for putting objects 'in' wherever possible, and 'on' otherwise, was exactly as predicted by E. Clark (1973b). Wilcox and Palermo deliberately chose pairs of objects that were conventionally related to each other: trucks which go on roads (although, for some reason, they always asked the child to manipulate the road, not the truck), boats which go under bridges over rivers, and teapots which go on tables. Despite this bias in favor of under instructions (for the road-truck and boat-bridge pairs), the youngest children usually responded by putting the piece of road 'in' the truck, and by putting the boat 'on' the bridge. The third pair of objects, the teapot and the table, involved in and on, and here all the children (aged 1;6 to 3;0) did better with on. (This was probably because the table did not really provide any container-space.) By age 2;6 or so, however, the children's knowledge of the conventional relations had begun to have more influence so the children appeared to do better with under than with in or on for the road-truck and boat-bridge pairs. These data provide further support for the argument that contextual factors (i. e. perceived containers and surfaces) play a critical role in the child's nonlinguistic strategies (E. Clark 1973b).[6]

The child's general knowledge and his context-based strategies allow him to go a long way in appearing to understand when he actually has only partial knowledge about word meanings. The problem is that his 'correct' responses may mislead us into thinking he knows more about meanings than he does. It is essential, then, to identify the child's strategies in different contexts and see when he relies on them. Once that is done, we shall be more certain of being able to distinguish responses based on full semantic knowledge from those based on partial semantic knowledge.

4. Children's strategies: Same or different? When children know little or nothing about the conditions of application for a word, they consistently rely on strategies for responding. These strategies are based on their nonlinguistic knowledge about objects and relations. (The children may even be ignoring strange words altogether.) As children learn something about a word meaning, though, their strategy for responding may change. At the earliest stage, for

example, the child's strategy might lead him to make one kind of mistake in his responses; at a later stage, however, his strategy might change as a result of what he now knows about the word meaning, so that the kind of error he makes also changes. The patterns of errors resulting from children's use of strategies provide a guide to different stages in the course of acquisition. The question I want to turn to next is how consistent children are in the actual strategies they choose. Do they all pick on the same strategy at a particular stage, or do they sometimes follow alternative routes in working out the conditions of application for new words? Clearly, if the latter is the case, the identification of stages in acquisition becomes much more complex.

Many studies have noted considerable uniformity in the strategies chosen by children with little or no knowledge of the relevant word meaning. For example, children all seem to rely on order of mention to talk about or to interpret temporal relations between events. The first event mentioned is treated as the first event to occur, both in production (E. Clark 1970) and in comprehension (E. Clark 1971; Ferreiro 1971; Keller-Cohen 1974). The priority of containers over surfaces also appears to be uniform in dealing with spatial relations between objects. Whenever there is a container available, the young child will put an object inside; otherwise, he will place a second object on some horizontal supporting surface. These strategies are used not only by very young children (1;6-3;0) but also by older children with more complex locative prepositions (E. Clark 1973b, unpublished data).

A similar uniformity in the initial strategy chosen was found in children's interpretations of deictic verbs--come, go, bring, and take (Clark and Garnica 1974). The younger children consistently chose the person at the goal of the motion when asked to identify the speaker or addressee of utterances containing these verbs. As a result, in the contexts given, come and bring always appeared to be 'correct' while go and take were always wrong. A change in the children's strategy to focus on the contrast between speakers and addressees revealed that the children had at most only a partial meaning ('motion') for all four verbs. Later stages in the acquisition of these verbs also seemed to elicit uniform strategies on the part of the children (Clark and Garnica 1974).

The same uniformity of strategy has also appeared in many studies of syntactic relations. For example, children consistently choose as actor the thing designated by the first noun in Noun-Verb-Noun sequences. Young children, as a result, make consistent mistakes on reversible passives: they interpret The cat was chased by the dog as The cat chased the dog (Bever 1970; Slobin 1966). Somewhat older children consistently identify the object named in the nearest noun phrase as the subject of the complement verb. For example, in John promised Bill to leave, the children assume that Bill is the one to go (e.g. Chomsky 1969; Cromer 1970). All the studies I have mentioned found considerable consistency across children both in terms of the initial strategies adopted and in terms of subsequent developmental changes.

But some evidence of variation is also beginning to emerge. There are several studies in which some children appear to have chosen one strategy and others another when first beginning to map word meanings or work on sentence structure. This kind of variation suggests that there are sometimes alternative routes to the same end--to an adult-like knowledge about meaning.

The first example of a context in which children might be taking alternative routes comes from comprehension data on before and after (E. Clark 1971). At the intermediate stage between relying solely on order of mention (the youngest) and displaying adult-like understanding, I found two groups of children. Both had acquired the meaning of before. But when it came to after, some children continued to apply the order of mention strategy (after correct about half the time) while others appeared to treat after as if it meant the same as before (after wrong all the time). In my original study, I suggested that these two groups represented two separate, ordered substages in acquisition. However, it is also possible that the two patterns of error on after were the result of children choosing different options rather than reflecting sequential stages. This question can probably only be resolved by looking at longitudinal data.

A much stronger case appears in some recent studies of deixis. Clark and Sengul (1974) found that children used several different routes in acquiring the contrasts between here and there, and this and that. Here and this, for adults, both indicate something near the speaker; there and that, something that is not so near, unless the contrast is cancelled by an accompanying gesture. We tested children's comprehension of these terms in two contexts: when the speaker was sitting beside the child and when the speaker was sitting opposite. The child was then asked to move one of a pair of animals on the table in front of him in response to instructions containing one of the four deictic terms.

Overall, there were three stages in acquisition: (1) no contrast between here-there or this-that; (2) a partial contrast (i.e. in one context only); and (3) full contrast. Analysis of the 'no contrast' stage showed that the children were using one or other of four distinct strategies. Some children always chose the object near themselves; others always chose the object near the speaker; a few chose the object away from themselves, and a few the object away from the speaker. The first two options were the most frequent, but all four occurred. Furthermore, the starting point chosen also appeared to determine whether the child at the 'partial contrast' stage first got the contrast right when beside or when opposite the speaker. The acquisition of deictic contrasts provides a clear example of children following alternative routes to an adult-like understanding.

This use of alternative routes in acquisition has also been noted in a few other studies. Kuczaj[7] has reported that in the acquisition of always and never, some children go through a stage of treating both words as positives, while others at the same age treat both as if they are negatives. Other kinds of variation have also been observed. For example, Brown (1968) found considerable variation in the frequency of instantiation for different question-types for different children. Bloom, Lightbown, and Hood (1975) found variation in the structural options children used at the beginning of the two-word stage. Some children begin combining a pronominal form with a content word; others begin by combining two content words.

To conclude, there do seem to be various ways of getting from the child's first strategies to the final stage in the acquisition of meanings. This forces one to be more cautious in identifying stages in acquisition. The particular route that each child follows in each case may well depend on the consistency with which the child himself views his world. His view, of course, may also change as he acquires more language. What is now needed is to find some a priori way of establishing when and why children are likely to take the same route, and when they are likely to choose different routes.

5. Where do strategies go? Children begin on the mapping problem by applying whatever nonlinguistic strategies seem appropriate in context. In the course of acquisition, though, as the child learns the meanings of particular words, he appears to relinquish many of the strategies he relied on earlier. For example, by the age of 3;0 or so, children no longer put an object inside a container when given instructions with the prepositions on or under (E. Clark 1973b). Likewise, when children have learned the conditions of application for the verbs go and take, they stop identifying the position of the speaker with the goal of the motion (Clark and Garnica 1974). The question is: What happens to the strategies that the children used to rely on earlier?

First of all, the child's nonlinguistic strategies do not simply vanish because they are no longer applied wholesale. Instead, their use becomes restricted to particular contexts. Take the first example which was considered as an illustration: Most 3;0 year-olds respond appropriately when asked to put something on or under a container (e.g. a box or a truck). In other words, they understand both on and under. At an earlier stage, though, they appeared to rely on their knowledge of containers alone in deciding how to respond to similar instructions, and generally placed the object inside the containers. What the 3;0 year-olds have done is restrict the domain in which they apply their earlier strategy. They use it when the instruction contains the preposition in. That particular strategy, then, could be regarded as the procedure relevant to meeting the conditions of application for the preposition in. The child's acquisition of the conditions of application for particular words, in fact, seems to go hand-in-hand with his giving up an over-broad use of his nonlinguistic strategies.

Even when the child has restricted the use of some strategies in certain contexts, he may still use them very broadly in others. For example, take the child's treatment of containers and surfaces during the acquisition of in, on, and under. By age 3;0, the child has learned to restrict his container and surface strategies to contexts with in and on respectively. However, these same strategies continue to apply very broadly when it comes to instructions that the 3;0 year-old does not yet understand. Thus, faced with prepositions like above or behind, the child resorts to his earlier strategies: objects are placed inside containers where possible, or else on the top surface (E. Clark, unpublished data). Children, then, continue to rely on their general strategies whenever they do not understand new words.

Young children are not the only ones to rely on such general nonlinguistic strategies; adults do it too, and in analogous situations. For example, if an adult has not been listening and yet realizes he has been asked to do something, he looks at the context and tries to guess what it was he could have been asked to do. Imagine he was handed a plate by the speaker. His strategy might be to place it on the table, if in the dining room; in the sink, if in the kitchen and if the plate was dirty, or in a cupboard if the plate was clean. Such reliance on the context to decide what had probably been requested is exactly analogous to the young child's use of what I have called nonlinguistic strategies.

A second situation in which the adult relies on the same general strategies is when he is immersed in a foreign language setting with little or no knowledge about the language. The adult, in such a setting, is forced to resort to just those general strategies that the young child uses when he tries to work out what other people are talking about. The adult pays close attention to the physical context in his efforts to understand what is going on. This situation seems even closer to the young child's than the first I described. This is because the adult, like the young child, is almost completely dependent on his nonlinguistic knowledge. This is unlike the case of inattentiveness where the adult always has the option of asking the speaker to repeat himself.

Nonlinguistic strategies, then, are used by the inattentive listener (whether adult or child) and by the learner of a second language in 'immersion' situations, as well as by the young child embarking on his first language. These strategies are probably best viewed as general organizational principles for dealing with objects and relations in the world. As such, these cognitive principles play an important role in the acquisition of meaning in language.

6. Conclusion. I have argued in this paper that the child relies on what he already knows when he tackles the mapping problem in language acquisition. By the time the child begins to acquire language, he has spent a year or more amassing knowledge about objects and their properties, and about possible relations between objects. His knowledge appears to take the form of general cognitive principles about how things are organized. These principles are what guide his first attempts to work out what words mean.

These principles underlie the strategies the child relies on when responding to language that he does not fully understand. In some contexts, the child's strategies may make it appear that he understands a good deal, while in others it is clear that he still knows little or nothing about particular word meanings. As the child learns something about a word meaning--about the conditions of application for that word--his strategies may change. The study of the child's nonlinguistic strategies, therefore, can tell a good deal both about his a priori knowledge and about the different stages he goes through in the course of acquisition.

The data on children's overextension, for example, provide fairly detailed information about the kinds of meanings children first attach to words. One can infer from the overextensions, whether they are full or partial ones, that a particular word has at least those features attached to it that are held in common by the objects the child applies it to. The investigation of first meanings, though, is complicated by several factors. First, there seem to be certain asymmetries in children's production of overextensions versus their comprehension of them; and secondly, perceptual knowledge seems to play an important role in first meanings, but it is sometimes difficult to distinguish between perceptual and functional knowledge.

Studies of relational terms--prepositions, verbs, and some adjectives--have already uncovered a number of nonlinguistic strategies used by young children. In many instances, their choices of strategy seem to be remarkably uniform. In others, there is some evidence that children may follow alternative routes and rely on different strategies in the course of acquisition.

Finally, the child's acquisition of the conditions of application for particular words is closely linked to his gradual restriction of the domain in which particular nonlinguistic strategies may apply. In many cases, the child's strategies seem to take on the role of the procedure required to meet particular conditions of application.

In summary, recent research on the acquisition of meaning by children has shown that the acquisition process cannot be considered in isolation. One must take into account what the child knows, what the context of the utterance is, and what kinds of nonlinguistic strategy the child may resort to when he still knows very little about what words and utterances mean.

NOTES

This research was supported in part by a grant from the National Science Foundation, GS-30040. I would like to thank Herbert H. Clark for his valuable comments on an earlier version of this paper.

1. What the speaker actually said was 'The shepherd has four dogs'.

2. 'Conditions of application' is simply a way of talking about the procedures that are used by speaker and addressee in deciding what it is in context that word X designates or how object Y should be designated. Harrison (1972) has made some suggestions about the form such procedures might take.

3. The criterial properties picked out, in these instances, would presumably be those that were most salient in general, or most salient in context. While developmental research strongly suggests that some perceptual features like verticality are very salient for the young child (e.g. Braine 1972), the question of whether some properties are more salient or more central conceptually and hence more likely to occur in overextensions needs further investigation (see Rosch, in press; E. Clark 1974b).

4. The word form is used here as a shorthand for all perceptual attributes of shape, size, movement, texture, sound, etc.

5. I am grateful to David Palermo for supplying me with the original data from this study from which the conclusions that follow can be drawn.

6. Wilcox and Palermo (in press), however, seem to view their data as counter-evidence to the arguments put forward in E. Clark (1973b).

7. Stanley A. Kuczaj, personal communication.

REFERENCES

Andersen, E. S. 1975. Cups and glasses: Learning that boundaries are vague. Journal of Child Language 2.

Bever, T. G. 1970. The cognitive basis for linguistic structures. In: Cognition and the development of language. Edited by J. R. Hayes, 279-352. New York, Wiley.

Bloom, L., P. Lightbown, and L. Hood. 1975. Structure and variation in child language. Monographs of the Society for Research in Child Development 40.

Braine, L. G. 1972. The apparent upright--Implications for copying and for perceptual development. Paper presented at the 20th International Congress of Psychology. Tokyo, Japan.

Brown, R. 1968. The development of Wh questions in child speech. Journal of Verbal Learning and Verbal Behavior 7.277-290.

Chomsky, C. S. 1969. The acquisition of syntax in children from 5 to 10. Cambridge, Mass., MIT Press.

Clark, E. V. 1970. How young children describe events in time. In: Advances in psycholinguistics. Edited by G. B. Flores d'Arcais and W. J. M. Levelt, 275-284. Amsterdam, North-Holland Publishing Company.

_____. 1971. On the acquisition of the meaning of before and after. Journal of Verbal Learning and Verbal Behavior 10.266-275.

_____. 1973a. What's in a word? On the child's acquisition of semantics in his first language. In: Cognitive development and the acquisition of language. Edited by T. E. Moore, 65-110. New York, Academic Press.

_____. 1973b. Nonlinguistic strategies and the acquisition of word meanings. Cognition 2.161-182.

_____. 1974a. Some aspects of the conceptual basis for first language acquisition. In: Language perspectives--Acquisition, retardation and intervention. Edited by R. L. Schiefelbusch and L. L. Lloyd, 105-128. Baltimore, Md., University Park Press.

_____. 1974b. Classifiers and semantic acquisition: Universal categories? Paper presented at the 73rd Annual Meeting of the American Anthropological Association. Mexico City, Mexico.

_____ and O. K. Garnica. 1974. Is he coming or going? On the acquisition of deictic verbs. Journal of Verbal Learning and Verbal Behavior 13.559-572.

_____ and C. J. Sengul. 1974. Deictic contrasts in language acquisition. Paper presented at the 49th Annual Meeting of the Linguistic Society of America. New York, N.Y.

Clark, H. H. 1970. The primitive nature of children's relational concepts. In: Cognition and the development of language. Edited by J. R. Hayes, 269-278. New York, Wiley.

_____. 1973. Space, time, semantics, and the child. In: Cognitive development and the acquisition of language. Edited by T. E. Moore, 28-63. New York, Academic Press.

Cromer, R. F. 1970. 'Children are nice to understand': Surface
structure clues for the recovery of a deep structure. British
Journal of Psychology 61. 397-408.

Dewey, J. 1894. The psychology of infant language. Psychological
Review 1. 63-66.

Donaldson, M. and G. Balfour. 1968. Less is more: A study of
language comprehension in children. British Journal of Psychology 59. 461-472.

_____ and R. J. Wales. 1970. On the acquisition of some relational
terms. In: Cognition and the development of language. Edited by
J. R. Hayes, 235-268. New York, Wiley.

Ferreiro, E. 1971. Les relations temporelles dans le langage de
l'enfant. Geneva, Droz.

Harrison, B. 1972. Meaning and structure: An essay in the
philosophy of language. New York, Harper and Row.

Huttenlocher, J. 1974. The origins of language comprehension. In:
Theories in cognitive psychology. Edited by R. L. Solso, 331-368.
Potomac, Md., Lawrence Erlbaum Associates.

Keller-Cohen, D. 1974. The expression of time in language acquisition. Paper presented at the 49th Annual Meeting of the Linguistic
Society of America. New York, N. Y.

Klatzky, R. L., E. V. Clark, and M. Macken. 1973. Asymmetries
in the acquisition of polar adjectives: Linguistic or conceptual?
Journal of Experimental Child Psychology 16. 32-46.

Labov, W. and T. Labov. 1974. The grammar of Cat and Mama.
Paper presented at the 49th Annual Meeting of the Linguistic
Society of America. New York, N. Y.

Nelson, K. 1973. Some evidence for the cognitive primacy of
categorization and its functional basis. Merrill-Palmer Quarterly
19. 21-39.

Palermo, D. S. 1973. More about less: A study of language comprehension. Journal of Verbal Learning and Verbal Behavior
12. 211-221.

Rosch, E. In press. Classification of real-world objects: Origins
and representations in cognition. Special issue of Bulletin de
Psychologie. Edited by S. Ehrlich and E. Tulving.

Slobin, D. I. 1966. Grammatical transformations and sentence
comprehension in childhood and adulthood. Journal of Verbal
Learning and Verbal Behavior 5. 219-227.

Smith, N. V. 1973. The acquisition of phonology: A case study.
Cambridge, Cambridge University Press.

Thomson, J. R. and R. S. Chapman. 1975. Who is 'Daddy'?
The status of two-year-olds' over-extended words in use and
comprehension. Paper presented at the 7th Child Language
Research Forum. Stanford University, Stanford.

Wilcox, S. and D. S. Palermo. In press. 'In', 'On', and 'Under' revisited. Cognition.

IF AND WHEN TRANSFORMATIONS ARE ACQUIRED BY CHILDREN

DAVID INGRAM

The University of British Columbia, Vancouver

Abstract. Most discussions on language acquisition in children
assume that the child has acquired most of the grammar of a language by age 5. Even the recent work of Chomsky (1969) suggests
that development between 5 and 10 is predominantly in comprehension
of the more idiosyncratic patterns of English. This paper argues
that not only are some exceptional patterns not acquired by age 5,
but also many rule-based general rules of grammar. Specifically,
it argues that most of the transformations of English are only acquired between the ages of 6 and 12. These are the transformations
that have to do with the embedding of one sentence into another. The
evidence for this comes from both theory and facts. The facts come
from the observation of children's complex sentences between 2 and
12. The structures up to 4 are primarily simple sentences. Those
from 4 to 6 show complex structures, but most propositions are still
simply juxtaposed to each other. Piaget's theory of cognitive development predicts that this should be the case. To relate two structures
to each other, the child needs to be capable of performing concrete
operations. This ability is only developed between the age of 6 and
12.

To discover appropriate conditions for a grammar to satisfy,
we need to investigate texts to inventory what possibly relevant linguistic data they contain. Texts appear to contain
much usable information about structure that would not be
contained in an unordered list of utterances (Braine 1973, 422).

1. Purpose. It is a common assumption that children have acquired most of the grammar of English by age 5 or 6. This assumption is stated quite clearly by Dale (1972:98) in his recent introduction to child language:

> Past the age of five or six, differences between the child's grammar and adult grammar are not obvious from spontaneous observation of free speech. There are a few characteristic difficulties that remain . . . However, these are relatively minor features. The basic syntactic structure of most of the child's sentences appears to be that of the adult grammar.

This position is also similar to the one expressed in C. Chomsky (1969:2) on the acquisition of syntax between the ages of 5 and 10.

> Our study deals with the later period, after age 5. Clearly, by this age the rate of acquisition of syntactic structures has decreased markedly, and differences between the child's grammar and the adult grammar are no longer so readily discernible in the child's spontaneous speech.

The differences that may still exist, Chomsky claims, are in the child's ability to comprehend adult structures. Those structures that do show errors, however, are not the more common ones in the language.

> Structures which have potential for late acquisition would be those, for example, which deviate from a widely established pattern in the language, or whose surface structure is relatively inexplicit with respect to grammatical relations, or even simply those which the linguist finds particularly difficult to incorporate into a thorough description . . . (C. Chomsky 1969:4).

These statements capture the current thinking about the acquisition of syntax in general and transformations in particular. They can be summarized as follows: (1) The child, by age 5 or 6, shows in his spontaneous speech essentially the same grammatical patterns as found in adult speech; in other words, he has acquired the major transformations of English. (2) There may still exist errors in the child's comprehension of certain specific adult structures; but the structures that show error are those that are either exceptional or unusual in some way.

The purpose of this paper is to challenge these assumptions. I argue that the spontaneous language of children around age 5 and 6 is still unlike that of the adult. More important, I suggest that the changes that occur between 6 and 12 are not simply reflections of the acquisition of the more idiosyncratic grammatical patterns. Rather, they are the result of the acquisition of much of the transformational structure of English. That is, while some of the transformations of English appear to be productive up to age 5, many are not until after that time. The child's grammar goes through an active period of 're-structuring' during this period. It is during this process that the child creates what is essentially the transformational component of his grammar.

Two kinds of evidence are put forth to support this position. One is data from texts of the spontaneous speech of children between the ages of 5 and 12. These data show that children are only beginning to use productively the ability to embed one sentence into another. The other evidence is data from cognitive development which shows that children before this age are generally incapable of performing cognitive operations of this kind. This point is demonstrated by showing that Piaget's theory of cognitive development is a reasonably good prediction of linguistic development. In short, the development of transformations between 5 and 12 coincides with the use of concrete operations during the same age period. Linguistic operations appear to be closely related to cognitive ones.

2. Preliminary remarks on rule productivity. Before discussing the acquisition of transformational rules, it is necessary to establish a criterion for determining when a rule can be said to be acquired. While this is a difficult thing to do, there have been some suggestive findings on the acquisition of rules by young children.

The simplest criterion would be to say that a rule exists when the product of that rule occurs in the child's language. This can be exemplified with the production of the English plural morpheme /-s/. It is possible to say that a child has a productive rule of plural formation when plurals are first used on English nouns. This, however, makes the unwarranted assumption that at every step the child's grammar operates similarly to the adults'. There are ways that plurals may be used nonproductively. The child may simply memorize two forms for each noun, one for the singular and another for the plural. This is the way that pairs like <u>foot-feet</u>, <u>man-men</u> are learned. Also, the child may use the plural sporadically, indicating that it is in the process of being acquired. It is difficult to see how a rule that is inconsistently used can be said to be part of the child's grammar.

A stronger criterion would be to say that a rule is acquired when it is used productively. This reflects Chomsky's definition of a grammar as a set of rules that can produce new instances of structure. The problem is to determine a way to decide when a rule has become productive. Cazden (1968) has found a very useful procedure to do this. In examining the occurrence of grammatical morphemes in the speech of Adam, Eve, and Sarah (cf. Brown 1973), she calculated a percentage for the times a morpheme was used in contexts where it was obligatory by adult standards. Doing this produced a very important finding. The occurrence of overgeneralizations for the plural morpheme did not occur until the morpheme was being supplied in obligatory contexts around 70 to 85 percent of the time. The occurrence of these indicates that the rule has become productive for the child. She states '. . . systematic errors and overgeneralizations provide convincing evidence that the child has a productive rule' (228). The finding indicates that a rule may not be productive until its rate of occurrence is quite high.

This observation casts serious doubts on the claim that the child has a productive grammatical rule because a structure may occasionally be used. With grammatical morphemes, it is relatively easy to determine contexts where the form should be used. This is not the case with the study of transformations. For example, it is difficult to say where the Passive transformation should be used by the child but hasn't been. Here we usually have to rely on frequency of occurrence. There are, however, ways that this can be done for some of the English transformations. (1) shows the first four sentences of a story told by Thecla R, 3,7 (taken from Pitcher and Prelinger 1963: 68).

(1) Once there was a little girl. She ate too many raisins. She got sick. The doctor had to come.

This is a case where the first two sentences could have been combined to produce one complex sentence as in (2).

(2) Once there was a little girl who ate too many raisins and got sick.

Later on in the story, Thecla uses the sentence in (3).

(3) Then that girl that was playing with her slept for the night.

(3) shows that the child does have relative clauses in her speech. If the pattern in (1) is the predominant one, however, we cannot speak of Relative Clause Formation as necessarily a productive rule in her language.

A related point to productivity is the way in which any particular structure is produced by the child. In the example with plural /-s/, the alternative to rule-based behavior was memorization. That is, the child could simply memorize the plurals as different from the singulars. With syntactic constructions, there are two ways that the construction can be produced by rules. The first would be through the use of phrase structure rules. The second is by transformations. This is the relevant issue in determining the acquisition of transformations. There is evidence (to be cited) suggesting that the first complex-looking syntactic constructions that children use are produced by phrase structure rules in the child's grammar. Only later do they become reanalyzed as complex structures produced by transformations. Because of this, it is not sufficient to say that a transformation is acquired when a certain number of constructions appear in the child's speech that would be produced by it in the adult language. A transformational rule can only be said to be productive if (1) constructions occur that look like adult complex structures, and (2) there is evidence that a transformation is at work in the child's grammar.

This shift in the child's grammar from a phrase structure treatment to a transformational treatment of a grammatical construction can be referred to as 'restructuring'. This term is taken from Kiparsky (1968:175) who states that 'it refers . . . to a discontinuous linguistic change arising from the difference between the grammar constructed by a child and the grammar of those whose speech constituted his linguistic experience'. As the child approaches the adult language, he is constantly changing the structure of his grammar. A transformational rule will be productive only after such a restructuring has occurred, and the rule is applied frequently in the child's language (relative to frequent use by adult standards).

Having expressed these clarifications on rule acquisition, I can now state the position of this paper more precisely: Between the ages of 5 or 6 and 12, the child restructures his grammar of English from a predominantly phrase structure grammar to a predominantly transformational one. The word predominant is important here. Before this age, the young child will produce a number of constructions that would be produced by transformations in the adult language. Many of these, however, are not the result of transformations in the child's system. Several can be explained by the child's use of a phrase structure grammar. Others may be in the midst of restructuring without the transformation yet being established. Some of the structures are produced by transformations, but there are only certain ones that are well documented. These are the rules like Subject NP-Aux Inversion in questions and Negative Placement in simple negative sentences. The transformations that appear to be productive before 5 or 6 are those that operate within simple sentences. The restructuring that occurs around age 6 can be said to involve predominantly rules concerning one sentence being embedded into another. Up to age 5 or 6, the child develops a phrase structure grammar along with a set of transformations that operate within a simple sentence. In the next six years, this grammar is restructured to include a set of rules that create complex sentences.

3. The development of complex sentences between 2;0 and 12;0

3.1 The first appearance of complex sentences. The first appearance of sentences that are complex in the adult language occurs in children's speech by age 3. Brown (1973) describes five stages of syntactic development based on MLU (mean length of utterance). He states that Stage IV is the one in which children begin to embed one sentence into another. Eve, Adam, and Sarah reached Stage IV at approximately 2;0, 3;0, and 3;6 respectively. This compares favorably with Nice (1925) who observed that children around age 3 begin to show longer and more complicated sentences. Stern and Stern (1907) date the onset of more complex structures after 2;6. In a recent report on complex structure in the speech of three children, Limber (1973) also found instances of these before age 3. Menyuk (1969) has done the most extensive study to date on the development of these sentences. 'The basic transformations postulated as being present in the fully developed grammar are used by varying numbers of children throughout the age range during the period of 3 to 7 years' (Menyuk 1969:76).

The fact that these structures appear for the first time does not mean that they have the same grammatical origins as their adult counterparts. It takes a great deal of time before this is true. For example, take the period Brown refers to as Stage I, roughly the period between the ages 1;6 and 2;0. Much has been made of this time as one in which the first two-word utterances representing grammatical relations occur. The point that is consistently undermined is that the most frequent utterance during the stage is the one-word utterance. While multiple-word utterances develop during this time, it is only in the next stage that they can be considered highly productive structures.

The same can be said for the child's grammar of complex sentences around age 3. These are still relatively infrequent and only beginning to develop. As for their structure, they are non-transformational in the first uses. Miller (1973) was one of the first to note this. In examining the early structures used by a young girl, Susan, at 2;2-3;6, he states:

. . . these three transformations--yes-no inversion, the negative, and verb ellipsis--appeared to develop as a group, and a
general pattern can be observed. The child first used a formula, or better, a phrase structure rule, that enabled him to
produce sentences which were transformations in adult grammar (Miller 1973:387).

This reflects a general principle of language acquisition--new functions are marked by old forms. Adapting to this paper, transformationally produced structures are first produced as phrase structures by the young child.

Francis (1969) has made similar observations on her son between
2;7 and 2;10. She argues that these early productions that look complex at first glance are actually the result of combining two phrase
structure systems. (4) provides three structures she produces to
account for her son's sentences.

(4) I want to + Verb Phrase
     I like to + Verb Phrase
     $\begin{Bmatrix} \text{Look} \\ \text{See} \end{Bmatrix}$ what + Noun Phrase (verb ing)

She also provides some interesting frequency counts on the occurrence
of these complex structures. The number of utterances that would be
produced by generalized transformations constituted less than 10 percent of the child's speech in either monologue or dialogue. Not only
are they not transformationally based, they are also not frequent.

A comparable finding occurred in Ingram (1972), where I wrote on
the development of phrase structure rules in the speech of 15 children
from corpora of approximately 150 multi-word utterances per child.
The children were spread across five stages of MLU grossly comparable to those of Brown (1973), with three subjects at each stage. The
first finding was that there were five stages in the development of
phrase structure rules. The first verb complements appeared at
Stage 3 which characterized the language of three subjects (age 2;8,
2;7, and 3;0 respectively). The Verb Phrase rule for these children
was as in (5).

(5) $VP \rightarrow VB \begin{Bmatrix} (S_2) \\ (NP) \ (NP) \end{Bmatrix}$

     Constraint on rule: $S_2 \rightarrow VP$

In discussing the constraint on this rule, I commented 'The children at
Stage 3 do not use complement sentences with a different subject than

that of the main clause, i.e. they do not use constructions like (27ii)' (Ingram 1972:75). (27ii) was sentence (6).

(6) John wanted me to go.

These did not appear until the next stage. Like Francis' son, these children did not appear to use adult rules of embedding but instead the combining of two verb phrases. Rule (5) could also have been stated as (7), without reference to S.

(7) VP → VB (VP)

A recent article by Ruth Clark (1974) has demonstrated the non-transformational nature of these early structures. She reports on the language of her son Adam during the period from 2;9 to 3;0. The gist of her argument is that performance is an important dimension of development and that through it competence is established. She calls her paper 'Performing without competence', suggesting that these early structures are not the result of abstract linguistic competence but instead performance factors. Her data also suggests that even an elaborate phrase structure analysis may be unwarranted.

Clark reports on strategies for producing utterances. One of these was a copying strategy. Here the child simply used an unanalyzed utterance of the adult for specific situations. For example, sit my knee was copied over from adult speech and used when he wanted to sit on someone's knee. 'Many sequences in Adam's speech, which would be assumed to have internal syntactic structure if the utterances were produced by an adult, may instead be well-practiced routines, of which no part is substitutable' (Clark 1974:5).

Another important strategy and one that will be emphasized throughout this paper is that of juxtaposition of two structures, much in the way mentioned by Francis. This juxtaposition may result either through inclusion of part of a previous utterance, or through putting together two structures of separate earlier sentences. (8) gives examples from Clark (1974:6) of sentence buildups.

(8) Baby Ivan have a bath, let's go see Baby
Ivan have a bath.

Mummy you go

where? (Asked by his mother)

Mummy you go swings

(9) lists some examples of Adam's speech showing the juxtaposition of two of his structures. Clark (1974:5-6) underlines the second simple structure.

(9i)   I want <u>you get a biscuit for me</u>.
(9ii)   Let me down, <u>ride my bike</u>.
(9iii) That a bunny <u>taking a book home</u>.
(9iv) I want <u>I eat apple</u>.

Examples like these not only suggest that the structures are not produced by transformations, but also that they are not even the result of a very complicated phrase structure grammar.

The use of juxtaposition like this is reminiscent of Weir's (1962) insightful, but somewhat neglected, study of the way children use speech in sequences. She noted in the pre-sleep monologues of her son Anthony, age 2;2-2;4, that utterances would be built up across several utterances. Braine (1973:422) has especially emphasized one of these as a procedure for establishing structure, calling it replacement sequencing.

(10)   man car
       man in car
       man in the car

Francis (1969) discusses a similar one, <u>key ringing</u>, a term used to describe how children group objects on sorting tasks between 2 and 6. Whereas replacement sequences build up a single structure e.g. (10), key ringing reflects how several different utterances will be run together. (11) provides an example of key ringing from Francis (169: 299).

(11)   I made a polish
       Where's a polish?
       There's a polish
       I make a polish on the table.

The child will select one word and string a series of sentences tied to it.

All of these observations reveal an important aspect of the speech of young children around age 3. This is that the juxtaposition of one sentence or structure to another is the predominant strategy for the construction of both larger utterances and discourse. It appears to be this strategy that is behind the first complex sentences, rather than the embedding of one sentence into another.

3.2 Complex sentences between 3;0 and 6;0. From the previous observations, it is possible to hypothesize three stages in the development of complex grammatical constructions. These are:

(12) Stage 1. The juxtaposition of two separate structures.
     Stage 2. The generation of one structure through phrase structure rules.
     Stage 3. The generation of one structure from two through the embedding of one sentence into another with transformational processes.

The construction of the first complex structures in the child's grammar around age 3 operates in the first of these stages. Evidence suggests a relatively loose combining of two structures. At some point after age 3, these become more productive and closely fused. They become part of a more elaborately developed phrase structure. Between ages 4 and 6, the generation of complex structures has the following characteristics: (1) the child develops a phrase structure grammar that can generate sentence-like structures within sentences; (2) the most common treatment of two propositions or sentences, however, is to 'juxtapose' them, connected by the conjunction and; and (3) the child does not relate very well structures produced by phrase structure with those juxtaposed as separate sentences.

I would like to exemplify this last point. In (1) and (3) there were sentences presented from a girl of 3;7. These show that the girl did produce relative clause structures, but this process was not very productive. The point is that the phrase structure grammar that does produce the relative clauses in her sentences is probably a very restricted one. Also, sentences with clauses are not related to those like in (1) which could be complex. There are two separate entities in the child's grammar-propositions: those enclosed within a single phrase structure and those juxtaposed in separate sentences. Children only begin to relate the two around the age of 6, and develop this skill gradually over the next six years.

Recall that the main impact of proposing a transformational grammar was that it claimed the relatedness of sentences. It allows one to relate two separate structures to a single underlying structure. There are two aspects of this kind of relatedness that come into the discussion here. One is the ability to embed one sentence into another from two separate sentences. This implies that the speaker has implicit knowledge that two full sentences are reduced into one by transformational processes. Second, there is the ability to create two structures on the surface from a common structure. Rules like Extraposition produce one of the sentences in (13) from the other,

(13a) <u>That I wanted to go</u> was obvious
(13b) It was obvious <u>that I wanted to go.</u>

Another example is Extraposition from Relative Clauses, that creates (14a) from (14b).

(14a) The boy runs quickly <u>who is tall.</u>
(14b) The boy <u>who is tall</u> runs quickly.

My claim is that children show neither one of these two abilities to relate structures before ages 5 or 6, and that it takes to around 12 before it is completed.

3.2.1. The relation between propositions. Let me provide some evidence to support these claims. In regard to the relatedness of propositions, it is obvious from an examination of children's speech from 3 to 6 that the child gradually develops the ability to relate two propositions. At the beginning, the child's speech is a series of propositions that are loosely put together. These sentences are rarely connected by a conjunction of any kind, and may not be in the correct temporal order. Here's an example of a story told by a girl Laurie, age 2;11 (Pitcher and Prelinger 1963:38)

(15) Once there was a baby. She broke her arm. A big spider
      came. She fall down. A big big long spider came. She
      bumped her head on the floor. She fall right down again,
      and get her poor head broke. She's a bad, bad girl,
      cause she's a sick sick girl.

Between ages 4;0 and 6;0, these loose connections are drawn closer by the use of conjunctions, predominantly <u>and</u>. The child uses <u>and</u> consistently, as if in an attempt to show the relatedness between his sentences. (16) is the beginning of a story told by Ed, age 5;1.

(16) Once there was a bear. And he lived behind a curtain
      and he never climbed up a curtain. And he thought he
      was living in a jungle because the curtain was colored
      brown. And one day he thumb-tacked the curtain to a
      wall. And then he climbed up the curtain, etc.

These two processes of juxtaposition, and juxtaposition with a conjunction dominate the speech from 3;0-6;0.
    Earlier I mentioned that it is difficult to find obligatory contexts where complex structures should apply. There is, however, one situation that I have noted where Relative Clause Formation does

appear to be obligatory. This is in the first sentence of story-telling, where the adult convention is basically:

(17) Once (upon a time), there was a X who Y
      Time focus   Introduction   Qualification

For example,

(18) Once (upon a time), there was an old lady who lived in a shoe.

It is possible to observe a child's ability to form relative clauses by examining how he introduces his own stories.

Pitcher and Prelinger (1963) have provided a rich source of data by publishing children's stories told between the ages of 2 and 6. Table 1 gives the number of stories for four age ranges and the number of children at each age who offered a story.

TABLE 1. Number of children and number of stories they told at four age ranges (Pitcher and Prelinger 1963).

Age ranges	2;0-2;11	3;0-3;11	4;0-4;11	5;0-5;11
Number of children	30	60	60	60
Number of stories	60	120	120	60

TABLE 2. Distribution of patterns used to introduce stories in the 360 stories collected by Pitcher and Prelinger (1963).

Age groups	2;0-2;11	3;0-3;11	4;0-4;11	5;0-5;11
Pattern:				
Sentence	67%	48%	24%	17%
NP	13%	18%	20%	13%
'Once . . .'	13%	29%	40%	50%
'Once upon a time . . .'	7%	4%	16%	20%

For each age group except the last, each child told two stories, each at a different month of the year. I examined the first lines of each of these stories to see if children followed the convention in (17) and were able to relate propositions through the use of relative clauses.

The results show quite strikingly that children in this period from 2;0 to 6;0 are just acquiring the ability to closely combine two propositions through the use of relative clause structures. Regarding the development of the ability to use Time Focus and Introduction in (17), there were four developmental patterns. The use of these is given in Table 2.

It was predominantly the youngest children who started their stories with a sentence, without either a Time Focus or an Introduction of the main character. Here are some examples:

(19a) Cass 2;8
      Boy fell out of car. He went in car again.
(19b) Daniel 2;10
      Little boy played. He cried.
(19c) Lucetta 2;3
      A horsie eats some food. He plays.

This pattern decreases across the subjects from 67 percent for the two-year-olds to only 17 percent for the five-year-olds. The Introduction was acquired by some of the children through the use of a Noun Phrase at the beginning of their stories. Rather than jumping into the action, the children would use these to introduce the main person in the story.

(20a) Dale 2;8
      A bus. He went up a hill.
(20b) Kip 3;7
      A wolf. And he starts to fight.
(20c) Laurie 4;2
      A pig. He gets in the fence and beats the cow up.

This pattern increased in use for three- and four-year-olds, showing that it is related to the 'onces' that follow rather than to the first one which decreased over the age ranges.

The third and fourth patterns show the use of a Time Focus. The occurrence of once was the widest spread, although the use of Once upon a time increased to 20 percent of the stories of the five-year-olds. Since these two are so closely related, there is no need to make much of the difference between them.

(21a) Isaac 3;3
      Once there was a bear.
(21b) Diane 4;8
      Once there was a dog.
(21c) Eliot 5;1
      Once upon a time there were four cowboys.

The development of the third aspect of (17), that is, the Qualification, shows clearly that children at these ages do not yet have productive use of Relative Clauses. The children show three ways of relating the qualifying proposition to the introduction. These are by juxtaposition, juxtaposition with a conjunction, and embedding with a relative clause. Table 3 shows the occurrence of these across the stories.

TABLE 3. Percentage of stories showing each of three relations between the Introduction and the Qualification of story beginnings for four age groups.

Age groups	2;0-2;11	3;0-3;11	4;0-4;11	5;0-5;11
Relation:				
Juxtaposition	75%	57%	40%	25%
Conjunction	22%	40%	37%	40%
Relative Clause	3%	3%	23%	35%

Juxtaposition is the placing of the Qualification in a sentence following the first sentence of the story. This was by far the dominant pattern for the two-year-olds. (For comparative purposes, the three relations will all be shown with once as the Time Focus.)

(22a) Porteus 2;10
Once there was a house. Peter lived in the house.
(22b) Betsy 2;7
Once there was a baby pig. He played with his Mommy.
(22c) Dulcy 3;4
Once there was a little pussy. He went outside.

The use of this loose connection between propositions dropped to 25 percent for the five-year-olds.

The two propositions were more closely tied by the occurrence of a conjunction between them. This was a dominant pattern for the 3;0 to 6;0 year-old children, and it shows the lack of embedding. Here are several examples of this process. Notice that each could have been stated as a relative clause.

(23a) Kurt 3;1
Once there was a little boy and he went for a walk in the woods.

(23b) Marla 3;4
Once there was a little boy and he hit someone on the head.
(23c) Lewis 4;5
Once out in the woods there was a big hole and a wolf
lived in it.
(23d) Ed 4;11
Once there was a little man and he went into the woods.
(23e) Keith 4;7
Once about a time there was a little man and he decided
to go up in the woods.
(23f) Upton 4;11
Once upon a time there was a great mean giant and he
had a hard hat.

The occurrence of relative clauses is infrequent, although they
reach 20 percent occurrence for the five-year-olds. While this figure
could be higher by considering these only against other cases where a
relative clearly could have been used, they are not all clearly embedded. The most common pattern was a reduced relative with
named. Forty percent of the sentences with relatives for five-year-
olds had these:

(24a) Tina 5;0
Once there was a kitty named Cindy.
(24b) Lorna 5;3
Once upon a time there was a big boy named Jimmy.
(24c) Alice 5;0
Once upon a time there was a cat named zero.

Another common pattern was reduced relatives with with phrases.

(25a) Emmet 5;0
Once there was a big scarey man with lots of faces.
(25b) Tab 5;0
Once there was a terrible crocodile with sharp teeth.

Both of these could result from a phrase structure rule that does not
deal with a full sentence in the underlying structure. This fact reduces greatly the actual number of first sentences used by the children that follow (17). Here are a few.

(26a) Chloe 4;2
Once upon a time there was a little girl who went for a
walk to a restaurant.

(26b) Dora 4;3
   Once upon a time there was a little horsie who lived on
   a farm.
(26c) Deirdre 5;6
   Once upon a time there was a little pussy cat that wanted
   to be a Christmas present.

The children at age 5 are just beginning to acquire the productive use
of complex structures such as these.

3.2.2 Transformationally related sentences. Besides combining
propositions into a single structure, transformational rules can also
create alternative surface structures by moving elements around.
Here are some paired sentences that would share a common underlying structure. The first is considered more basic in each pair; the
rule noted creates the second structure.

Extraposition
(27a) That John came early bothered me.
(27b) It bothered me that John came early.

Raising
(28a) I believe that John is a fool.
(28b) I believe John to be a fool.

Passive
(29a) I believe John to be a fool.
(29b) John is believed by me to be a fool.

Tough Movement
(30a) It is easy for me to hit you.
(30b) You are easy for me to hit.

It Replacement
(30a) It seems that you are happy.
(30b) You seem to be happy.

Nominalization
(32a) To paint is fun.
(32b) Painting is fun.

Extraposition can be used as an example of how this ability
develops. The child at six will use structures like (27b), but this
does not mean that he has a rule of Extraposition. Structures like
(27a) will not be found. At this point, the surface structure of (27b)

reflects more or less what the underlying structure must be. Over the next few years, the child will experience sentences of the form of (27a) and relate these to those like (27b). At that point, the child will restructure his knowledge of English grammar so that forms like (27b) will be transformationally produced.

Menyuk (1969) summarizes several studies she has conducted over the years on the acquisition of transformations in children between 3 and 7. In her book, she refers to three groups specifically: nursery school, kindergarten, and first grade children. Her results show that while complex structures occur in the speech of children, there are certain restrictions on them. The fact that a structure occurs does not mean that it appears in other parts of the sentence, or that it can be transformationally moved to create a different surface form. For example, while 87 percent of the children use relative clauses on object nouns, only 46 percent use them on subjects. Or, although all of the children are using infinitival complements, e.g. you have to do this, only 17 percent are using two or more in a sentence, e.g. you have to do this to get it to work. While some see this as a performance problem, I see it as an indication of the child's incomplete grammar of English, one without a very productive set of transformational processes.

Menyuk's (1969:100) discussion of nominalizations as in (32) are insightful.

Nominalizations can also be subjects of sentences as in Painting can be fun, To eat frog's legs is my greatest desire. These types of structures are not found in the language sample of this population. Instead we find Infinitival Complement constructions such as I like to paint and I like to eat frog's legs and Object Nominalizations with Predicate Phrases such as It's good to eat and It's fun to paint. The latter occur rarely in the language sample and are possibly memorized formulas since we do not find any sentences with any Noun Phrases other than the pronoun it.

Observations like these reveal the limited productivity of complex sentence patterns in the six-year-old child.

3.3 Complex sentences between 6;0 and 12;0. That a great deal of syntactic development takes place during the first six years of school has been demonstrated quite nicely by O'Donnell, Griffin, and Norris (1967). They studied the syntax of 180 children, 30 at each of the following: kindergarten, 1st, 2nd, 3rd, 5th, and 7th grades. Speech samples were obtained by showing the children two silent cartoons and asking them to tell about them afterwards. The third, fifth, and seventh grades also provided a written sample of the films. The use of a common topic makes it possible to make some specific claims on the occurrence of various grammatical constructions across the children. The ages range from a mean of 5;10 for the kindergarten children to a mean of 13;3 for the seventh graders.

The results showed that the use of syntax increased across the grade levels. For example, one of the types of constructions they studied was the kind resulting from embedding a sentence inside of an NP with a head noun. This would include relative clauses and their various reduced versions. They state:

> The rate of occurrence of sentence-combining transformations in nominal constructions increased significantly in Grades 1 and 7, and the overall increment in the frequency of such transformations was also significant . . . (O'Donnell, Griffin, and Norris 1967:57).

Two particular results are noteworthy. The first is that there was a group of structures that particularly developed over the school years.

> Greatest overall increases and most frequently significant increments from grade level to grade level were found in the use of adverbial infinitives, sentence adverbials, coordinations within T-units, and modifications of names by adjectives, participles, and prepositional phrases. In the theory of transformational grammar, all these constructions are explained as being produced by the application of deletion rules (O'Donnell, Griffin, and Norris 1967:90).

Examples of these are presented in (33).

(33a) Adverbial Infinitives:
    The ant went out to get some food
(33b) Sentence Adverbials:
    I don't know why he did that
(33c) Coordinations within Clauses:
    The wind went first and blew off a house top
(33d) Noun and Adjectives, Participles, and Prepositional Phrases:
    cold rain
    bird in a tree
    the man wearing a coat

The fact that these processes resulting from deletion increased so greatly can be understood when comparing the acquisition of complex structures to the manner in which children acquire other structures. Erwin (1964) has noted that children show at least three stages in acquiring rules to produce inflections for irregular plurals. First, the child will learn a word such as <u>feet</u> correctly, but purely on memory. No plural rule will occur. Next, the child will acquire plural /-s/, and will say <u>foots</u>. Finally, <u>feet</u> will be relearned within the child's new rule system.

These same stages can be proposed for the acquisition of trans-formations. Let me use reduced relatives as an example. First, the child will learn to produce forms like <u>the man wearing a coat</u> or <u>the red coat,</u> but they will not be transformationally derived. Next, the child will learn how to form relative clauses. When this occurs, sentences like <u>the man wearing a coat</u> will appear as <u>the man who is wearing a coat</u>. The old pattern will be taken over by the new pattern. Finally, once the child knows that these structures are all related, transformational rules to reduce them can be developed by the child. The great gains in the use of reduced structure between kindergarten and seventh grade reflects the acquisition of knowledge about em-bedded sentences and the transformations that reduce them. One can say that it is during this period that children restructure their gram-mar to derive adjectives from relative clauses.

(34) is a sentence used by a 8;7 boy (Third Grade) in the O'Donnell, Griffin, and Norris study.

(34)   the North Wind came along and asked the sun to for them
       to have a test to see which one was the strongest and most
       powerfulest.

If the child is restricting his knowledge of infinitives as resulting from fully embedded sentences, one would expect cases like this where the normally deleted subject <u>them</u> appears. This child is in the process of acquiring the <u>for-to</u> construction and Raising.

The second finding of this study concerns the use of coordination between propositions. Children continued to put propositions together with conjunctions up to Grade 5, and then showed a decrease in Grade 7. This indicates that children were becoming better at merging their propositions together through embedding. This finding was re-lated to another important result. Recall that there were written samples to compare with the spoken ones for Grades 3, 5, and 7. It was found that in Grades 5 and 7, there were significantly more nomi-nally complex structures in written than spoken language. That is, children were better at using complex structures in written than in spoken language.

The use of writing requires one to combine as much information together as possible. Because of considerations of skill, it also imposes the requirement that one should not be repetitive. Factors like these are very conducive to developing elaborate syntactic means for both embedding sentences and also for having surface structure variants of the same underlying sentence. It appears that much of the complex syntactic patterning described in recent years by transformational linguists can be traced back to the influence of the writing system. It is a frequent complaint that the elaborate sentences used as linguistic examples are ones that are never spoken. That may be true, but it is probably because they are not as much part of the spoken language as of the written language. Linguists working with informants of unwritten Indian languages often have trouble eliciting complex structures. The informants usually state that the complex structures are possible, but not used. Without a written tradition, however, they are not necessary.

All of this suggests that the development of writing in grade school plays an important role in the child's learning of complex structures. The need to be concise and non-repetitive creates a circumstance conducive to the development of process of embedding and transforming structures.

4. Cognitive development and transformations

4.1 Cognitive theory. The child's development in the ability to relate one sentence to another is directly analogous to his cognitive changes between 3 and 12. These skills have been studied extensively by Piaget in numerous books and articles. I will first provide a brief overview of Piaget's stages of cognitive development over this period and then discuss how these relate to transformations.

Piaget (1962) refers to the time between ages 4;0 and 7;0 as a stage of Intuitive Thought. The child begins to seek an understanding of the world around him, but relies on perceptual judgments alone. At this period the child is not capable of abstract thought. Also, the child is not very advanced in the ability to reason out an explanation for events in the world. Because of this, the child relies on intuitions.

Two examples will suffice to demonstrate the intuitive nature of the child's thought. When presented with two containers with different shapes but the same amount of water, the child will 'intuit' that the container with the highest water level is the one with the most water in it. Here he relies totally on perception. As Piaget (1928:220) has said 'Immediate perception is the measure of all things'. Second, when the young child is asked to draw a picture of a bicycle, he will place the parts on the page without showing the relation between them. This is also true of pictures of people, where eyes, noses, and ears will be in assorted relations. The child deals with each one at a time, and does not unify them into a single structure.

The first example shows the inability of the child to perform a reversible operation. Piaget (1928:171) states: 'a mental operation is reversible when, starting from its result, one can find a symmetrically corresponding operation which will lead back to the data of the first operation without these having been altered in the process'. The child cannot retrace the steps to arrive at the conclusion that the water in the two containers was at one point the same amount. Because the child cannot do this, the child cannot relate very effectively one part or element to another. The second example shows this with the use of 'juxtaposition' in the pictures he draws. Since the child cannot hold aspects in relation, he simply juxtaposes them.

This state of affairs changes around age 7 with the onset of the period of concrete operations. The child develops the ability to perform reversible operations, and can begin to retrace the steps that have resulted in a particular state of affairs. Perceptual criteria are abandoned for more logical ones. As a result the child overcomes the simple strategy of juxtaposition.

It is not difficult to draw a parallel between the child's cognitive ability over this period of time and his linguistic ability to relate propositions. Between 3;0 and 6;0 or 7;0, the young child uses predominantly juxtaposition to relate one sentence to another. Likewise to transformationally relate two propositions requires the ability to perform a reversible operation. We have seen now that the data suggests that the use of complex structures is not very productive. There is now an explanation for this. The child at this time cannot yet perform reversible operations. He cannot very effectively take two propositions and relate them to each other through embedding them into a single structure. Reversibility would also be involved in the ability to relate the various pairs in (27) to (32). The fact that sentences like these only occur during Piaget's concrete operational period shows that the development of transformations is very closely related to the child's cognitive abilities.

4. 2 Evidence relating transformations to cognitive operations. Research from a Piagetian perspective on the development of the ability to relate propositions to one another has been done by Piaget (1928), Sinclair (1967), and Ferreiro (1971), the latter summarized in Ferreiro and Sinclair (1971). This work has generally shown that children before the development of concrete relations do not relate propositions very well. Here, I present some of the findings of Ferreiro on this topic.

Ferreiro was interested in seeing how children develop both the understanding and production of sentences which express a temporal order of relationship between two events. Regarding the possible ways that two events may be related, Ferreiro and Sinclair (1971:41) state:

> When two nonidentical events or actions are described, the
> presence of two verb-phrases is necessary, but there is no
> obligation to use a particular syntactic structure: subordi-
> nate clauses, coordinate clauses, or simple juxtaposition of
> two propositions are all equally appropriate.

Notice that these three alternatives have been described here regarding the use of first sentences in stories.

The ages and numbers of subjects at each age were:

Age:	4;0-4;11	5;0-5;11	6;0-6;11	7;0-7;11	8;0-8;11	9;0-9;11
Subjects:	32	31	19	16	14	11
Age:						10;0-10;5
Subjects:						7

In order to compare linguistic and cognitive skills, she first gave
the 130 children a standard Piagetian task for the conservation of
water. The child is first shown two similar glasses with equal
amounts of water. One of these is poured into a third container
which is taller and narrower than the first two. The child is then
asked if the new container has the same amount of water as the old
one. If the child says that the taller container has more water now,
he is asked to guess the water level of the original glass when the
water is poured back into it. This test grouped most of the children
into three groups which I refer to as: (1) nonoperational group (4
year-olds), (2) preoperational group (4 and 5-year-olds), and (3)
operational group (6 to 10-year-olds).

The nonoperational group would say that the taller glass had more
water in it. They could not perform a reversible operation in which
they would retrace the steps and ascertain that the amount of water
was still the same. The preoperational group also said that the
taller glass had more water, but they could guess where the water
level would be in the original glass. Here the child is on the way to
forming reversible operations but cannot yet make the final deduction.
Ferreiro refers to these as one-way mappings. The operational
group can perform the reversible operations necessary to conclude
that the amount of water has not changed.

Production-of-speech relating two events was done in several
ways. (I give only those discussed in Ferreiro and Sinclair.) In
one, the experimenter acted out two events and the child had to
describe them. This was called 'free-choice description'. Next,
the child was asked to describe the events by first mentioning the

agent of the second event. For example, if the events were a girl-doll washing a boy-doll and then the boy going up the steps, the experimenter would say, 'but this time, start by talking about the boy' (Ferreiro and Sinclair 1971:41). This was the 'inverse-order description'. Here the child would need to use a temporal marker of some kind since the order of mention of the events would be inappropriate. Third, the child was asked when-questions about the events, e.g. 'when did the girl wash the boy?'; 'when did the boy go upstairs?' (Ferreiro and Sinclair 1971:42). These were asked to determine if the child understood the temporal relations involved.

Each of the three groups differed in their responses to these tasks. The transition was from a very loose connection between the propositions to a closer one with the use of subordination. The nonoperational group responded in the following ways. On the free-choice description the children described the events in two independent and weakly linked propositions. For example, (35) is cited in Ferreiro and Sinclair (1971:42).

(35) Elle l'a nettoyé pi il a monté (age 4;2)
      'She cleaned him and then he went up'

Interestingly, the children would even give the events back sometimes in a different order than their occurrence. Order of the events did not seem important to them. On the inverse-order description, the events were simply given in one order or another without any temporal markers. In response to when-questions, they would say now or just this moment, relating the event to the moment of speaking rather than to the other event.

The responses of the preoperational group were especially revealing, and show the pretransformational nature of the syntax of five-year-olds. On the free-choice description, the children still loosely juxtapose propositions, but begin to use temporal adverbs like before or after. The events, however, are always given in their order of occurrence; that is, 'their order of enunciation is always the same as the temporal order of events' (Ferreiro and Sinclair 1971:43).

(36) La fille a nettoyé le garçon; après le garçon est monté
      en haut de l'escalier. (age 5;8)
      'The girl cleaned the boy; afterwards the boy went up to
      the top of the stairs'

While this appears to be a complex sentence, Ferreiro and Sinclair (1971:43) note that the clauses are loosely linked with the tenses usually the same. On the reverse-order description, the children will start with the agent of the second event, 'However, they are incapable of using the temporal indicators needed to describe the actual temporal succession'. They would use several strategies, one of which worked. One was to keep the same adverb but give the wrong order.

(37) Le garçon est monté en haut des escaliers et après la
      fille l'a nettoyé
      'The boy went up to the top of the stairs and afterwards
      the girl cleaned him'

The children were incapable of doing the reversible operation necessary to start with the second event. This showed that the complex structure of these sentences is questionable and that a transformation of Adverb Preposing did not exist. One could say that the children did not understand the words before and after. The responses to the when question, however, showed that the semantics of these words is intact. Here is an example from a child at 5;0 who gave the responses in (34) and (35).

(38) Adult: Quand le garçon est-il monté?
              'When did the boy go upstairs?'
      Child: Après que la fille l'a nettoyé.
              'After the girl cleaned him'.
      Adult: Quand la fille l'a-t-elle nettoyé?
              'When did the girl clean him?'
      Child: Avant qu'il est monté
              'Before he went up'

When the experimenter preserved the inverse-order description, however, the child could not describe the events by starting with the 'boy'. He finally says that you have to start with the girl to relate the two events. When asked to try again with 'boy', he says:

(39) Le garçon monte en haut des escaliers et après la
      fille le nettoie.
      'The boy goes up to the top of the stairs and afterwards
      the girl cleans him'.

The operational group of children between the ages of 6 and 10 are able to produce these constructions correctly. Also, almost all of the children's responses use subordinate clauses which were absent in the first two groups. (French uses après que and avant que to mark such subordinate clauses.) Also, the children usually use different tenses in the clauses. Ferreiro (1971:55) notes that the older children between 8;0 and 12;0 not only use the subordinate clauses, but also put the clause sentence initially.

(40) Après que la fille a lavé la figure du garçon, le garcon
a monté les escaliers.
'After the girl washed the boy's face, the boy went up
the stairs'.

This shows that the children at this age have a transformation of
Adverb Preposing.

The data from Ferreiro is the best evidence yet of the relation
between concrete operations in cognition and syntactic transformations. The nonoperational children are not yet capable of closely
relating two separate propositions. Even when the child gets better
at this and begins to use subordinate markers, these do not indicate
a complex structure in the child's grammar. Only after age 6 do
complex sentences result from productive rules. This coincides
with the child's cognitive ability to perform concrete operations.
When the child is capable of relating propositions through reversible
operations, the acquisition of transformations occurs.

Ferreiro and Sinclair (1971:45) are careful in the claims they make
about the relation of cognition and language. 'We have no intention of
completely reducing language to operational development'. What they
do show, however, is that language development is very closely related to the cognitive development of the child.

5. A note on morphophonemic development. If the development of
concrete operations reflects an increase in the ability to develop complex structures in syntax, one may ask whether or not it also influ-
ences phonological development. It turns out that there are similar
developments in the acquisition of the morphophonemic patterns of
English. That is, not only is syntactic development not complete by
age 6, but neither is phonological development. Since the main purpose of this paper is the acquisition of transformations, the evidence
is only briefly sketched here (cf. Ingram, in press, Chapter 2, for a
fuller discussion).

Morphophonemics refers to phonological changes that result from
the addition of one morpheme to another. Chomsky and Halle (1968)
provide an in-depth study of a number of the complex morphophonemic
patterns of English. The young normal child by age 6 can produce
most of the speech sounds of his language. The data to date suggests,
however, that morphophonemic development is just beginning (e.g.
Berko, 1958).

Two recent studies by Moskowitz (1973) and Atkinson-King (1973)
show this quite clearly. Moskowitz studied the acquisition of the
English vowel shift rule by children between 5 and 12 years of age.
Using nonsense forms, she found that five-year-olds did not show
any indication of a rule of vowel shift. As for the older children,

Moskowitz (1973:248) states:

> There is no doubt that these children have knowledge of vowel
> shift, since the data are almost overwhelming. The differences
> among the results for the three age-groups indicates that the
> acquisition of this information takes place gradually. Seven-
> year-olds and some 9-12 year-olds seem to tolerate any kind
> of alternation of vowel quality while other 9-12 year-olds toler-
> ate only the major alternation pattern of English.

The study by Atkinson-King (1973) focused on the stress rules of
English that result in the contrasts in (41).

(41) Noun compounds   Noun phrases
      gréen house   green hoúse
      red head   red héad
      hót dog   hot dóg

She tested these in several tasks, including picture identification.
The subjects were approximately 300 children between 5;0 and 13.
Her results show that these rules are only acquired between 6 and
12. 'In general a child of five does not yet show the ability with these
stress contrasts but a child of twelve does; and the closer to twelve
a child is, the more likely he is to have acquired it' (Atkinson-King
1973:v).

The acquisition of these morphophonemic rules is similar to the
acquisition of transformations that embed one sentence into another.
Just as one proposition has to be related to another for the two to be
embedded into one structure, so does one word have to be related to
another in order for a rule to be established which produces one for
the other. This suggests that words like divine and divinity are
first acquired separately, and then related to one underlying form.
The child needs to be capable of reversible operations in order to
relate pairs of words like these.

6. Conclusion. All of these observations lend support to the
position that language development is not completed by age 6. More
important, the patterns that have yet to be learned are not just the
idiosyncratic ones that characterize exceptions, but some of the
major rules of English. Specifically, it appears that most of the
transformational rules that concern English complex sentences are
acquired in this period. This fact is consistent with the child's cognitive abilities at this age. It is only between the ages of 6 and 12
that the child learns the ability to perform concrete operations. This
ability is needed to relate one proposition with another.

The Appendix presents the first part of a story told by a young girl of 5;6 about a movie entitled <u>Pippi Longstocking</u> which she had just seen. An examination of this text shows that this child obviously has a language problem. The text is far different from what one would hear from an adult speaker of English. This child's language problem, however, is not due to abnormality. She is a very normal child for her age. Her problem is that she has yet to develop a productive set of transformational rules to relate her propositions to each other. Complex structures occur, but most often juxtaposition is the major means used to relate two sentences. The next six years will be a very active and important period of language development for her. With the onset of concrete operations, she will acquire the major transformations of English.

APPENDIX

PIPPI LONGSTOCKING: A REPORT BY A GIRL OF 5;6

First the grandpop that in the pirate's cave sent bottles with messages in them and Pippi had a balloon and her bed was underneath it and they fought but then it couldn't fly anymore and then they made a airplane with a bicycle and after that broke they . . . what did they do? I don't know if they did that and then they were at the pirate ship and we were on an island they were on a island and they got stuck and there's alligators and everything and so when they saw the man and Pippi Longstocking is talking like a man and said 'the treasure's buried here, the treasure's buried here' and it wasn't and it wasn't it was in the water where grandpa and Pippi Longstocking made and then she got one of them and then she got four of them but one of them Pippi Longstocking got and that was a good one cause it had jewels and everything but the other one just had a plain old skeleton in it . . .

REFERENCES

Atkinson-King, Kay. 1973. Children's acquisition of phonological stress contrasts. UCLA Working Papers in Phonetics. No. 25.
Braine, Martin. 1973. Three suggestions regarding grammatical analyses of children's language. In: Ferguson and Slobin 1973: 421-429.
Brown, Roger. 1973. A first language. Cambridge, Mass. Harvard University Press.
Cazden, Courtney. 1968. The acquisition of noun and verb inflections. Child Development 39. 433-438. (Reprinted in Ferguson and Slobin, 226-240).

Chomsky, Carol. 1969. The acquisition of syntax in children from 5 to 10. Cambridge, Mass. The MIT Press.

Chomsky, Noam and Morris Halle. 1968. The sound pattern of English. New York, Harper and Row.

Clark, Ruth. 1974. Performing without competence. Journal of Child Language 1.1-10.

Dale, Philip. 1972. Language development: Structure and function. Hinsdale, Illinois, The Dryden Press.

Ervin, Susan. 1964. Imitation and structural change in children's language. In: New directions in the study of language. Edited by E. Lenneberg. Cambridge, Mass., MIT Press. (Reprinted in Ferguson and Slobin, 391-406).

Ferguson, Charles and Dan Slobin, eds. 1973. Studies of child language development. New York, Holt, Rinehart and Winston.

Ferreiro, Emilia. 1971. Les relations temporelles dans le langage de l'enfant. Geneva, Droz.

_____ and Hermine Sinclair. 1971. Temporal relations in language. International Journal of Psychology 6.39-47.

Francis, Hazel. 1969. Structure in the speech of a 2-1/2-year-old. British Journal of Educational Psychology 39.291-302.

Ingram, David. 1972. The development of phrase structure rules. Language Learning 22.65-77.

_____. (in press). Phonological disability in children. London, Arnold.

Kiparsky, Paul. 1968. Language universals and linguistic change. In: Universals in linguistic theory. Edited by E. Bach and R. Harms. New York, Holt, Rinehart and Winston. 171-202.

Limber, John. 1973. The genesis of complex sentences. In: T. Moore, ed. 169-185.

Menyuk, Paula. 1969. Sentences children use. Cambridge, Mass., MIT Press.

Miller, Wick. 1973. The acquisition of grammatical rules by children. In: Ferguson and Slobin. 380-391.

Moore, Timothy, ed. 1973. Cognitive development and the acquisition of language. New York, Academic Press.

Moskowitz, Arlene. 1973. On the status of vowel shift in English. In: T. Moore, ed. 223-260.

Nice, Margaret. 1925. Length of sentences as a criterion of a child's progress in speech. Journal of Educational Psychology 16.377-379.

O'Donnell, Roy, William Griffin, and Raymond Norris. 1967. Syntax of kindergarten and elementary school children: A transformational analysis. Champaign-Urbana, Illinois, National Council of Teachers of English.

Piaget, Jean. 1928. Judgment and reasoning in the child. London, Routledge and Kegan Paul.

_____. 1962. Play, dreams, and imitation in childhood. New York, Norton.

Pitcher, Evelyn and Ernst Prelinger. 1963. Children tell stories. New York, International Universities Press.

Sinclair, Hermine. 1967. Acquisition du langage et développement de la pensée. Paris, Dunod.

Stern, Clara and William Stern. Die Kindersprache. Leipzig, Barth.

Weir, Ruth. 1962. Language in the crib. The Hague, Mouton.

CHILDREN WITH LANGUAGE PROBLEMS: WHAT'S THE PROBLEM?

PAULA MENYUK

Boston University

The nature of the language development difference between children with disorders of the central nervous system and children who are developing normally has been a matter of great controversy lately. The question put is: Is there a qualitative or a quantitative difference in the language development of the two groups of children? That is, do these children acquire the same knowledge of language in the same order as do normally developing children, or does this knowledge differ in some way? Most of the controversy has been generated by linguists, not clinicians. The latter take the view that it is either an absurd question ('Of course there's a difference!'), or is totally non-germane to their task of remedying the language behavior of these children. 'For the clinician, however, the quantity/quality issue may be merely an academic one and of no functional use toward teaching or modifying the child's language behavior' (Yoder and Miller 1972:122). The statement itself contains two assumptions: (1) with these children, unlike normally developing children, language must be taught or modified; and (2) the method used to teach or modify is independent of the particular language state of children in this population or the particular language processing mechanisms they employ. Either position vis-à-vis the quality/quantity issue renders both assumptions clearly open to question. The following discussion will explore (1) whether or not there is a theoretical basis for either position; (2) what the little data that is available on the language behavior of these children tells concerning this issue; and (3) what implications conclusions about this issue have for both the researcher and clinician in understanding and possibly remedying the language behavior of children with language problems.

Theoretical bases for descriptions of language development

It is a fact that different schools of thought exist about the bases for language acquisition. Do these differing theoretical positions predict quantity or quality differences in the case of children with developmental disorders? One can, in very roughshod manner, categorize these schools of thought as LAD (Language Acquisition Device) (for example, Chomsky 1965) and CAD (Cognitive Acquisition Device) (for example, Braine 1971). The first position assumes that human infants not only have the biological potential to acquire language, but in addition, 'come to' the language acquisition task with notions about the possible 'form' of the human language. The necessary condition for learning language is a biologically intact organism. The role of the environment is to provide the necessary data: the language. The second position assumes that the human infant has the biological potential to learn and to learn in a particular manner. One of the things the human infant learns is language. The conditions that are necessary for learning are a biologically intact organism and a responsive environment.

The LAD position seems to have implicit in it the hypothesis that biological intactness, or some compensatory mechanisms which might circumvent deficit, will lead to a sequence of language acquisition which does not vary from child to child. The CAD position also seems to have implicit in it the hypothesis that biological intactness, or some compensatory mechanisms, plus a responsive environment will lead to a sequence of language acquisition which does not vary from child to child. Thus, except for the inclusion of the notions of a responsive environment, and except for the fact that language is a part of the repertoire of human behaviors, rather than distinct, CAD does not seem to differ strikingly from LAD. However, if one assumes that mere exposure to language is a constant, these latter two additional factors proposed by CAD introduce two other possible sources of variability and thus, hypothetically, increase the possibility of variability. Further, since both theoretical positions suggest that biological intactness is a necessary condition for development, biological insult without the 'appropriate' compensatory mechanisms could lead to differences in the language acquisition process.

In addition to the above theoretical positions concerning the bases for language acquisition, there is the theoretical description of language behavior, the variable rule (Labov 1969), which might be applied to the difference in language behavior one observes between children developing language normally and those who are not. That is, it might be the case that in all aspects of language behavior the 'same rules' of language use eventually become available to both groups of children, but that the frequency, conditions for, and consistency of use of particular rules vary between the two groups. One might consider the nature and degree of variability in use of linguistic rules either a quantitative difference or a qualitative difference, depending on whether or not one considers this variability to be a function of difference in knowledge of language (the grammar) or a difference in language performance.

The situation, then, appears to be that any theoretical explanation or description of the language acquisition process can predict either similarity (but delayed) or difference in the language development of children who are developing normally and those who are not. Each model can account for either similarity or difference in the manner indicated in Table 1.

TABLE 1.   Theoretical predictions of delay or difference.

Model	Prediction
LAD	
A. Biological intactness	
B. Compensatory mechanisms	Similarity
C. Exposure to language	
D. Significant variations of A, B, C	Difference
CAD	
A. Biological intactness	
B. Compensatory mechanisms	
C. Learning strategies	Similarity
D. Responsive environment	
E. Significant variation of A, B, C, D	Difference
LAD/CAD + Variable rules	
A. G + Variable rules	Similarity
B. Variable rules	Difference

It should be noted that the same possibilities for similarity or difference between normally developing children exist when one assumes the CAD position or the LAD position plus the notion of variable rules, and, indeed, one finds discussions of universals in language acquisition (Slobin 1973; Brown 1973) and individual or group variations (Bloom 1970; Bowerman 1973), in the sequence of acquisition of particular structures, with about equal frequency in the child language literature.   Universality in the sequence of acquisition of linguistic structures is explained by universal biological-cognitive constraints; individual variation is explained by individual cognitive-social-linguistic constraints. With children with developmental disorders one can either assume universality because of compensatory mechanisms or preclude universality because of deviation from biological-cognitive constraints.

A possible out for theoreticians may be that both similarities and differences exist between children with and without language problems. A reasonable explanation of similarity and difference might be that suggested by Chatsworth (1975):

> . . . many ethologists feel that if someone posits an innate mechanism for a behavior of a particular species it automatically implies in the mind of many psychologists that they are claiming that every member of the species has the mechanism and has it at the same strength. No respectable ethologist, however, believes this because it is in direct conflict with his own empirical observations as well as with what everyone else knows about natural behavior, namely, that it differs from individual to individual, sometimes widely, sometimes little . . . depending.

If this position has some validity, then one would expect to find children with language problems who differ little or who differ widely. The researcher's task, then, might be to pinpoint what similarities and differences exist in the language behavior of which children and why.

Given the current theoretical state of affairs, clinicians might very well agree with the previously cited statement that the issue is 'merely an academic one, and of no functional use toward teaching or modifying.' However, some resolution of these issues seems critical in determining what to do about teaching or modifying. If one assumes that the language acquisition process is similar for children with and without language problems, but slower for those with problems, one might decide to leave them alone to develop at their own pace, or one might decide that what they need is more of what normally developing children get (whatever that is) in an attempt to get them to accelerate their pace. In distinction to this, one might assume that the language acquisition process is different for children with developmental problems, determine what the differences are, attempt to explain the bases for the differences, and then design remedial programs which take into account what the children know about language and how they have achieved this knowledge. Clinicians have come to both, either, or neither of these conclusions (the latter arbitrarily decide what these children should know about language; for example, color names) because they appear to be in a quandary about what difference is a difference and then what to do about it.

Language behavior of children with developmental problems

What does the data on the language behavior of these children show? In the past, most studies of the language behavior of children with developmental problems were comparisons of their behavior with that of normally developing children on standard tests and standard measures of language performance. When the language behavior of populations of mentally retarded, aphasic, deaf, autistic, learning disabled, etc. children are compared to normally developing children of their own age on the standard tests and measures, one overall finding emerges. They lag behind their normally developing age peers on any aspect of language (semantic, syntactic, morphological, phonological) tested. Some recent studies using language samples for analysis indicate that it takes aphasic (Morehead and Ingram 1973) and mentally retarded (Lackner 1968) children a significantly longer time than it does normally developing children to increase their mean morphemes per utterance, and to acquire the same syntactic structures.

These are overall findings since there appear to be children within each 'diagnosed' population with whom this developmental delay is more or less marked than the average for the group. With the aphasic population it is suggested, however, that in other aspects of language development (semantic and phonological) differences exist in the structures used, and that there is a difference in the frequency of usage of certain structures. Further, as one observes the development of M. M. U. within the normal and aphasic population the age difference between the populations increases. Thus at M. M. U. 3+ there is approximately a 37-month difference, at M. M. U. 4+ a 54-month difference, and at M. M. U. 5+ a 71-month difference, which may indicate that some structures are never acquired. With the mentally retarded children, although the sequence of development of syntactic structures follows the pattern observed with normally developing children, it was observed that severely retarded children may become arrested in their language development and remain at a 'lower' stage. There is, thus, within these populations, the possibility of (1) some aspects of the language being acquired at a later age than that of normally developing children, (2) some aspects not being acquired at all, and (3) some aspects being acquired differently.

In other studies (Menyuk 1971) it appears to be the case that those aspects of sentence types or structures which are acquired later than their simpler counterparts, or are used relatively infrequently by the normally developing child, cause particular difficulty for the child with developmental problems. Some examples with particular populations are the following:

(1) /Id and Iz/ tense and plural rules--mentally retarded children
(2) Auxiliary/modal expansion--aphasic children
(3) Derivatives (in written language)--deaf children
(4) Conjunction and embedding--aphasic and mentally retarded children

In other words, some aspects of the language are acquired at a much later age. Finally, as was suggested by Piaget (1970), and researched by Cromer (1974), delay itself without the appropriate intervening stages may in some way distort the nature of the structure that is acquired although, on the surface, it may appear to be the same. For example, if children do not go through the process of making generalizations about a structure, it may be that their understanding of these structures is different from that of children who have made these generalizations. Cromer points to the lack of the development of an object strategy in achieving understanding of structures in which the subject is not named ('The doll is easy to see'). I analyzed the spontaneous speech and sentence repetition of children aged 3 to 6 years who were developing language normally and those labelled as retarded in language development for unknown causes (Menyuk 1964). It was found that omission of a base structure category and a morphological marker was the most frequent and consistent behavior observed with the delayed language group throughout the age range, whereas developmental changes occurred within the normally developing population, and substitutions and redundancies became more frequent with maturation. The frequency of omissions as compared to generalizations in the generation of structures and sentences has also been found in other studies of language delayed children (Leonard 1972). The question that these results suggest is: If these children are taught how to produce complete sentences or structures, and succeed in doing so, is their knowledge of these structures the same as that of children who go through the intervening generalization stages?

In summary, despite the overall findings of simple developmental delay, one can find behaviors that at least suggest difference as well as delay. Developmental delay itself has at least three components, and possibly five:

(1) Late onset and acquisition of structures A
(2) Even greater delay with structures B
(3) Never acquired structures C
(4) Different categorization of structures D?

(5) Different (or absent) transitional stages in the acquisition of structures E?

Is it the case that one can discuss 'them', that is, all children who display a deviance in language acquisition, as if both the behavior observed and the explanation for this behavior were the same for all these children? Is it the case that the same categorization of structures into A, B, C, D and E can be found with all children who have developmental problems? That is, are all the structures that are delayed, markedly delayed, etc. the same for all these children? The answer to these questions is not known since so little research carried out with these children has carefully examined what they know about language, much less why.

Hypothesize for a moment that something is known about the brain and behavior, and, in particular, about the developing brain and language behavior. It has been suggested that the developmental process, in cases of children with suspected neurological abnormalities, is distorted by cerebral trauma which then may give rise to a large variety of dysfunctions (de Hirsch 1972). These dysfunctions are not only limited to language but are observed in all areas of physiological and psychological functioning. Bilateral involvement seems to be suggested. This general trauma, it is said, interferes with the normal maturational process, and results in difficulties with integration and organization of input information. Along with these overall dysfunctions the organism is able to develop some compensatory mechanisms. It is suggested that, unlike adult aphasics, these children do not exhibit circumscribed pathologies related to particular structural lesion. From this hypothesis it is difficult to account for 'a large variety of dysfunctions' or a 'clinical picture that varies from child to child'. It is the case, however, that variety does exist within this population as well as within mentally retarded and autistic populations. Perhaps this variety can be fully accounted for by differential experience from the cradle onward to educational settings. It has been noted, but not clearly researched, that mother-child interaction is either deficient and/or distorted in the case of children with developmental disabilities. However, it is equally possible that particular structural lesions might account for the variety of behaviors observed or that, indeed, both conditions might exist, separately and together: overall trauma and specific lesions. Finally, differences in the compensatory mechanisms available to the child could account for the variety which might include differences in structural mechanisms available and also in experience.

If it is the case that a variety of clinical pictures is presented by the child with developmental disabilities and that possibly there is a variety of neurological substrates, compensating mechanisms, and experiences, which underlie the variety of clinical pictures, then it seems difficult to accept the notion that language development for these children is simply a slowing down of the normal developmental process. A review of the rather sparse data on the language behavior of children with developmental problems suggests that both similarities and differences in the language development of these and normally developing children may exist within and across populations of these children and, indeed, within a single child. The initially presented hypothesis concerning the neurological substrate of this language behavior, overall trauma, does not seem to account adequately for the varieties of behavior observed. We suggest, then, that various neurological substrates are possible and that the varieties of language behavior observed are indications of this possibility. When the language processing abilities of children with suspected neurological abnormalities was examined in a variety of tasks, at least three groups of children were observed (Menyuk 1975a), and simple observation indicates the possibility of a fourth group. Table 2 indicates the different groups that have been identified thus far.

TABLE 2. Comparison of language performance among aphasic children and with normal children.

| | Sentence reproduction | | Speech sound identification | | Spontaneous speech | |
	Language	Speech	Perception	Production	Language	Speech
Group 1	delayed	delayed	delayed	delayed	delayed	delayed
Group 2	arrested	different	different	different	delayed	different
Group 3	same	different	same	different	?	different
Group 4a					some block	same
Group 4b					blocked	different

Group 1 appears to be simply delayed in language development. In a sentence and phonological repetition task, and in a task requiring perceptual and productive categorizations of minimal pair words, their behavior is quite similar to the behavior observed with younger, normally developing children. That is, they benefit from the immediate sentence model and reproduce sentences in somewhat better form than they spontaneously produce them, but their reconstitution of structures is still similar to that of much younger children. Their phonological reproductions and categorization errors are similar to those found with a younger population of normally developing children. Group 2 within this population appears to be arrested in their sentence repetition performance (they do not benefit from the model and repeat at the level of their spontaneous production of these sentence types); their phonological recoding of words in sentences is different from that observed with younger, normally developing children; and they have marked difficulty in productively and perceptually categorizing minimal pair words.

The Group 3 children appear to comprehend sentences, insofar as one is able to measure this, and perceptually categorize minimal pair words, in a manner almost commensurate with that of their age peers. However, their production of language is markedly different from normally developing children in terms of phonological categories and rules, and their productive categorization of minimal pair words is significantly different from that of language delayed and normally developing children. It should be noted that Group 1 and Group 2 children do not show marked differences in terms of the syntactic structure of the sentences they spontaneously produce but do so in terms of repetition of sentences (both syntactically and phonologically) and in the perceptual and productive categorization of minimal pair words. The potential Group 4 children are those who have been described as having a 'word finding' problem. These children seem to fall into two categories of language behavior: those who have difficulty in generating any sentence at all, and those who in spontaneous speech run into difficulty sometimes, and only show real deficiency when confronted with a naming task per se (that is, naming pictures or objects). In just one probe with one child who was having difficulty in generating any sentence at all, it was found that when an acoustic-motor cue to the initial sound or syllable of the word being searched for was provided, the child could complete the word but could not go on to complete the sentence.

It may be the case that children who only occasionally display difficulty in finding a word when producing language and always have difficulty when naming pictures, might also benefit from a speech cue in the naming task, but for a different reason. Possibly these latter children use the semantic cues of the structure of the sentence to help them retrieve a word when speaking spontaneously but, of course, do not have the cues when naming pictures. The speech cue may help them in lexical retrieval. The children who have difficulty in generating any sentence at all may have a motor planning problem rather than a lexical retrieval problem and, therefore, are continuously blocked in their generation of sentences.

There appears to be a sufficient number of similarities in the language behavior of these children and the language behavior of adult aphasics to suggest that the neurological substrate of their behavior, like that of adult aphasics, may vary and not simply be a function of overall trauma. The differences between the children and adults may be in the capacity of a developing organism to overcome lesion or trauma by some compensatory mechanisms.

The variety in language behavior observed with children with suspected neurological abnormalities can also be found within other populations: mentally retarded and autistic children. Some of these behaviors are similar to those found with children who are diagnostically categorized as aphasic, and others are dissimilar. Most of the difference, thus far, has been described in terms of degree of involvement. For example, autistic children are said to behave as if they were partially blind and deaf, mentally retarded, and congenitally aphasic (Wing 1969). However, there is a group of children within this population who are said to be 'echlalic' in their language behavior while others are not. In addition to being delayed in language development a subgroup of the mentally retarded children (Downs-Syndrome children) appear to be much more inconsistent in their phonological performance and make unique substitutions when compared to other mentally retarded children (Cromer 1974). It is possible that if similar patterns of language behavior are observed between subgroups of populations of children with developmental disorders, the processing mechanisms employed by these children are also similar, if not the neurological substrates of the behavior. What these children can and cannot do linguistically may provide good cues to the processing mechanisms they are employing to understand and produce language. Differing neurological substrates should logically lead to differences in the processing mechanisms of children with developmental disabilities. Determining possible differing neurological substrates is at the present moment an academic question since there is nothing one can do to repair physically either general cerebral trauma or specific lesions. The hope is, however, that something might be done about the faults in processing mechanisms.

Several suggestions have been made about underlying processing faults, and these suggestions are in all instances partially substantiated by experimental data. The following are the suggested faults with one exemplar source indicated:

(1) Deficit in auditory discrimination, categorization, and integration (Eisenson and Ingram 1972)
(2) Impaired rate of processing auditory input (Tallal 1974)
(3) Short-term memory deficit (Menyuk 1969)
(4) Long-term memory deficit (Cromer 1974)
(5) Deficit in attention, perception, and retrieval routines (Weiner 1972)
(6) A general representational deficit (Morehead and Morehead 1974)

Some items have been left off the list, but the foregoing are representative statements. Although there appears to be a fair degree of variety in the suggestions made for processing faults, what is being suggested by all these statements is that the raw data of language presented in its natural context (a communicative interaction in a particular situation) is not being processed by children with central nervous system involvement in the same way as that of normally developing children. It is being further suggested that these processing faults exist for nonlanguage as well as language stimuli. The process of perception, both linguistic and nonlinguistic has been divided into stages (for example, Gibson 1969). Different processing mechanisms appear to be involved in the perceptual process at each stage, as indicated in Table 3.

TABLE 3. Perceptual stages.

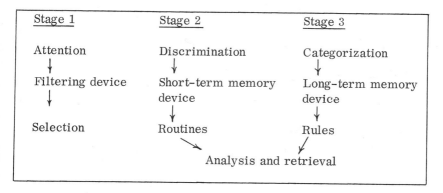

Some children with developmental problems may simply have difficulty in recasting what they know (the rules) into particular motor movements. Others may have difficulty in attending to those aspects of the input stimuli which are crucial to decision making. Others may have difficulty in decision making (observing differences and similarities), and still others in developing rules for the decisions they have made. If no filtering device is available to the child, then it is clear that no further operations on the input data can be carried out. Some autistic and possibly mentally retarded children appear to have this difficulty. Simultaneous attention to what is being said and the context in which it is said is required in communicative interaction. Autistic children who have developed some language have difficulty with this task and are observed to produce utterances that are inappropriate to the context. Some children can make decisions in line with a model immediately present, but cannot develop rules and thus cannot analyze and apply this knowledge to new instances. Again, some autistic and some mentally retarded children (although the latter have been observed to generalize in proscribed domains) appear to have this difficulty. Some children eventually develop rules, but because of a fault in the short-term memory device they either need a great many more samplings of the data to come up with these rules or, indeed, they come up with rules that are different from those of normally developing children because the information they are receiving is distorted. Both the amount and the complexity of the information to be processed within a given time will affect the success with which the task is carried out. Some aphasic children appear to have this difficulty. Other aphasic children, on the other hand, only appear to have difficulty in recasting these rules into patterns of motor movement.

Is it necessary to establish appropriate processing strategies (if one can do this) in the nonlinguistic domain before establishing these strategies in the linguistic domain? This does not seem to be the case for two reasons. The first is based on some data, the other on logical possibilities. Although it is the case that aphasic children continue to have difficulty in discriminating between and sequencing pure tones and speech syllables, unless they are allowed more time than the normally developing child needs to process this information (Tallah 1974), they indicate in their language behavior that they are not 'stuck' at segmental processing. They appear to be using sentential information (semantic and syntactic) to process the acoustic data, not simply the acoustic data. On logical grounds it is clear that nonlinguistic processing abilities are not sufficient to establish linguistic processing abilities. Are they necessary? It appears to depend on the processing abilities referred to; that is, the ability to attend to, discriminate, and categorize nonlinguistic information as well as linguistic information seems necessary for the appropriate use of language, and that nonlinguistic information will be used to interpret linguistic information. It is not clear that the ability to seriate objects in an array, for example, is necessary for the development of word order rules. Given the fact that the processing abilities of children with developmental disorders may vary within and across populations, it seems necessary to explore their behaviors, both linguistic and nonlinguistic, in various situations, before coming to any conclusions about what language behaviors are dependent on what factors (environmental, cognitive, and linguistic).

Implications for language remediation

The theoretician's and researcher's questions might be resolved by more and more insightful assessments of the behavior of children with problems. One might achieve both a better understanding of the bases for language acquisition and of the particular problems of these children. One would not, however, completely resolve the questions of the clinician, that is: if to intervene and when? what to do and how to do it? There are several notions that have been culled from the research literature on language acquisition that have been adopted by clinicians, but in varying ways. The language intervention programs can be roughly divided into two camps: (a) the behavior modifiers and (b) the cognitive-Freudians. Both camps use the conclusions that have been drawn about the child's development in general, and language in particular, in totally different ways. If we take each of the clinician's questions separately, the two approaches seem to separate on all of them. It should be noted that in addition to the approaches indicated above there have been suggestions that they be incorporated (Schiefelbusch and Lloyd 1974). The following is a brief summary of how the two positions appear to bifurcate on the questions.

(1) On the first two questions: if and when to intervene? (a) Behavior modification takes place naturally from birth. We can, however, control the environment in much better ways than naturally exist and, therefore, intervention should take place at any time, the earlier the better, with any individual or group of individuals. (b) Intervention should take place when development deviates markedly from the norm. The degree of deviation requiring intervention remains an open question. However, the earlier one intervenes, the better the prognosis for normal development.

(2) On the third question: what to do? (a) Teach behaviors that are functionally important to the human (language is one of them) by breaking down the parts that compose the behavior and then systematically build the behavior. (b) Present the child with learning activities in stages that reflect those observed in normal development and in situations that reflect, as far as possible, those situations observed in normal development.

(3) On the fourth question: how to do it? (a) Establish stimulus-response-reward chains for any piece of behavior. (b) Allow the child to operate on appropriate stimuli and thus to establish rules about the domain of behavior.

The overriding criticisms of the behavior modification approach to language remediation in the case of the child with developmental problems have been that the child does not appear to achieve independence and apply what is learned in the laboratory-teaching session outside the rigid domains of that teaching situation, nor does he incorporate the chain established into the language system as a whole. The criticisms of the cognitive/Freudian approach to intervention have been that to attempt to replicate the 'normal' situation seems futile because if these children could have taken advantage of the normal situation why have they not done so and, further, the 'normal' process has yet to be clearly described. What is very surprising, given the heat of the arguments concerning which approach to use in language remediation, is that there is very little data available on the long-term effects of either approach, or any other, on the language state and progress of these children.

The current state of affairs seems to be the following. The data available now on how children with developmental disorders process language indicates that their processing of language inputs is different from that of normally developing children and, indeed is different among children within these populations. The language behavior end product of these differences may be similar (but delayed) to that of normally developing children in some instances and dissimilar in others. These similarities and differences can, perhaps, be accounted for by differences in compensatory mechanisms among these children, and their language behavior per se can provide good cues to the extent and nature of these compensatory mechanisms. If this is the case the questions of the clinician: if to intervene and when? what to do and how to do it? are not simply resolved.

The answers to the first questions, by common consensus, appear to be always if there is any predicted as well as real problem evident, and as early as possible. This may be questionable until we have more data on the development of language by children with developmental problems, although, hopefully, it is a safe rule of thumb. Determining processing differences can indicate feasible ways of carrying out the 'how' of intervention, but one must determine what these differences are in any instance or group of instances. This, in turn, requires the development of appropriate assessment techniques. The 'what' of intervention is composed of both the function and content of the child's present language state and what are developmentally feasible next steps, but, again, techniques for determining the language state of the child need to be developed. Finally, having decided on a course of action, there is a great need to provide data on the long-term effects of any intervention strategy. Despite the fact that a great deal has been written, said, and concluded about the language behavior of children with developmental problems, it clearly is the case that there is a great need to derive fuller descriptions of the language development process of these children before one can answer the questions of 'what's the problem?' and 'what should be done about it?'

REFERENCES

Bloom, L. 1970. Language development: Form and function in emerging grammars. Cambridge, MIT Press.

Bowerman, M. 1973. Early syntactic development: A cross-linguistic study with special reference to finish. Cambridge, Cambridge University Press.

Braine, M. 1971. On two types of models of the internalization of grammars. In: The ontogenesis of grammar. Edited by D. Slobin. New York, Academic Press, Inc. 153-188.

Brown, R. 1973. A first language. Cambridge, Harvard University Press.

Chatsworth, W. R. 1975. Developmental psychology and human ethology. SRCD Newsletter, 5-6.

Chomsky, N. 1975. Aspects of the theory of syntax. Cambridge, MIT Press.

Cromer, R. 1974. Receptive language in the mentally retarded: Processes and diagnostic distinctions. In: Language perspectives: Acquisition, retardation, and intervention. Edited by R. Schiefelbusch and L. Lloyd. Baltimore, U. Park Press. 237-268.

Eisenson, J. and D. Ingram. 1972. Childhood aphasia: An updated concept based on recent research. In: Papers and reports on child language development, No. 4. Edited by D. Ingram. Stanford University. 103-120.

Gibson, E. J. 1969. Principles of perceptual learning and development. New York, Appleton-Century-Crofts.

deHirsch, K. 1972. Early language development and minimal brain dysfunction. Paper presented at the New York Academy of Science Conference: The minimally brain damaged.

Labov, W. 1969. Contraction, deletion, and inherent variability of the English copula. Lg. 45.715-762.

Lackner, J. R. 1968. A developmental study of language behavior in retarded children. Neuropsychologia 6.301-320.

Leonard, L. B. 1972. What is deviant language? Journal of Speech and Hearing Disorders 37.427-446.

Menyuk, P. 1975a. The language impaired child: Linguistic or cognitive impairment. Paper presented at the New York Academy of Science Conference: Developmental psycholinguistics and communication disorders.

_____. 1975b. Bases of language acquisition: Some questions. Journal of Autism and Childhood Schizophrenia 4.325-345.

_____. 1971. The acquisition and development of language. Englewood Cliffs, N.J., Prentice-Hall, Inc. Chapter 7.

_____. 1969. Sentences children use. Cambridge, MIT Press.

_____. 1964. Comparison of grammar of children with functionally deviant and normal speech. Journal of Speech and Hearing Research. 7.109-121.

Morehead, D. and D. Ingram. 1973. The development of base syntax in normal and linguistically deviant children. Journal of Speech and Hearing Research 16.330-352.

Morehead, D. and A. Morehead. 1974. From signal to sign: A Piagetian view of thought and language during the first two years. In: Language perspectives: Acquisition, retardation, and intervention. Edited by R. Schiefelbusch and L. Lloyd. Baltimore, U. Park Press. 153-190.

Piaget, J. 1970. Piaget's theory. In: Carmichael's handbook of child psychology, vol. I. Edited by P. H. Mussen. New York, John Wiley and Sons, Inc. 703-732.

Slobin, D. 1973. Cognitive prerequisites for the development of grammar. In: Studies of child language development. Edited by C. Ferguson and D. Slobin. New York, Holt, Rinehart and Winston, Inc. 175-208.

Tallal, P. 1974. Is developmental aphasia primarily a defect of perception, not language? Paper presented at Neuropsychological Conference, Boston.

Weiner, P. S. 1972. The perceptual level functioning of dysphasic children: A follow-up study. Journal of Speech and Hearing Research 15.423-438.

Wing, L. 1969. The handicap of autistic children: A comparative study. Journal of Child Psychology, Psychiatry 10.1-40.

Yoder, D. and J. Miller. 1972. What we may know and what we can do: Input toward a system. In: Developing strategies for language interaction. Edited by J. E. McLean, D. Yoder, and R. Schiefelbusch. New York, Holt, Rinehart and Winston, Inc. Chapter 5.

AN UPDATE ON
THE LINGUISTIC DEVELOPMENT OF GENIE

SUSAN CURTISS, University of California at Los Angeles
VICTORIA FROMKIN, University of California at Los Angeles
DAVID RIGLER, Los Angeles Children's Hospital
MARILYN RIGLER, Pacific Oaks College
STEPHEN KRASHEN, Queens College

The case of Genie has by now been widely discussed among linguists. Papers have been published on her linguistic development (Fromkin et al. 1974; Curtiss et al. 1974; Curtiss et al. 1973a) and presented before countless scholarly meetings (Fromkin 1972; Curtiss et al. 1972a, 1972b; Krashen et al. 1972a, 1972c, 1972d; Curtiss et al. 1973b). It is not the purpose today to repeat what is in these papers, but some background may be helpful for those hearing of Genie for the first time.

The case history of Genie is of interest to all concerned with the effects of sensory deprivation. While certain experiments concerned with sensory deprivation have been conducted using consenting adults as subjects, it is obvious why no experimental studies have used children. If we could ignore the cruelty and inhumanity of such a study we might wish to replicate the apocryphal experiments of Psammeticus or King John. One could then start by separating the child from social input, e.g. put her into a room away from others, keep the doors closed to muffle the passage of sounds, limit the intensity and variety of visual experiences, keep all social contact to a bare minimum, and immobilize the child to reduce opportunity for kinesthetic feedback. One might reduce stimulation further by bathing the child infrequently, by making interruptions for toileting unnecessary, and by feeding the child only infant food. In addition, one might beat the child if she produced any sounds.

The experiment described is unfortunately the one experienced by Genie for most of her first 14 years. Genie is now almost 18 years old. Yet, one might say that her life really began on November 4, 1970, when at 13 years 7 months she was hospitalized on orders from the Los Angeles Superior Court. It is surprising that she survived at all. It is not surprising that she was malnourished, unable to stand erect, unable to speak or comprehend spoken language--a primitive and unsocialized victim of unprecedented deprivation and social isolation. Many things have taken place during these 4-1/2 years. She now expresses love, pleasure, and anger; she laughs and cries. She has learned many social skills: she can eat with utensils, chew her food, dress herself, brush her teeth, wash her hair, and tie her shoelaces. She rides a bus to school and sews on a sewing machine. She runs and jumps and throws basketballs. And she speaks and understands--imperfectly, to be sure.

This real life experiment is not finished. We do not yet know the extent of the damage which her isolation and sensory deprivation has wrought. She is still learning, still developing. Many aspects of her development provide information on a number of key issues of interest to linguists. We will try to discuss some of these today.

This report is based on the eight months Genie stayed at the Children's Hospital Rehabilitation Center and the subsequent years in a foster home. During the entire period she has been observed, tested, recorded, and videotaped. Standardized tests have been administered (psychological, linguistic, cognitive development, and perceptual tests), as well as various linguistic comprehension tests developed particularly for her. In addition, dichotic listening and T-scope tests have been used to determine her cerebral dominance for language and certain other abilities. She may be the most tested subject in history.

Language acquisition

All the evidence at our disposal revealed that at the time of her emergence Genie had not acquired language. The big question, then, was: could she? Was she too old? She was already pubescent and according to Lenneberg's hypothesis already past the age when one can acquire a first language through normal (or even non-normal) means.

An example of the extent to which Genie is acquiring language is shown by the following dialogue, part of a larger interchange of February, 1975:

Marilyn and Genie: 2-19-75

G: Marsha give me square (referring to a piece of fabric that she held).

M: When?

G: In the class.
Marsha give me in the class.
Marsha in the class.

M: Which class?

G: 1 class, 2 class, 3 class.

M: What does Marsha do in class?

G: Draw.

M: What does Marsha draw?

G: Sun.

M: Did Marsha come to your class, or did you go to Marsha's class?

G: Go {in / ing} Marsha class.

M: Oh! You're changing classes. That's something new. Do you have a new teacher?

G: Jill. Marsha have Jill.

M: Marsha has Jill, too. Is Marsha in your class, or are you in Marsha's class?

G: Marsha class. Go in Marsha class.

M: You went in Marsha's class.

G: Marsha's class.

A further example of the extent to which Genie is acquiring language is shown by the complex negation test, first administered to Genie on October 17, 1973. In this test Genie is presented with sentences such as the following: (a) Point to: The book that is not blue is on the table. (b) Point to: The book that is blue is not on the table. In this test she had before her four pictures: (a) a red book on a chair, (b) a red book on a table, (c) a blue book on a chair, (d) a blue book on a table. Her score was 83 correct and 1 incorrect, demonstrating that even under controlled conditions of presentation she understands the notion of 'scope'.

It is interesting to compare these results with her processing of complex sentences with embedded relatives not involving negation. She has no difficulty with sentences such as The boy is looking at the girl who is frowning, where the relative is on the object, or The boy who is frowning is looking at the girl, with a relative on the subject, when the relative clause does not end in an NP. But in a sentence such as The boy who is looking at the girl is frowning, where the relative clause ends in an NP followed directly by the main verb, she always interprets the noun closest to the verb as the subject. This conforms to Bever's and Mehler's findings and suggestion regarding the NVN processing strategy (Bever 1970, 1971; Mehler 1971).

What is very strange is that one would certainly expect Genie also to interpret all simple active NVN sentences as actor-action-object sentences; yet this is not so. At first (1971, 1972) her responses were random on a word order test, when asked to point to the picture showing The girl pulls (or is pulling) the boy vs. The boy pulls the girl. She did no better with active sentences than with passive. More recently she responds either 100% correct or 100% wrong. She seems to be attempting to figure out the word order strategy but so far without success.

In addition to the anomalous responses to actor-action-object active sentences, she is still not using word order to distinguish between such sentences as What is on the blue box ? vs. What is the blue box on ? Yet in contrast to this, along with the complex sentences, she appears to be using the NVN strategy to process simple sentences on a pronoun test frequently given to her. The test consists of a set of pictures and test sentences, each of which describes only one of the pictures. Although until recently Genie did not appear to comprehend any of the third person pronouns, and made many errors on the pronoun test, it is interesting that with the sentences where all NP's are nouns, her errors are not reversals of subject and object. For example, Genie is presented with sentences such as The girl is feeding the boy, as well as She is feeding him. On the sentences where subject and object are both nouns, she has made only one error which was a subject-object reversal, and in that instance she immediately corrected herself. All other instances of noun subject-verb-noun object on this test have been interpreted correctly.

These data seem to be contradictory; she does use the word order strategy in the case of the pronoun test and the relative clauses. In addition, her own spontaneous utterances show great constraints on word order including agent-action-object order and have done so from the beginning. On the other hand, she does not use the word order strategy on any of the word order tests.

Bever suggests that with children 'there is a steady improvement in interpreting reversible passives until about the age of four; at this age, there is a temporary increase in the tendency to interpret the first noun as the actor and the last noun as the object.' Bever points to a

general relation between cerebral dominance and the utilization of perceptual strategies . . . (in) that those children with a preference for stimuli presented to the right ear have a greater dependence on the linguistic perceptual strategy than children without such an ear preference.

Since, as I will discuss subsequently, it appears that Genie is using her right hemisphere for language as well as other processes, it may be the case that this has an influence on her variable use of this perceptual strategy.

The importance of temporal ordering relations is revealed in Genie's responses to sentences involving before and after. When the sentence order follows the temporal order of events, she has no difficulty. Thus she never errs on commands such as Touch your nose before your ear or After you touch your nose, touch your ear. Long after she could process these sentences correctly, she was still having difficulty with sentences which do not follow temporal order of events, such as Touch X after you touch Y, or Before you touch X, touch Y. There seems to be increasing understanding, however, and interestingly enough, in the last six months, her responses to the after sentences in which the temporal order is reversed are for the most part wholly correct, while she still frequently errs on the before sentences. This does not support the hypothesis that before [the feature [+prior] on adverbials] is learned earlier than after (Clarke 1971).

It is interesting to see the kinds of shifts she makes in her understanding and knowledge. Until recently, in tests involving the distinction between some, one, and all, the sentences with some were interpreted as all. Thus, when asked to put some of the beads in the dish, she would put all of them in. She has now made a shift and some is interpreted as one, which in some sense is more correct than her earlier interpretation.

Her confusions on prepositions are also revealing. She has no problems with in, on, next to, in front of, and in back of. Earlier she had no difficulty with over and under. But now she errs on under, as disjunct items with no relationship between them, and when the relationship was understood, a confusion between them set in. This is supported by the fact that she often confused in front of and in back of--again only with each other. The errors may then show increased understanding rather than retrogression.

Syntactic understanding of tense and aspect still seems to be missing. We use tests with pictures with which normal children have no difficulty. Genie in discussion about the pictures seems to understand conceptually what they stand for, but is unable to point to the correct picture distinguishing between, for example, The girl will open (is opening/opened) the umbrella.

Yet she usually responds correctly to The girl is going to/is gonna open the umbrella and always correctly to The girl finished opening the umbrella. Her ability to interpret the 'finished' sentences correctly, and her inability to respond to the morphologically marked past tense parallels her relative sophistication for the concepts underlying sentences as compared to their syntactic reflection.

She seems to be beginning to learn the pronoun system of English--
but just beginning. At first, responses on this test were random, and
mostly incorrect. Most of her responses to sentences using third
person subject and object pronouns are now correct, e.g. <u>The girl is
feeding him</u> or <u>her</u> or <u>She/he is feeding the girl</u>, and even <u>She is feeding him</u> vs. <u>He is feeding her</u>, but she is still making errors. Interestingly though, she comprehends the reflexive and reciprocal markers (self, each other). Her errors on the sentences containing re-
flexives are only where the subject NP is a pronoun and she misinterprets that pronoun--i. e. where <u>He is feeding himself</u> is misunderstood as <u>She is feeding herself</u>. Since she does not err when
the subject is a noun, this shows that she knows the meaning of <u>self</u>
but ignores the pronoun marker on the reflexive altogether and relies
on her comprehension of the subject NP to determine her response.

While third person subject and object pronouns are receiving increasingly more correct responses, this is not so with possessive
pronouns; <u>his</u>, <u>her</u>, <u>my</u>, <u>your</u>, <u>our</u>, <u>their</u> are all undifferentiated at
this point. [Test: 'Point to his arm', 'Point to her shoe', etc. . . .]

Despite the huge gaps in Genie's knowledge of syntax, it is clear
that she has learned a great deal. Acquisition is painfully slow but it
continues.

Comprehension vs. production

It is also clear that like most normal children, for the most part
Genie's comprehension exceeds her production. First it should be
said that she still speaks very little, or comparatively little. Her
articulation remains very faulty, despite the fact that in imitation
she does very well. Her phonological system is far simpler than
her phonetic ability. She still simplifies consonant clusters, deletes final consonants, centralizes and laxes vowels, etc. It is still
an effort for her to speak. The amplitude of her speech has improved
greatly, however, and her pitch has decreased somewhat. Furthermore, there is greater pitch variation beginning to approach what one
could call sentence intonation. One hears one primary stressed
syllable in each utterance, with the stress realized by both pitch
and amplitude. Nonetheless, it is still very difficult to understand
her if you have not been with her for a period of time.

There is great contrast between her knowledge of the phonological
and phonetic representation of words and her production of them.
The fact that Genie is able to distinguish between singular and plural
nouns in a comprehension test shows her ability to distinguish between final simple consonants and clusters, although for the most
part in speaking she still deletes or simplifies final clusters in her
speech.

This contrast between her knowledge of the phonological and phonetic representation of words and her production of them is further
evidenced by her ability to understand and produce rhyming words.
In one test she was presented with a picture and then with three other
pictures and asked to point to the picture that 'rhymes'. Prior to the
test in game playing she had shown she could rhyme or at least we so
concluded and wished to make sure. For example, she might be
shown a picture of a pear and then pictures of a peach, a pie, and a
bear. She has no difficulty with pointing to the rhyming bear.

Her simplified phonological system is perhaps the source of a
number of items that mark the great disparity between Genie's comprehension and production of syntax as well. For example, as stated
previously, there is no doubt that she comprehends pluralization on
nouns, but since she deletes (or simplifies) final consonants and
consonant clusters, plural markers do not appear in her spontaneous
production of nouns. It is the same with possessive markers. She
comprehends the possessive, but it does not appear in her own production. Past tense and third person singular marking also involve
final clusters; so here, too, Genie's phonological system may mask
what grammatical features of language she intends to mark on the
surface.

Despite absence of such forms, her spontaneous utterances are
becoming increasingly more complex. Prepositions are now used at
times as is the copula, and many utterances include what one may
call 'serial verb constructions', or complex sentence types. Examples of such sentences are:

Eat lunch on plate.
Genie have a tantrum at school.
Genie angry at teacher.
I am going see dentist on Friday.
Is buttoning coat.
I want go school.
I want think about Mama riding bus.
Think about going dentist on Friday.
Mama said don't spit.
Mr. Vaughan say put face in swimming pool.

The disparity between comprehension and production runs two ways.
As we described above, there are elements of language which she
comprehends but does not produce, e. g. plural and possessive.
Perhaps the most striking example of this difference is with questions, however. She comprehends all question types--yes/no questions or who, what, when, which, where, why, and how questions.
Yet she does not ask any questions, except those she has been trained

to say. On the other hand, there are elements in her production which at least under formal test conditions, she does not appear to comprehend. For example, as some of the foregoing example sentences show, she uses the present progressive. Yet she does not seem to be able to respond correctly to such sentences in the tense/ aspect test described earlier. Moreover, as stated earlier, she does not appear to consistently comprehend N-V-N sequences as subject-verb-object on the word order tests, even though her own sentences show fixed word order: possessor + possessed, modifier + noun, and subject-verb-object.

Language vs. cognitive development

The relationship between cognition and language may be revealed by the semantic system. To investigate the kinds of semantic features Genie utilizes, a number of classification tasks were administered. She is presented with a number of picture cards for each such test and asked to put the pictures together that belong together. In one test the pictures are all of humans, some male and some female; in another the pictures are all animate but divided into human/non-human categories; in a third test the pictures are human and non-human divided into animate/inanimate classes; in a fourth test all the objects depicted are inanimate divided into edible/inedible groups, and in the final test the distinction is between whole body vs. part of body. When these tests were first administered about a year ago, Genie sorted 'correctly' except for the categories human/non-human and part/whole. Within a short time and as of now she has no difficulty in sorting any of these categories.

The independence of cognitive development from linguistic development seems to be clearly shown in the case of Genie. In her isolated state there was little input of any kind. She was closed off from the world of machines, buildings, flowers, toys, animals. Yet after her emergence her ability to generalize specific objects to general categories was very rapid. She seemed to learn simultaneously the generic terms and the names for the members of a class. Tory, the name of the household dog, was reserved for him but all other dogs were immediately recognized as dogs, as, of course, was Tory. One did not need to teach her, as she learned the words for dress, socks, shoes, tie, coat, sweater, that these were all clothes, nor that a toy which moved was not animate.

It is strange that some of her first words were color words and very early she could differentiate between different colors and different shapes and understood size relationships, pointing unerringly to the 'big red circle' vs. 'small red circle' vs. 'big yellow circle' etc. According to Church (1971): 'disadvantaged 4-year-olds are likely not to know color names; yet even at her stage in language development where she was responding only to single words, Genie knew colors.

Further illustration of Genie's cognitive advance over linguistic development is that as soon as she began to understand and answer wh_-questions she responded to why and how questions which usually come much later in normal children's development. As I pointed out, however, although Genie understands all questions she has not once asked a question herself, which may involve emotional problems as well as linguistic ones.

We have not discussed her psychological problems but clearly these impinge on every aspect of her life and development. While she has learned much language and seems to continue in her acquisition, she does not use language for communication where she can avoid it. She has little understanding of the social functions of language. Her emotional difficulties therefore also prevent us from getting a clear picture of what she is capable of producing linguistically.

Psychological testing with Genie has consistently yielded results that may be described as polarized. On certain related functions she achieves very low scores. For example, on WISC she has never achieved a verbal subtest score greater than two. On performance subtests, in contrast, she has achieved subtest scaled scores as high as eight and nine. Similarly, in May, 1973, her Leiter mental age was nearly twice that achieved on the Peabody and in February, 1974, on the ITPA her Psycholinguistic Age for 'visual association' was twice the age for 'verbal expression'. Qualitatively, the impression one gets of Genie is of a child whose gestalt and visuo-spatial perception is greatly superior to her capacity to process stimuli sequentially. She demonstrates great facility in remembering faces and names, possesses a large and continually growing vocabulary, and has no difficulty finding her way about in real space. It is interesting, however, that as she develops sequential skills, she may be losing some of her parallel non-sequential abilities to process the same stimuli. For example, at first Genie responded quickly and accurately when asked how many pennies appear in a random display of 0 to 7 pennies, gestalting the number as she did not yet know how to count. When she began to learn to count, she did so only with errors and distress and continued to rely on her ability to gestalt numbers. Now that she can count certain amounts accurately and fairly fluently, she appears to have 'lost' the ability to gestalt these amounts and will guess wrong when asked to do so.

Hemispheric dominance

Contemporary concepts of cerebral activity suggest that most language functions are localized in the left hemisphere, whereas perception of spatial relationships is substantially determined by activities in the right hemisphere. While this is undoubtedly an oversimplified formulation, it has been reflected in empirical findings and in neurological theory for over a century.

There are further speculations and hypotheses concerning the relationship between language acquisition and lateralization. This is further related to the 'critical age hypothesis'. It is interesting that Alajouanine and Lhermitte (1965) have been unable to demonstrate any critical period in their study of 37 children who sustained brain injury ranging from about 18 months to about 11 years. Krashen (1972b) has shown that the data reported in the literature support a completion of lateralization by the age of 5. If language learning continues after this, then the relationship between lateralization and language acquisition is not simple.

Bever (1971) suggests that 'the fact that functional dominance appears to develop simultaneously with the perceptual strategies (noted earlier) raises the possibility that cerebral lateralization is itself critically dependent on certain kinds of experience.'

The study of Genie may support this proposal. Genie appears to do very poorly on tasks that reflect normally left hemisphere activity, whereas on right hemisphere tasks she performs quite well. Since there is no gross neurological deficit we have speculated on a relationship between her years of isolation and lack of exposure to language stimulation, and on the other hand, her physical immobilization and sensory deprivation in an unchanging, monotonous environment during the usual period in which language is acquired and lateralization develops.

As has been reported in detail in the literature (Krashen 1973; Fromkin et al. 1974; Curtiss et al. 1974), the dichotic listening tests administered to Genie by Krashen showed an overwhelming left ear advantage for verbal stimuli but not for environmental sounds. What was even more surprising was the relative magnitude of her left ear advantage for verbal stimuli, far beyond that of other normal subjects and comparable only to patients with hemispherectomy or with split-brains.

One possible interpretation of these results is that Genie is indeed lateralized but not in the ordinary sense--in which there is a division of functions between the two hemispheres. Rather it may be that Genie is primarily using her right brain and that the lack of linguistic input blocked the normal lateralization development. Since her primary input was visual and tactile, as little as those stimuli were, it was the right brain which developed.

There is no question about her ability to perform what are normally considered 'right hemisphere' tasks. In the Mooney faces test (Mooney 1957)--considered to be the most reliable and most widely used test for gestalt perception ability and which has shown strong right hemisphere processing--Genie's responses are extraordinary. (The test involves silhouetted type figures and one must state whether they are real or false faces.) There are 70 stimuli, and of these, 50 are of real faces. Genie's identification of these was 100% correct. She missed only 6 of the 20 'incorrect faces'. This is far above the responses of a normal adult.

Similar results are shown on the Street Test, the Thurstone Gestalt Perception Test, and in the Harshman Figures Test (see Curtiss, forthcoming).

I could cite many other examples of her almost uncanny ability for special location memory, facial memory, etc.

What is not known is whether she is indeed using her right hemisphere for these tasks or whether she is a case of reverse lateralization. The environment-sounds dichotic listening test result suggests that this is not the case but much more evidence is needed. We are now in the process of administering a number of Tachistoscopic tests to see if we can answer this question. But such tests are not easy to administer to Genie. Although she is instructed each time to fixate on a star in the center, we cannot be sure that she is doing this. There are also other difficulties. We have so far administered a dot location test, a rhyming test, and a homonyms test using a T-scope.

The results so far are not conclusive and more testing is needed. But the results to date suggest a reversal in dominance. The dot location test is processed better in the left hemisphere, the verbal tests, better with the right (Curtiss, forthcoming).

It is still possible that she is using both hemispheres for these 'right hemisphere tasks' and only the right for the language tasks. It is also possible that as she develops linguistically the nonlanguage abilities will lessen, as has been shown to be the case with children and as Levy (1969) has demonstrated with left-handers who appear to have bilateral representation of language. Or it may happen that with greater language acquisition the left hemisphere will begin to show language processing ability.

Whether or not Genie will be able to answer many of the questions which are of interest to us concerning language acquisition, cerebral dominance, language and thought, etc., what is perhaps more important is that Genie, the human being, continues to learn, to grow, to live in the world.

NOTE

The work reported on in this paper was supported in part by a grant from the National Institute of Mental Health, U.S. Department of Health, Education, and Welfare, #MH-21191-03.

REFERENCES

Alajouanine, T. and F. Lhermitte. 1965. Acquired aphasia in children. Brain 88.653-662.
Bever, Thomas G. 1970. The cognitive basis for linguistic structures. In: Cognition and the development of language. Edited by John R. Hayes. New York, Wiley.
_____. 1971. The nature of cerebral dominance in speech behavior of the child and adult. In: Language acquisition: Models and methods. Edited by R. Huxley and E. Ingram. New York, Academic Press. 231-254.
Church, J. 1971. Methods for the study of early cognitive functioning. In: Language acquisition: Models and methods. Edited by R. Huxley and E. Ingram. New York, Academic Press. 175-192.
Clarke, Eve. 1971. On the acquisition of the meaning of before and after. Journal of Verbal Learning and Verbal Behavior 10.226-275.
Curtiss, Susan. Forthcoming. The case of Genie: A modern day wild child. Doctoral dissertation, UCLA.
_____, V. Fromkin, S. Krashen, D. Rigler, and M. Rigler. 1972a. The development of language in Genie. Paper presented at the American Speech and Hearing Association, San Francisco.
_____. 1972b. The syntactic development of Genie. Paper presented at the Linguistic Society of America, Winter meeting, Atlanta.
_____. 1973a. Language acquisition after the critical period: Genie as of April, 1973. Proceedings of the Ninth Regional Meeting of the Chicago Linguistics Society.
_____. 1973b. The case of Genie: Some questions, some answers. Paper presented at the Linguistic Society of America, Winter meeting, San Diego.
_____. 1974. The linguistic development of Genie. Lg. 50.528-554.
Fromkin, Victoria A. 1972. The development of language in Genie. Paper presented at the American Psychological Association, Honolulu.
_____, S. Krashen, S. Curtiss, D. Rigler, and M. Rigler. 1974. The development of language in Genie: A case of language acquisition beyond the 'critical period.' Brain and Language 1.81-107.
Krashen, Stephen and R. Harshman. 1972a. Lateralization and the critical period. Paper presented at the 83rd meeting of the Acoustical Society of America.
Krashen, Stephen. 1973. Lateralization, language learning, and the critical period: Some new evidence. Language Learning 23.63-74.
_____. 1972b. Language and the left hemisphere. Working Papers in Phonetics 24. UCLA.

Krashen, Stephen, V. Fromkin, S. Curtiss, D. Rigler, M. Rigler, and S. Spitz. 1972c. Language lateralization in a case of extreme psychological deprivation. Paper presented to the 84th meeting of the Acoustical Society of America.

_____, V. Fromkin, and S. Curtiss. 1972d. A neurolinguistic investigation of language acquisition in the case of an isolated child. Paper presented to the Linguistic Society of America, Winter meeting, Atlanta.

Lenneberg, Eric H. 1967. Biological foundations of language. New York, Wiley.

Levy, Jerre. 1969. Possible basis for the evolution of lateral specialization of the human brain. Nature 224. 614-615.

Mehler, Jacques. 1971. Studies in language and thought development. In: Language acquisition: Models and methods. Edited by R. Huxley and E. Ingram. Nex York, Academic Press. 201-224.

Mooney, Craig M. 1957. Age in the development of closure ability in children. Canadian Journal of Psychology 11. 219-226.

POSTSEMANTIC PROCESSES
IN DELAYED CHILD LANGUAGE
RELATED TO
FIRST AND SECOND LANGUAGE LEARNING

CAROLYN KESSLER

Immaculata College of Washington

Abstract. Recent studies increasingly substantiate the similarities
in the acquisition of a first and second language, particularly with
reference to the sequencing of specific structures.   This study in-
vestigates a third component in child language studies, that of
deviant or delayed language.

Longitudinal data for a group of 18 children ranging in age from
three years, two months (3;2) to ten years, two months (10;2) undergoing therapy for deviant language provided the basis for investigating
the acquisition of a set of ten grammatical structures.   The order of
acquisition closely resembles that which has been reported for first-
language learners and for children learning English as a second language.   The postsemantic processes applying to the conversion of
semantic configurations into linear structures are examined for each
member of the set of acquisitions within the framework of Chafe's
(1970, 1971) model of semantic structure.

1. 0 Introduction. Without denying that fundamental differences
exist between the child's first discovery of linguistic phenomena and
the learning of a second language with its presuppositions of cognitive development along with linguistic experience, recent research
increasingly substantiates some basic similarities between first and
second language acquisition.   Focus in determining these similarities
has largely been directed towards the sequence in which specific
grammatical morphemes or functors are acquired.   First language

studies by Brown (1973) and the de Villiers (1973), for example, give an order of structural acquisitions that has been preserved with remarkable consistency in second language research of Dulay and Burt (1974c), Bailey, Madden, and Krashen (1974) and, more recently, Fathman (1974, 1975). In other studies as those by Tremaine (1975), Milon (1974) and Ervin-Tripp (1974) similarities between the development of first and second languages are reported. In a study of first language bilingualism, Kessler (1971) found that children acquiring two languages simultaneously appeared to be developing structures common to both languages in the same order and at the same rate.

The concern of this paper is to report a study investigating a third component in child language studies, that of deviant or delayed language, and its relationship to normal first and second language learning. The term 'delayed language' implies, as Menyuk (1971:201) defines it, 'delay in onset, slowness of the process, termination of the process before average adult linguistic performance is reached.' As Menyuk further points out, the language delayed child is presumed to follow the course of development observed for children acquiring language normally. This paper examines that presumption more closely.

For normal first language development Brown (1973) describes the acquisition of 14 grammatical morphemes in the speech of three children studied longitudinally. Using a cross-sectional approach, the de Villiers (1973) examined the presence or absence of these same 14 morphemes in the speech of 21 children aged 16 to 40 months. Taken together, the rank orderings obtained for the structures in these two studies demonstrate a high degree of correspondence.

Among studies of children acquiring a second language are those of Dulay and Burt (1974a, 1974b). Examining the acquisition of English as a second language for a group of 60 Spanish-speaking and 55 Chinese-speaking children, aged 7 to 9, they found that the order of acquisition of 11 morphemes was virtually the same for both groups of children. Errors made by children learning English as a second language generally reflected the same developmental structures used by children acquiring English as their first language. In an earlier study, Dulay and Burt (1973) presented evidence that three different groups of 5- to 8-year-old Spanish-speaking children acquired a subset of Brown's 14 morphemes in approximately the same order. From this, Dulay and Burt conclude that a common order of acquisition operates in second-language acquisition.

Some modifications in Dulay and Burt's sequencing may be found in comparing a subset of structures examined by Brown with that included in two recent studies of Fathman (1974, 1975). These have concentrated on the acquisition of English as a second language by two groups of children, Spanish-speaking and Korean-speaking. In one study of 6- to 10-year-old children learning English in a natural

setting, apart from a structured ESL program, Fathman reports an
ordering which closely parallels that of Brown for a set of seven
structures. Fathman replicated this order in another study (1975)
with 120 children ages 6 to 14. Of these, 60 were Spanish-speaking,
60 Korean-speaking. Table 1 gives a comparative rank sequencing
for Brown's first-language and Fathman's second-language studies.

TABLE 1. Order of acquisition for seven structures: First and
second language learning.

Structure	First-language learners (Brown 1973)	Second-language learners (Fathman 1974, 1975)
1. progressive -ing	1	2
2. preposition	2	3
3. plural	3	1
4. possessive	4	6
5. article	5	4
6. present regular	6	7
7. present irregular	7	5

Clearly there is a close relationship between the order in which
children normally acquire their first language and that which is
followed by children acquiring a second language. Similarity becomes even more apparent if the seven structures are subdivided
into two groups: the progressive -ing, preposition, plural in one;
possessive, article, present regular and present irregular in the
other.

For children manifesting language delay, Wilcox and Tobin (1974)
found that the difference in linguistic performance of hard-of-hearing
and normal-hearing children was one of degree rather than kind.
Their results provide support for the theory that language delayed
children develop language along the same route as that followed in
normal first language acquisition.

Morehead and Ingram (1973) studied matched groups of 15 young
normal subjects aged 19 to 37 months, the period when children
normally acquire a base syntactic system, and 15 linguistically
deviant children whose intellectual or physiological impairment was
not sufficient to be the cause of their difficulties in acquiring language. The linguistic levels determined by the mean number of morphemes per utterance were comparable for both groups. Results of
this study demonstrate that the grammars reflecting a base syntactic

development were nearly identical for both groups on each of five linguistic levels.

The study reported here also examines development of some of the structures investigated by Morehead and Ingram. Focus, however, is on a subset of the rules accounting for inflectional morphology and selected lexical items representing minor syntactic categories. To be included in the study specific structures were determined on the basis of those which could be compared to Brown's first language studies of normal children and Fathman's of second language learning. The order of acquisitions reported by both Brown and Fathman is based on children's oral production of the language rather than on any type of strict comprehension or receptive language task. Brown's longitudinal data for three children was gathered from naturalistic settings. Fathman's order is determined from scores obtained on The Second Language Oral Production English Test (SLOPE Test).

After determining the order of acquisition of a set of structures for language delayed children and comparing that order with first and second language learning, the further question is raised which asks if there is any linguistic explanation for the observed sequencing.

2.0 Method. The set of 10 structures investigated includes: (1) articles in an obligatory context for the or a(n), (2) progressive -ing suffix as in the context girl paint or girl is paint, (3) contractible auxiliary as in girl painting, (4) noun plural, regular form, as in the context two boy, (5) subject pronoun as in the context her eat, (6) possessive pronoun as in the context him shoes, (7) contractible copula as in that my book, (8) present tense, regular verb forms as it hurt, (9) present, irregular, as she have, (10) preposition as in the context go pool.

2.1 Linguistic model. The linguistic model adopted for this study is that proposed by Chafe (1970, 1971). This view of language design, which preserves the concern for the language user's ability to transform configurations of ideas into configurations of sounds, takes as its basis conceptual or semantic configurations. These structures undergo various postsemantic processes in the progression towards linearly ordered surface structures, which are ultimately converted into phonetic structures.

Pertinent to the application of Chafe's model to language acquisition studies is the distinction between semantic configurations and postsemantic processes. Semantic structures are the simultaneous collocations of three major types of units: inherent, lexical, and contextual features. This simultaneous arrangement of units is illustrated by listing them in a vertical dimension as in the example:

V
process   (inherent features)
action
<u>break</u>   (lexical unit)
progressive   (contextual feature)

Semantic structure is built around the centrality of the verb.
Accompanying nouns are related to it in specific ways. These noun-
verb relations consequently form the core of semantic structure.
Semantic influence, in other words, radiates from the verb to the
noun.

Three postsemantic processes of particular significance in this
study are linearization, deletion, and semantic change. Linearization converts the nonlinear configurations of meaning to a linear
arrangement. Deletion processes result from a drive towards
economy of phonetic outputs. Processes which add and redistribute
semantic and postsemantic units are summarized under that of
semantic change. Literalization is a general term for any postsemantic process which converts a semantic unit into another
semantic unit or a configuration of semantic units. These intermediate postsemantic structures then undergo further processes to
convert them into surface structures.

This semantic view of language design is summarized in the following schematization (Chafe 1970:49):

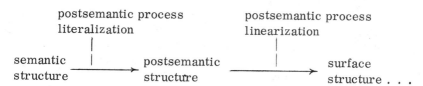

Postsemantic processes are followed by symbolization and phonological processes producing the phonetic structure.

2.2 Subjects. The subjects in this study were 18 children undergoing therapy for language deviancy at the Institute for Childhood
Aphasia, formerly at Stanford University School of Medicine. The
children ranged in age from 3 years, 2 months to 10 years, 2 months
(3;2 to 10;2) at the time data collection began. No one medical diagno-
sis was common to the group. Some children indicated emotional
disturbances. Others gave indication of hearing problems or some
minimal cerebral dysfunction. Excluded from the study were children
whose language difficulties could clearly be traced to severe

physiological impairment or mental retardation. Table 2 gives a general profile for the children, giving IQ as determined from the Leiter International Performance Scale and medical impressions given at the time data collection began as well as the chronological age span during which data was collected.

2.3 Procedure. Language samples were collected under standardized conditions for each child through procedures developed by Ingram (1973). Each child was sampled when first entering the Institute for Childhood Aphasia and at three-month intervals thereafter. Time intervals for each of the 18 children varied in that some were sampled for only one three-month period, others for almost two years. Within each three-month sample point, three separate subsamples were collected at weekly intervals. Any sample point, then, covered a three-week period. Language samples were elicited by showing the children a set of 90 pictures during the course of each three-week sampling period. The pictures evoked either a spontaneous comment from the child or a response in answer to a question from the investigator. The same set of pictures was repeated for each consecutive sample period. For each language sample the mean length of utterance (MLU) was calculated through procedures described in Tyack (1973). All sampling was done under the same conditions, including the same room at the Institute for Childhood Aphasia, with samples elicited and transcribed by the same investigator, who also calculated the MLU's for each sample. The linguistic level as defined by Brown (1973:56) was then established for each sample point.

2.4 Scoring the data. The presence or absence of a structure in obligatory contexts was tallied for each child at each linguistic level in which the structure occurred. A minimum of three obligatory occasions for a specific structure to occur at a given level was required for the structure to be counted. Criteria in determining obligatory contexts generally followed those used by Brown (1973: 259-269). The specific procedures are here given for each structure.

(1) noun plural, regular. Obligatory presence of allomorphs /-s~-z~-ɨz/ was determined from linguistic criteria as in the frame two ____, they are ____, or some + count noun. Examples of omissions taken from the data are two boy, those are cloud.

(2) pronoun, subject and possessive. Obligatory contexts were determined by the presence of a pronominal form. Absence was counted as the failure to produce the required form as in her eat soup, for subject pronouns. Absence for possessive

TABLE 2. Profile of children with language delay.

Child	I. Q.	C. A.	Medical impressions
Child 1	155	3;2-3;9	possibly mild neurological dysfunction
Child 2	81	4;2-5;9	none available
Child 3	104	3;5-4;7	some emotional problems; no evidence of neurological deficit
Child 4	120	3;11-4;9	some difficulty in fine motor coordination
Child 5	79	7;11-8;3	organic, emotional problems; difficulties with coordination, perception; normal electroencephalogram
Child 6	66	9;11-10;1	articulation problems; strength in receptive language understanding
Child 7	128	6;4-7;4	emotional problems; potentially superior abilities
Child 8	--	10;2	possibly some cerebral dysfunction; hard-of-hearing
Child 9	113	7;9-8;11	emotional problems; no significant neurological problems
Child 10	--	5;2-5;5	none available
Child 11	109	6;0-6;9	minor coordination problems; abnormal electroencephalogram suggests dysphasic problem
Child 12	--	5;2-5;5	none available (twin to Child 10)
Child 13	110	5;10-6;3	no evidence of specific neurological dysfunction
Child 14	--	9;4-10;6	no evidence of neurological dysfunction; some articulation difficulty
Child 15	120	6;0-6;9	delayed motor functioning; residual hearing loss; some neurological dysfunction
Child 16	--	9;10-11;5	minimal cerebral dysfunction; gifted functioning in non-verbal tasks
Child 17	121	5;11-7;6	minimal evidence of physiological dysfunction associated with language, emotional deviations; conducive hearing loss temporarily present
Child 18	--	9;7	possibly minimal cerebral dysfunction; emotional problems; normal intellectual potential

pronouns is observed in <u>put on she shoes</u>. No count was made of the use of <u>you</u> or <u>it</u> since these forms do not carry subject vs. object case distinctions.

(3) article. Articles <u>the/a(n)</u> were tallied together for presence or absence in obligatory contexts. Absence is noted in expressions as <u>under tree</u> or <u>boy talk phone</u>

(4) preposition. Unlike Brown's study which limited prepositions to the obligatory contexts for <u>in/on</u>, the obligatory context for any preposition was counted. Absence is observed in <u>go pool</u> or <u>he play the ocean</u>.

(5) third person singular present tense verb, regular and irregular. The obligatory presence of the regular form with its three allomorphs /-s~ -z~ -ɨz/ was limited to stative verbs. Absence was counted in contexts as <u>he want</u>, <u>it hurt</u>, <u>she like it</u>. These verbs occurred infrequently. Of somewhat greater frequency were irregular forms as <u>says</u>, <u>has</u>. Absence was counted for the uninflected forms.

(6) copula, contractible. Contexts for obligatory presence of the copula were almost exclusively limited to contractible forms possible in such expressions as <u>that my mommy</u>, <u>it fat</u>.

(7) progressive -<u>ing</u> suffix. The two markers needed to realize the present progressive of verbs, the -<u>ing</u> suffix and the auxiliary <u>be</u>, were tallied separately. Obligatory presence of -<u>ing</u> was determined from the nature of the verb. Most of the pictures evoked verbs with the inherent features of process or action. Absence was counted in contexts as <u>girl paint</u> or <u>girl is paint</u>.

(8) auxiliary <u>be</u>, contractible. Obligatory contexts were determined from process or action verbs as <u>she eating cake</u>, <u>boy jumping</u>.

Overgeneralizations were noted but not counted. Attempts to include other structures as the past tense of verbs, irregular plurals of nouns, noun possessives, object pronouns, uncontractible copula and auxiliary were discounted because of the extremely low frequency of these forms.

3.0 Results. The ratio of presence to total possible realizations in obligatory contexts was calculated for each structure at each linguistic level in which it occurred. These ratios were then averaged to determine the mean score. Table 3 gives the mean scores in percents for occurrence in obligatory contexts of the 10 structures.

TABLE 3. Rank order of acquisitions.

Structures	Ratio of actual occurrences to possible occurrences in percents
1. subject pronoun	81
2. plural, regular	78
3. progressive -ing	70
4. preposition	70
5. article	62
6. present tense, irregular	62
7. possessive pronoun	54
8. present tense, regular	53
9. copula, contractible	52
10. auxiliary, contractible	40

The rank ordering is given in Figure 1 by plotting mean scores in percents against structures. This, then, gives the overall pattern of the sequencing of acquisitions.

Several structures attained the same mean score. The ordering of these and contiguous structures such as regular present tense, contractible copula, and contractible auxiliary is undoubtedly arbitrary. The differentiation in scores is not sufficiently great to give support to reliable sequencing. However, for structures at either end of the graph the reliability of sequential arrangements is probably more positive. For example, subject pronouns, regular plurals, and progressive -ing may be expected to develop before third person present tense markers, or the copula and auxiliary verbs.

4.0 Discussion. Mean scores reflect the relative accuracy of the children's attempts to apply linguistic rules. The sequencing of specific structures gives some indication of the acquisition of the processes that relate underlying structures of meaning to surface manifestations. In other words, the acquisition of specific structures implies that the child has acquired postsemantic processes linking underlying semantic configurations with surface manifestations.

A high degree of correspondence is observed between the ordering found in structural acquisitions by language delayed children and the sequencing reported by Brown for normal first language and Fathman for second language. Table 4 gives the comparative rank orders in the three studies.

FIGURE 1. Delayed language sequencing of acquisitions.

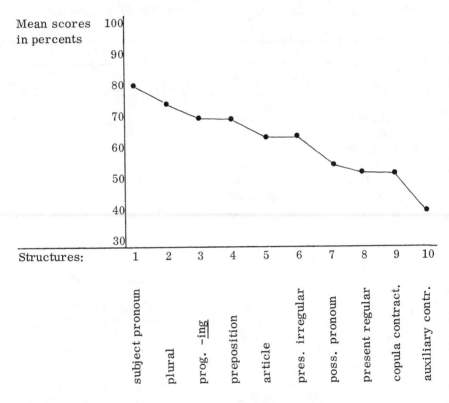

TABLE 4. Rank order in language delay compared with first
and second language learning.

Structure	First language (Brown)	Second language (Fathman)	Delayed language
1. subject pronoun	–	1	1
2. plural	4	2	2
3. progressive -ing	2	3.5	3.5
4. preposition	3	3.5	3.5
5. article	5	5	5.5
6. present, irregular	–	6	5.5
7. possessive pronoun	–	7	7
8. present, regular	8	–	8
9. copula, contractible	9	–	9
10. auxiliary, contractible	10	–	10

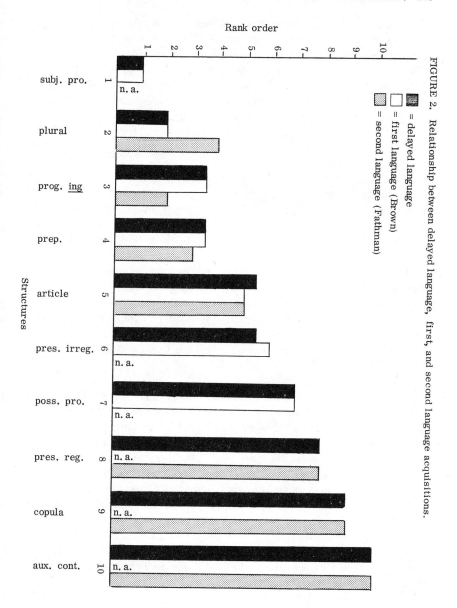

FIGURE 2. Relationship between delayed language, first, and second language acquisitions.

Figure 2 displays the relationship between the 10 structures in the language delay study, and 8 structures from Fathman's second language study, and 7 from Brown's first language sequencing.

The notable exception is the rank order of the plural in Brown's study. In a study by the de Villiers (1973), however, the plural is tied in rank with the present progressive and preposition on, thereby giving a closer approximation to the second language and delayed language ordering. Minor discrepancies as this possibly suggest that there is no one correct rank order of acquisitions, but that groups of structures are acquired together.

In searching for possible determinants for the order of acquisition, Brown turned to grammatical complexity as one possibility after finding a nonsignificant correlation between the order of acquisition for first language and the frequency of the forms in the speech of the parents to the child. Using a transformational model of grammar, Brown found that the cumulative number of transformations required for a particular structure gives rise to a partial ordering. A third possible determinant of sequencing is semantic complexity. Admittedly a difficult task since no general semantic theory is yet available that would permit determination of relative complexity of all of the elements studied, Brown concludes, however, that a cumulative index of semantic complexity does give rise to a partial account of the ordering.

5.0 Linguistic perspectives. Chafe's semantic model of language permits a perspective that takes into account the semantic-syntactic interface of the 10 structures studied. Since this model looks at the relationship between surface syntactic structures and the underlying semantic configurations, surface manifestations are viewed as the product of postsemantic processes operating on semantic configurations. Postsemantic processes then are the link between configurations of meaning and their linear arrangement on the surface. Chafe's model changes the focus from looking at the acquisition of grammatical morphemes as manifestations of syntactic development to reflections of semantic development. It is this change of perspective that motivates the use of this model for the linguistic analysis of the 10 structures investigated in language delay.

Chafe (1971:58) states:

It is useful to imagine thoughts as being present in a huge and multidimensional conceptual space. Semantic structure is then a kind of grid that allows us ultimately to convert at least part of what is present in conceptual space into sound.

Acquisition of structures as plural markers, progressive suffixes, auxiliary verbs, copulas, prepositions, pronouns, articles is, therefore, a process of filling in some of the cells in the matrix or grid. In turn, this grid allows the conversion of semantic concepts to linear arrangements conforming to the rules of the language. In accounting, then, for the order in which structures are acquired semantics plays a crucial role. It is the position taken here that without a knowledge of semantic structures underlying structures as prepositions, articles, or inflectional markers, one can know little of the 'why' of observed sequencings. Chafe (1970:84) argues that nothing but a superficial understanding of language will ever be possible unless we view semantic structure as the area in which the well-formedness of sentences is determined.

In applying Chafe's model, a set of semantic structure formation rules and postsemantic process rules accounts in broad terms for the acquisition of the structures described in the preceding sections. Rules presented do not claim to be complete specifications of the semantic configurations. Rather, they attempt to focus on those units, inherent and contextual, which appear to play a central role in surface realizations and, consequently, in the language acquisition process. Some of the rules treat formation of the semantic structure; others the postsemantic processes modifying them. Semantic configurations and postsemantic processes are discussed in two categories: those which apply to verbs and those which apply to nouns.

5.1 Semantic configurations and postsemantic processes for verbs. Playing a central role in the realization of the copula and progressive form of the verb is the inherent feature 'state'. Formation of the semantic configuration for the copula is given in the following semantic rule (S1).

(S1)

$$V \xrightarrow{} V \begin{array}{l} \overline{} \text{patient} \\ \quad\quad N \end{array}$$

state   state
             be

This rule states that a verb having the inherent feature 'state' obligatorily becomes a complex semantic unit in which a patient is associated with the verb. A single-headed arrow reads as 'becomes'. If the root is the verb be, realization of the copula must take place to appear in utterances as it's fat. Early stages of child language typically reflect omission of any postsemantic process resulting in copula manifestations.

Only verbs not specified as 'state' can include the contextual unit 'progressive'. A semantic formation rule gives this as:

(S2)   V — — $\gg$ progressive
      −state

This rule is read that only verbs not specified as 'state' can include the contextual feature 'progressive'. The double-headed arrow is read as 'associated with' and the broken line as 'optionally applies'.

Postsemantic processes of literalization, a form of semantic change, and linearization operate in stages to ultimately produce the suffix -ing on the main verb, add the semantic configuration for auxiliary and, later, provide for the linearization of the contextual feature 'progressive' followed by linearization of the auxiliary be. That postsemantic processes operate in stages is evident in the non-simultaneous acquisition of the various components of progressive verbs. The marker -ing is acquired considerably earlier than the auxiliary be.

Children apparently acquire the distinction between 'state' and 'non-state' rather early. Data revealed no attempts to form progressives with stative verbs.

A verb will acquire postsemantic specification for the present tense marker, third person singular, if the semantic configuration for the verb includes the contextual feature 'non-past'. In addition, the verb must be accompanied by a subject noun which is neither first, second, nor plural. A postsemantic process operating on a semantic structure to form an intermediate configuration is rule (S3).

(S3)   V ——$\gg$ present/N^{subject}
    state   −first
    root   −second
    −past   −plural

This rule says that non-past state verbs carry a present tense marker as in it hurts, he has. The distinction between regular and irregular forms is proper to a later component of the grammar which takes into account phonological representation.

The inherent feature 'locative' can also be associated with some stative verbs. Rule (S4) accounts for semantic configurations with 'locative' for both inherently locative verbs and those which are not.

(S4a) state — — $\rightarrow$ locative

This rule states that some stative verbs optionally include the inherent feature 'locative' in their semantic configurations. These verbs have surface realizations as in or on.

(S4b)   V ⎯ ⎯ ⎯→   V
          -locative   locative
          root   root + locativizer

This rule converts certain verbs into locatives as crawl to crawl under, for example. The postsemantic linearization of 'locative' associates the verb with an accompanying noun, giving realizations as ride on a bike. Preposition omission as in boy walk car may indicate that the child has not applied the semantic structure rule with the inherent feature 'locative'.

Semantic structure and postsemantic process rules discussed to this point have dealt with verbs. The following rules pertain to nouns.

5.2 Semantic configurations and postsemantic processes for nouns. Of particular relevance to nouns are the contextual features 'plural' and 'definite'. Although a full treatment of noun pluralization in English is far beyond the scope of this discussion, the formation of a semantic structure with the feature 'plural' underlies the surface manifestation of this marker. Rule (S5) gives formation of the semantic structure.

(S5) N ⎯ ⎯ ⎯≫ plural
      count

This rule states that 'plural' may optionally appear in the semantic configuration for count nouns. Contextual units by their nature do not influence the choice of lexical units and do not carry with them the redundancy that often holds between inherent features and lexical units. Linearization of 'plural' accounts for realizations as two boys or three girls. Pluralization is apparently an early acquisition. Of note, however, is that failure of this rule to apply was most often in the context of a number as two or three followed by a noun, two boy or three girl.

Although much attention could be given the definite and indefinite article, for purposes of simplicity rule (S6) allows the contextual unit 'definite' to be associated with the noun.

(S6a) N ⎯ ⎯ ⎯≫ definite

This rule states that the contextual feature 'definite' is optionally associated with some nouns. It does not, however, take into account the inherent feature 'aggregate' associated with a class of elements treated as an undifferentiated whole. Indefinite articles originate in configurations that indicate the non-presence of 'aggregate' and 'plural' on count nouns. This is given in rule (S6b).

(S6b)   N ⟶⟶⟶≫ -definite
           count
           root
           -aggregate
           -plural

This rule obligatorily gives rise to the surface form a(n). Lineari-zation processes give either the definite or indefinite article as in see up in the sky or that's a girl. Failure to take into account the non-presence of 'aggregate' and 'plural' may be the source of the sometimes indiscriminate mixing of a/the in child language.

Noun roots are also subject to the postsemantic process of dele-tion if they are not carrying new information. Certain nonlexical units retained in the surface structure after postsemantic processes apply come to be symbolized as pronouns. Pertinent to this study are those units resulting in subject and possessive pronouns. In the process leading from semantic configurations to surface structures, 'genders' and 'cases' are introduced postsemantically. At some point nouns can be specified with inherent units 'masculine', 'feminine', 'neuter'. In the course of postsemantic processes nouns are further specified as 'subjective', 'objective', 'possessive'. This occurs after the subject or possessive relations have been introduced, but before linearization. Rule (S7) is a rough approximation of the deletion pro-cess producing an intermediate semantic structure. In (S7) X is a cover symbol for 'gender' and 'person'. Deleted inherent features are represented by Y; deleted contextual units by Z.

(S7)   N   — — →   N
           ⎧subjective⎫   ⎧subjective⎫
           ⎨possessive⎬   ⎨possessive⎬
           ⎩objective ⎭   ⎩objective ⎭
           X   X
           Y   (plural)
           root
           -new
           (plural)
           Z

This rule states that the semantic configuration on the left-hand side can optionally be rewritten as that on the right. Acquisition of the subject pronoun before the possessive may reflect that the possessive needs to take into account more structural information than does the subject form.

6.0 Conclusions. Although the manner in which oral production data was elicited differed appreciably from that of Fathman's study for second language learning and Brown's for first language, the general sequencing of structures examined in this study was remarkably similar to both first and second language acquisition. The composite picture emerging is that some type of language processing mechanism is universally operative in language acquisition. These organizing principles function under varied conditions: normal first language acquisition, adding a second language, acquiring two languages simultaneously, or acquiring language on a delayed schedule.

One could argue that the sequencing of acquisitions in language delay is attributable to the therapy program in which the children were engaged. Studies by Gottsleben, Tyack, Buschini (1974) showed that children apply certain grammatical rules more frequently after training than at the onset of therapy. Fathman (1975) found that the order in which children acquired English as a second language was independent of the order of structural presentations in ESL programs. If this is true for the second language learner, it may well be true for the delayed language child undergoing therapy.

Within the limitations of this study one may conclude that language delayed children in certain respects, at least, follow the normal path for first language acquisition. This applies with regard to certain surface manifestations that find their source in the semantic structure of the language. It does not address the fact that other rules operative in language delay most probably have origins in cognitive development. If one agrees with Chafe (1971:57) that there is good reason to regard semantic structure as the formalization of human knowledge, a closer look at language delay may reveal that some of the deviant structures find their source in the child's view of the world or in the way he has structured that knowledge for whatever reason and to whatever degree.

Linguistically, realization of specific surface structures reflects acquisition of an underlying semantic configuration and the post-semantic processes operating on it. Processes as deletion, semantic change, and linearization are the link between the underlying semantic configuration and surface structure. Postsemantic processes hold a central role in associating surface structures, such as grammatical morphemes, with abstract configurations of meaning. The child's acquisition of surface forms is consequent to the acquisition of the underlying semantic structures. If the child is unable to specify fully these configurations, he cannot be expected to produce surface realizations. Surface manifestations can occur only if he discovers how to process the configuration. Delay in language acquisition may well have some of its roots in failure to construct the underlying semantic structures, specifying all of the necessary units related to noun and verb roots. This will result in an inadequate application of postsemantic processes, or in no application at all. Or the child may be able to construct the underlying forms but not be able to apply the linking postsemantic process that gives the surface form. Failure of either type of rules to apply, semantic or postsemantic, will prevent surface realizations.

Creative construction of semantic configurations and the postsemantic rules that operate on them is viewed here as a general process functioning in language acquisition, regardless of the condition-- first, second, or delayed. It does not yet address the much larger unknown. What are the configurations and processes operative in the formalization of human knowledge? What, then, is the relationship between language acquisition and cognitive development? Awareness of the similarities in the acquisition of a sub-set of semantic structures and processes does not give answers but, hopefully, provides insights that can lead to further explorations into the theory of the language acquisition process.

NOTE

This research was supported in part by the National Institute of Neurological Disease and Stroke Grant 5 PI5 NS07514 NSPB. The author is grateful to Jon Eisenson, director of the Institute for Childhood Aphasia, formerly at Stanford University School of Medicine and now at San Francisco State University, and David Ingram, University of British Columbia, for their part in making this study possible.

REFERENCES

Bailey, N., C. Madden, and S. Krashen. 1974. Is there a 'Natural Sequence' in adult second language learning? Language Learning 24. 235-243.

Brown, R. 1973. A first language: The early stages. Cambridge, Mass., Harvard University Press.

Chafe, W. 1970. Meaning and the structure of language. Chicago, University of Chicago Press.

_____. 1971. Linguistics and human knowledge. In: Georgetown University Round Table on Languages and Linguistics 1971. Edited by R. J. O'Brien, S.J. Washington, D.C., Georgetown University Press.

Dato, D. 1971. The development of the Spanish verb phrase in children's second-language learning. In: The psychology of second language learning. Edited by P. Pimsleur and T. Quinn. Cambridge, Cambridge University Press.

DeVilliers, J. and P. de Villiers. 1973. A cross-sectional study of the acquisition of grammatical morphemes in child speech. Journal of Psycholinguistic Research 2. 267-278.

Dulay, H. and M. Burt. 1973. Should we teach children syntax? Language Learning 23. 235-252.

_____. 1974a. Errors and strategies in child second language acquisition. TESOL Quarterly 8. 129-136.

_____. 1974b. Natural sequences in child second language acquisition. Language Learning 24. 37-53.

_____. 1974c. A new perspective on the creative construction process in child second language acquisition. Language Learning 24. 253-278.

Eisenson, J. 1972. Aphasia in children. New York, Harper and Row.

_____ and D. Ingram. Childhood aphasia: An up-dated concept based on recent research. Acta Symbolica (in press).

Ervin-Tripp, S. 1974. Is second language learning like the first? TESOL Quarterly 8. 111-127.

Fathman, A. 1974. The relationship between age and second language productive ability. Paper presented at the annual meeting of the Linguistic Society of America, New York.

_____. 1975. Language background, age, and the order of acquisition of English structures. Paper presented at the annual TESOL Convention, Los Angeles.

Gottsleben, R., D. Tyack, and G. Buschini. 1974. Three case studies in language training: Applied linguistics. Journal of Speech and Hearing Disorders 39. 213-224.

Ingram, D. and J. Eisenson. 1972. Therapeutic approaches III: Establishing and developing language in congenitally aphasic children. In: Aphasia in children. Edited by J. Eisenson. New York, Harper and Row.

Ingram, D. et al. 1973. Language samples of children with language disorders. San Francisco, Institute for Childhood Aphasia, San Francisco State University.

Kessler, C. 1971. The acquisition of syntax in bilingual children. Washington, D. C., Georgetown University Press.

_____. 1973. Postsemantic processes in children with language delay. Paper presented at the annual meeting of the Linguistic Society of America, San Diego.

Menyuk, P. 1971. The acquisition and development of language. Englewood Cliffs, N. J., Prentice-Hall.

Milon, J. 1974. The development of negation in English by a second language learner. TESOL Quarterly 8. 137-143.

Morehead, D. and D. Ingram. 1973. The development of base syntax in normal and linguistically deviant children. Journal of Speech and Hearing Research 16. 330-352.

Tremaine, Ruth V. 1975. Syntax and Piagetian operational thought: A development study of bilingual children. Washington, D. C., Georgetown University Press.

Wilcox, J. and H. Tobin. 1974. Linguistic performance of hard-of-hearing and normal-hearing children. Journal of Speech and Hearing Research 17. 286-293.

THE DEVELOPMENT OF CEREBRAL DOMINANCE AND LANGUAGE LEARNING: MORE NEW EVIDENCE

STEPHEN D. KRASHEN

Queens College

As recently as a month ago (at the time of the New York Academy of Science Conference on Developmental Psycholinguistics), at least certain questions concerning the development of cerebral dominance and its relation to language acquisition seemed to me to be more or less settled. Our hypothesis (Krashen and Harshman 1972; Krashen 1973a) that cerebral dominance was established by around five had been confirmed by clinical data, dichotic listening data, and other kinds of evidence, and there was reason to suspect that this process was related to first language acquisition (Krashen 1973b). This position differed from that presented by Lenneberg (1967) in his Bio-logical Foundations of Language . The development of cerebral dominance, according to Lenneberg, was complete at puberty, and its completion was directly related to a critical period for language acquisition. Citing data from Basser (1962) and other case histories of brain damaged children, Lenneberg had argued that the infant brain was 'equi-potential'--language could develop in either hemisphere in case of unilateral damage to the other side. Signs of cerebral dominance are detectable by around two, and full laterali-zation occurs at around puberty.

Three kinds of evidence seemed consistent with this hypothesis: (1) Right sided brain damage was connected with language disorders more often in children than in adults, indicating a relatively greater right hemisphere contribution to language and more diffuse lateralization in children. (2) Unilateral hemispherectomy, when performed as a result of lesions incurred during childhood, did not seem to

179

result in aphasia, regardless of which side was removed. This also suggests less lateralization in children. (3) The prognosis for recovery from acquired aphasia resulting from unilateral lesions is much better in children under puberty than in adults. This could be interpreted as consistent with the lateralization by puberty hypothesis if two assumptions are made: First, recovery must involve the minor hemisphere, and second, the minor hemisphere's ability to assume the language function is directly dependent on at least some degree of minor hemisphere representation of language.

In a previous paper (Krashen 1973a), it was pointed out that the data utilized to support points (1) and (2) were also consistent with the hypothesis that the development of cerebral dominance was complete by around five, rather than puberty. Right lesions producing speech disturbance appear to be limited to ages five and under in the studies Lenneberg cites. Moreover, the literature (Alajouanine and Lhermitte 1965, Guttman 1942) indicates that the percentage of cases of speech disturbance associated with right damage in children older than five is approximately the same as that seen in adults, a result that is inconsistent with lateralization by puberty. A review of the hemispherectomy literature shows that in the vast majority of cases the lesion was incurred before five. It does seem to be the case that in such instances we do see good recovery of language; cases in which the lesion was incurred after five and before puberty are, however, rare, and hemispherectomy data does not help decide between the lateralization by five and lateralization by puberty hypotheses. [1]

The hypothesis that lateralization is established by five was further strengthened by dichotic listening studies. Dichotic listening is a relatively simple procedure for determining cerebral dominance for auditorily presented stimuli. In dichotic listening, subjects are presented with simultaneous, competing stimuli and are asked to report what they have heard. When verbal stimuli are presented to normal, right-handed adults, a slight but significant right ear advantage in accuracy of recall usually emerges. Kimura (1961) was the first to discover this. She prepared a tape that presented sets of three pairs of digits, separated by .5 seconds. Her right-handed subjects showed a right ear advantage, and a group of left-handed subjects with known right hemisphere representation for language showed a left ear advantage. Kimura concluded that the right ear advantage reflected left hemisphere specialization for language and that a left ear advantage reflected right hemisphere dominance. The task Kimura gave her subjects involved a considerable short-term memory load. Others, most notably Studdert-Kennedy and Shankweiler (1970) demonstrated that a right ear advantage in normal right handers would be found for single pairs of short nonsense syllables, such as consonant contrasting CV syllables.

Several dichotic listening studies had been done using children as subjects (Kimura 1963, Geffner and Hochberg 1971, and Knox and Kimura 1970 all used sets of digits as stimuli). All of these studies showed an apparent decrease of the right ear advantage with age, a result which seems to conflict with both the lateralization by five and the lateralization by puberty hypotheses. We argued (Krashen and Harshman 1972) that this apparent decrease was a statistical artifact; as children get older their ability to guess and their short-term memory capacity increase. This causes an increase in overall accuracy and a resultant decrease in ear difference when measured by subtracting the left ear score from the right ear score (a ceiling effect). We suggested that a measure that was free of accuracy variations and unaffected by changes in guessing rate would show no change in ear difference after age five.

More recently, dichotic listening has been done with children using tasks that require less memory load. Berlin, Hughes, Lowe-Bell, and Berlin (1973), Goodglass (1973), and Dorman and Geffner (1973) all presented children five and older with single pairs of CV's, as in Studdert-Kennedy and Shankweiler (1970), and all reported no change in right ear advantage after five.

The above data, then, all seems to point to age five, with the possible exception of the finding that recovery from aphasia tends to be better before puberty. This, however, could be due to other factors, like an age related general decrease in the ability of areas in the injured hemisphere to assume language functions. Such cases of ipsilateral recovery have been documented for adults (Penfield and Roberts 1959; Milner, Branch, and Rasmussen 1968).

Implications of the age five hypothesis

The development of cerebral dominance had been linked to the close of a critical period for language acquisition, in that 'interhemispheric plasticity' (the ability of language to 'transfer' hemispheres) was suggested to be related to the 'plasticity' necessary to acquire a second language completely and naturally. While these two senses of plasticity seem only vaguely related, the data from brain damaged children cited above indicates that the development of cerebral dominance and thus complete transfer may occur only at or before five anyway.

It should be pointed out, however, that placing the completion of the development of lateralization earlier than puberty does not mean that a critical period does not exist. Puberty does seem to be an important turning point with respect to language learning. Child-adult differences appear to exist with respect to the product of language learning, linguistic competence (especially in the domain of phonology; see e.g. Oyama 1973; Asher and Garcia 1969; Seliger, Krashen, and Ladefoged, in press; Krashen and Seliger, in press) and with respect to optimal learning environments (see e.g. Krashen, in press, for a review). There are, on the other hand, some interesting similarities: There is evidence that children and adults utilize similar learning strategies, as shown in error analysis research (see Richards 1971, for a review) and in a recent study of grammatical morphemes in adult second language learners, which showed a difficulty ordering in adults not significantly different from that found in children learning English as a second language (Bailey, Madden, and Krashen, 1974; see also Madden et al. 1975). While it is possible that some physiological changes underlie the close of the critical period, it seemed unlikely that the development of cerebral dominance was responsible. If such an obvious change in the brain did take place at this time and was related to the critical period, moreover, one might expect child-adult differences to be much greater than they are.

The age five hypothesis has encouraged investigators to look for some other phenomena to explain or relate to child-adult differences in language learning. Schumann (forthcoming), Taylor (1974), and Stevick (1974) have all suggested investigation in the so-called 'affective domain', the psychological changes that occur at around puberty. Ellen Rosansky and I (Krashen, in press) have independently been considering changes in cognitive development that occur at around puberty, namely the onset of Inhelder and Piaget's 'formal operations' stage. Elkind (1970) has argued that formal operations and the psychological changes may be related (for discussion, see Krashen, in press) and it is of course possible that there are neurological events related to all of these. The completion of the development of cerebral dominance, it seemed, was not a 'biological barrier' to language acquisition, however.

Age five appears to be a pivotal time. In Western countries, children start school at this age, and a great deal of first language acquisition is complete: two facts that are probably related. It has been suggested (Krashen and Harshman 1972, Krashen 1973b) that the development of cerebral dominance and first language acquisition might also be related. Specifically, first language acquisition might depend on the previous maturation and lateralization of certain mental abilities localized in the left hemisphere. Consistent with this hypothesis are reports that developmental dyslectics, children who are poor readers but seem to be normal in other respects, tend to show a weaker right ear advantage in dichotic listening than normal subjects. Such children could be examples of late lateralization and maturation of certain crucial abilities necessary for normal reading.

Lateralization by zero

Very soon after the conclusions just summarized were reached, new data emerged to support a third position, that cerebral dominance was established at birth. Molfese (in press) presented speech stimuli (CV syllables and the words boy and dog), musical stimuli (C major chord), and a 'noise burst' to adults, children (age 4 to 11), and to infants (age one week to ten months) and obtained auditory evoked responses. He found that the 'AER to the speech stimuli was greater in the left hemisphere in nine of the ten infants, while the response to the piano chord and noise were greater in the right hemisphere in all ten infants'. Similar findings were obtained for the older children and adults; the apparent degree of lateralization seemed, in fact, to be slightly greater in the infants than in the older subjects.

More evidence for early lateralization came from Gardiner, Schulman, and Walter (1973) who found results similar to Molfese's, using an EEG technique with five- and six-month-old babies. The presence of morphological asymmetries in the brain has been reported in both premature and full-term infants similar to those found in the adult brain (Witelson and Pallie 1973, Teszner 1972). Wada, Clark, and Hamm (1973), moreover, reported such asymmetries in fetal infants as young as 29 weeks post-gestational age!

There appears to be some inconsistency between this data and the clinical data that supports the lateralization by five hypothesis. Richard Harshman attempted to bring both sets of data together (Harshman and Krashen 1973) to be consistent with one picture of the development of cerebral dominance. In this view if the adult brain is considered 'fully lateralized' (assume about 90% of the language function represented in the left hemisphere and 10% in the right; assume also that lateralization is a holistic phenomenon), the infant brain is partially lateralized (e.g. 60% in the left and 40% in the right). We hypothesized a development of lateralization from zero to about five, which is quite consistent with the clinical data that indicates a right hemisphere contribution to the language function before five and with dichotic listening data indicating no change in right ear advantage after five.

Electrophysiological data (EEG and AER) is consistent according to the following argument. (1) Our measures of cerebral dominance are 'surface' measures and are only indirectly related to the true state of cerebral dominance in the brain. Evidence is the fact that in dichotic listening we find only slight right ear advantages in subjects known to be 'fully lateralized'. In the typical dichotic listening experiment, the right ear gets about 60% of the correct responses and the left ear about 40%, while the true division of labor for the kind of stimuli used (see Zaidel 1975) is about 90%-10%. Similarly, with auditory evoked response the differences between hemispheres, while significant, is not as great as we think the actual division of labor is. (2) In certain kinds of subjects, the 'surface' measures are much closer to the actual state of affairs. In split-brain subjects, for example, the right ear advantage in dichotic listening is gigantic, with the left ear getting virtually nothing correct (Milner, Taylor, and Sperry 1968; Sparks and Geschwind 1968). Some electrophysiological research has been done using split-brain subjects (Gott, Rossiter, Galbraith, and Saul 1973) and it appears to be the case that 'greater differentiation of function can be detected (in split-brain subjects) by means of evoked potential analysis' (Gott et al. 1973:33).[2]

Such results are presumably due to the lack of a functioning corpus callosum in these subjects. In normals, the presence of a functioning corpus callosum and the greater interhemispheric communication it allows might equalize responses from the two hemispheres and thus attenuate the measured degree of lateralization.[3] (3) In some sense, young children might be like split-brains. It seems to be the case that the corpus callosum is incompletely developed at birth (Hewitt 1962) and that myelinization of the corpus callosum is not complete until about age six (Yakovlev and Lecours 1967). The lack of interhemispheric communication in infants, then, might result in a closer relationship between surface measures and true scores for measures of cerebral dominance. Molfese found the typical moderate adult level (or slightly greater) degree of measured lateralization in his infant subjects. Our hypothesis interprets this result as indicating a moderate (60-40?) true degree of lateralization.

Lacunae and current developments

The above explanation of the development of lateralization from zero to five clearly allows John Gilbert's recent results (personal communication) of a 'normal' degree of lateralization in three-year-old children using dichotic listening. Some studies, however, show a development of the right ear advantage in children under five. Ingram (1975) presented three- to five-year-old children with single pairs of consonant contrasting short words, and her data indicates an increase of degree of lateralization with age, especially for her male subjects. Bever (1971) also reports an increase in right ear advantage with age in children less than five. His results indicate that the more linguistically mature subjects are more lateralized. The fact that some studies show a developmental trend from three to five and others do not is a serious problem. (Note that we are, however, prepared with an explanation of electrical and dichotic measures in young children no matter how they come out! An increase in lateralization we cheerfully welcome as confirming the lateralization by five hypothesis, and no change, or a decrease we can blame on the development of the corpus callosum, a classic case of a solution to a problem that is no real explanation.)

Despite this problem, the data up to a few months ago seemed to point clearly to lateralization by five, developing with or slightly before language acquisition. Very recent experiments and observations, however, indicate that the picture is not as simple as we thought it was (a common development in most areas of scientific inquiry).

First, Kinsbourne, in his presentation at the New York Academy of Sciences earlier this year, reported that the only cases of language disturbance or delay in young children he found invariably involved injury of the left hemisphere. He explains other investigators' findings of right damage associated with language disturbance as not true unilateral injury. A more careful examination, he concludes, would reveal at least some degree of left hemisphere injury as well.

This argument in favor of a full lateralization at birth or earlier hypothesis is tempered by new evidence in favor of the old lateralization by puberty hypothesis. (Unfortunately one cannot merely settle on five as a compromise.) Satz, Bakker, Goebel, and Van der Vlugt, in a study to appear in Brain and Language,[4] did a dichotic listening experiment using children aged 5 to 11 as subjects. Stimuli were digits, presented in sets of four pairs at a time, involving a very large memory load. They found that the right ear advantage for their subjects increased with age, becoming significant at 9 and leveling off at 11. This result is consistent with Bryden's (1970) finding. He reported an increase in the number of right-handed children showing a right ear advantage after age 5 to around puberty, using two and three pair sets of digits in dichotic listening.

Satz et al. argue for a developmental hypothesis, with some degree of lateralization by 5 and full lateralization at puberty, a hypothesis which they claim is consistent with 'incidence and recovery in speech disturbances in brain damaged children'. As we have seen above, it does seem to be consistent with what is known about recovery from aphasia, which appears to be better when the lesion is acquired before puberty. As mentioned above, however, this recovery may be due to factors other than an incomplete lateralization and available right hemisphere language. Satz et al.'s hypothesis, however, is inconsistent with what we know of the incidence of aphasia in children older than five. For this age group, aphasia is rarely the result of right hemisphere lesions, just as in adults.

To summarize thus far, some dichotic studies (those using single CV's as stimuli) report no change in ear difference after five, while others, using two or more sets of digits, do. (The situation was not at all clarified by Sobotka, reported in Porter and Berlin, in press, who used both Berlin's CV tapes and a three pair per set digits tape prepared in Satz's laboratory. The experiment was a logical one; both sets were presented to 7-, 9-, 11-, and 13-year-old children. A right ear advantage was found; but in neither case was there an interaction of the right ear advantage with age!) If, however, the increase with age for the digits-with-memory load task does prove to be reliable, and it is confirmed that no increase occurs after five with single competing CV's, some possible explanations are available.

Both Porter and Berlin (in press), and Harshman, Remington, and Krashen (forthcoming) have suggested that 'different (dichotic) tasks tap different levels of language processing' (Porter and Berlin).[5] CV's may tap 'auditory and/or phonetic processing', word and sentence recognition tasks may involve semantic and syntactic levels, and 'linguistic short-term and long-term memory processes may be reflected in tests requiring memory. Also, lateralization of vocal tract control may exist' (Sussman 1971). Porter and Berlin also suggest that each of these 'stages may be lateralized to a different degree, and each may develop ontogenetically at a different rate', auditory/phonetic processing may develop and lateralize early, by five, which is consistent with those studies that find no increase in the right ear advantage with CV stimuli after five. The Satz et al. and Bryden studies reveal 'a developmental increase in REA because the task tapped lateralized language processes which mature late and show significant changes between 4 and 12 years'.

There is some indirect evidence that at least the two 'stages' at issue here (auditory/phonetic processing and linguistic short-term memory) are independently lateralized. We have recently discovered an adult male-female difference in lateralization; males being significantly more lateralized than females in a CV single pair dichotic test (Remington, Krashen, and Harshman, 1974; Harshman, Remington, and Krashen, forthcoming). Subsequent to that discovery, a thorough literature survey and reanalysis of other data revealed that a feature of dichotic tests that do not show a sex difference is that the task involved a significant memory load; that is, sets of either three or four pairs of digits. Harshman et al. have thus suggested that 'the sexes might differ with respect to lateralization of some . . . (lateralized) processes but not others'. They also point out that 'the presence or absence of a sex difference might even help to distinguish one type of lateralized process from another'.

In addition, Yeni-Komshian, Isenberg, and Goldberg (1975) have also provided evidence for the independent lateralization of linguistic short-term memory. In their study, longer S-R intervals led to an increased REA on a verbal dichotic listening task.

The demonstration of independence of two lateralized processes lends some credence to Porter and Berlin's hypothesis of a separate ontogeny for auditory/phonetic processing and linguistic short-term memory (or whatever else is involved in digit perception).

Porter and Berlin do not attempt to connect their hypothesis to the clinical data or to the critical period hypothesis; and I will conclude with some attempt at these tasks. Consider the case of a normal eight-year-old, who, according to Porter and Berlin, is fully lateralized for auditory/phonetic processing but who has some degree of bilateral representation (but mostly left hemisphere) for whatever stages underlie performance on a digits dichotic listening task. The clinical data indicates that a right hemisphere lesion will have little effect on language. This is not inconsistent with Porter and Berlin, as according to their hypothesis some processes are fully lateralized ('safe' in the left hemisphere) while others are, at worst, just mostly represented in the left hemisphere at this age. It is thus not surprising that right hemisphere damage will not grossly affect language performance as most of the language faculty is left lateralized. The clinical data also indicates complete recovery from acquired aphasia at this age when it is the result of unilateral damage. If this recovery involves 'transfer', or right hemisphere assumption of the language faculty (which it need not--see my previous remarks), one could hypothesize that what language there is in the right hemisphere at this age, certainly more than is found in the adult, is sufficient to allow complete 're-growth' of language. This assumes, of course, that processes that are not represented in the right hemisphere at this age, can redevelop along with those that are represented. (See note 3.)

The kind of research called for by the Porter-Berlin hypothesis is clear. We would expect more rapid recovery of those processes that are lateralized later. Developmental dichotic and electrophysiological studies using a variety of stimuli should be done and their results compared with careful descriptions and testing of language recovery in older children. If the Porter-Berlin hypothesis is confirmed, such studies, along with further sex difference studies, might tell us a great deal about how language is represented in the brain.

It is difficult even to speculate about the relationship of lateralization to the critical period while so many questions remain open about the developmental course of lateralization. Rather than hide behind a statement like 'more research is necessary before conclusions can be drawn', I will make a guess. If, as Harshman and I have suggested earlier, the maturation of a function goes along with its cortical lateralization, those aspects of language lateralized by puberty may correspond to the mastery of more abstract levels of language; for example, those gaps in first language acquisition described in Hatch (1969), Atkinson-King (1973), C. Chomsky (1969), and by Ingram (this conference). The development of lateralization may thus 'still' go along with first language acquisition, or rather, the maturation of abilities necessary for language acquisition. While Lenneberg's hypothesis that the completion of lateralization marks the end of the critical period should be re-evaluated in light of the new evidence, we still have as yet no real evidence that full lateralization means the loss of any real ability.

NOTES

I thank Richard Harshman for detailed discussion and criticism of nearly every point in this paper. I am also indebted to Sheri Berenbaum and Susan Curtiss for their helpful comments.

1. Pia (1962), a German neurologist, recommends that such operations should not be performed in patients who incur brain damage after five, because of the possibility of a permanent aphasia!

2. It should be pointed out that evoked cortical potentials need not be in exact proportion to actual language processing activity; such responses invariably contain nonlinguistic bilateral auditory components.

3. This argument assumes that language is first processed in the left hemisphere and that any right hemisphere response results from information getting 'back' to the right hemisphere after initial left hemisphere processing. This model may not be entirely correct for all aspects of language. Research by Blumstein and her associates (Blumstein 1974) shows that the acoustic to phonetic conversion for some features may take place in the right hemisphere or at lower levels. Studdert-Kennedy and Shakweiler (1970) have shown, however, that for the CV stimuli used in the studies described here, processing is in the left hemisphere.

4. I thank Dr. Harry Whitaker, editor of <u>Brain and Language,</u> for making these and other studies available to me.

5. See Harshman and Krashen (1973) for similar suggestions.

REFERENCES

Alajouanine, T. and F. Lhermitte. 1965. Acquired aphasia in children. Brain 88.653-662.
Asher, J. and R. Garcia. 1969. The optimal age to learn a foreign language. Modern Language Journal 53.334-41.

Atkinson-King, K. 1973. Children's acquisition of phonological stress contrasts. Working Papers in Phonetics (UCLA) 25.

Bailey, N., C. Madden, and S. Krashen. 1974. Is there a 'natural sequence' in adult second language learning? Language Learning 24. 235–243.

Basser, L. 1962. Hemiplegia of early onset and the faculty of speech with special reference to the effects of hemispherectomy. Brain 85. 427–460.

Berlin, C., L. Hughes, S. Lowe-Bell, and H. Berlin. 1973. Dichotic right ear advantage in children 5 to 13. Cortex 9. 393–401.

Bever, T. 1970. The nature of cerebral dominance in speech behavior of the child and adult. In: Biological and social factors in psycholinguistics. Edited by Morton. Urbana, University of Illinois Press.

Blumstein, S. 1974. The use of theoretical implications of the dichotic technique for investigating distinctive features. Brain and Language 1. 337–350.

Bryden, M. 1970. Laterality effects in dichotic listening: Relations with handedness and reading ability in children. Neuropsychologia 8. 443–445.

Chomsky, C. 1969. The acquisition of syntax in children from 5 to 10. Cambridge, Mass., MIT Press.

Dorman, M. and D. Geffner. 1974. Hemispheric specialization for speech perception in six-year-old black and white children from low and middle socioeconomic classes. Cortex 10. 171–176.

Elkind, D. 1970. Children and adolescents: Interpretive essays on Jean Piaget. New York, Oxford University Press.

Gardner, M., C. Schulman, and D. Walter. 1973. Facultative EEG asymmetries in babies and adults. UCLA Brain Information Service Conference Report 34.

Geffner, D. and I. Hochberg. 1971. Ear laterality performance of children from low and middle socioeconomic levels on a verbal dichotic listening task. Cortex 7. 193–203.

Goodglass, H. 1973. Developmental comparison of vowels and consonants in dichotic listening. Journal of Speech and Hearing Research 16. 744–752.

Gott, P., V. Rossiter, G. Galbraith, and R. Saul. 1973. Hemispheric evoked potentials to verbal and spatial stimuli in human commissurotomy patients. UCLA Brain Information Service Conference Report 34.

Guttmann, E. 1942. Aphasia in children. Brain 65. 205–219.

Harshman, R. and S. Krashen. 1973. On the development of lateralization. UCLA Brain Information Service Conference Report 34.

Hatch, E. 1969. Four experimental studies in syntax of young children. Technical Report 11, Southwest Regional Laboratories.

Hewitt, W. 1962. The development of the human corpus callosum. Journal of Anatomy 96.355-358.

Ingram, David. 1975. If and when transformations are acquired. Georgetown University Round Table on Languages and Linguistics 1975. Edited by Daniel Dato. Washington, D.C., Georgetown University Press.

Ingram, Diana. 1975. Cerebral speech lateralization in young children. Neuropsychologia 13.103-105.

Kimura, D. 1961. Cerebral dominance and the perception of verbal stimuli. Canadian Journal of Psychology 15.166-171.

_____. 1963. Speech lateralization in young children as determined by an auditory test. Journal of Comparative and Physiological Psychology 15.899-902.

Kinsbourne, M. (in press). The ontogeny of cerebral dominance. In: Developmental psycholinguistics and communication disorders. Edited by Aaronson and Rieber. New York Academy of Science.

Knox, C. and D. Kimura. 1970. Cerebral processing of nonverbal sounds in boys and girls. Neuropsychologia 8.227-237.

Krashen, S. 1973a. Lateralization, language learning, and the critical period: Some new evidence. Language Learning 23.63-74.

_____. 1973b. Mental abilities underlying linguistic and nonlinguistic functions. Linguistics 115.39-55.

_____. In press. The critical period for language acquisition and its possible bases. In: Developmental psycholinguistics and communication disorders. Edited by Aaronson and Rieber. New York Academy of Science.

_____ and R. Harshman. 1972. Lateralization and the critical period. Working Papers in Phonetics (UCLA) 23.13-21.

_____ and H. Seliger. In press. Maturational constraints in the acquisition of a second language and a second dialect. Language Sciences.

Lenneberg, E. 1967. Biological Foundations of Language. New York, Wiley.

Madden, C., N. Bailey, and S. Krashen. 1975. Acquisition of function words by adult learners of English as a second language: Evidence for universal strategies. Papers from the Fifth Annual Meeting of the North Eastern Linguistics Society (NELS), 234-245.

Milner, B., C. Branch, and T. Rasmussen. 1968. Observations on cerebral dominance. In: Language. Edited by Oldfield and Marshall. Penguin Modern Psychology Readings.

_____, L. Taylor, and R. Sperry. 1968. Lateralized suppression of dichotically presented digits after commissural section in man. Science 161.184-186.

Molfese, D. In press. The ontogeny of cerebral asymmetry in man: Auditory evoked potentials to linguistic and nonlinguistic stimuli. In: Cerebral evoked potentials in man. Edited by J. Desmedt.

Oyama, S. 1973. A sensitive period for the acquisition of a second language. Unpublished doctoral dissertation, Harvard University.

Penfield, W. and L. Roberts. 1959. Speech and brain mechanisms. Princetown, University Press.

Pia, H. 1962. Die Hemisphärektomie bei infantiler Hemiplegie. Therap. Genenw. 4.162-170.

Porter, R. and C. Berlin. In press. On interpreting developmental changes in the dichotic right-ear advantage. Brain and Language.

Remington, R., S. Krashen, and R. Harshman. 1974. A possible sex difference in degree of lateralization of dichotic stimuli? Journal of the Acoustical Society of America 55.434 (A).

Richards, J. 1971. A non-contrastive approach to error analysis. English Language Teaching 25.204-219. Also in: Focus on the learner: Pragmatic perspectives for the language teacher. Edited by Oller and Richards. Rowley, Mass., Newbury House.

Satz, P., D. Bakker, R. Goebel, H. Van der Vlugt. In press. Developmental parameters of the ear asymmetry: A multivariate approach. Brain and Language.

Seliger, H., S. Krashen, and P. Ladefoged. In press. Maturational constraints in the acquisition of a native-like accent in second language learning. Language Sciences.

Sparks, R. and N. Geschwind. 1968. Dichotic listening in man after section of neocortical commissures. Cortex 4.3-16.

Stevick, E. 1974. Why is a foreign accent? Linguistics and psychoanalysis: Some interfaces 1.1-2.

Studdert-Kennedy, M. and D. Schankweiler. 1970. Hemispheric specialization for speech perception. Journal of the Acoustical Society of America 48.576-594.

Sussman, H. 1971. The laterality effect in lingual-auditory tracking. Journal of the Acoustical Society of America 49.1874-1880.

Taylor, B. 1974. Toward a theory of language acquisition. Language Learning 24.23-35.

Teszner, D. 1972. Etude anatomique de l'asymetrie droit-gauche du planum temporale sur 100 cerveaux d'adults. Unpublished doctoral dissertation, Université de Paris. (Cited in: Molfese, in press).

Wada, J., R. Clark, and A. Hamm. 1973. Asymmetry of temporal and frontal speech zones in 100 adult and 100 infant brains. Paper presented to the 10th International Congress of Neurology, Barcelona. (Cited in Molfese, in press).

Witelson, S. and W. Pallie. Left hemisphere specialization for language in the newborn: Anatomical evidence for asymmetry. Brain 96.641-646.

Yakovlev, P. and A. Lecours. 1967. The myelogenetic cycles of regional maturation in the brain. In: Regional development of the brain in early life. Edited by Minkowski. Oxford, Blackwell.

Yeni-Komshian, G., D. Isenberg, and H. Goldberg. 1975. Cerebral dominance and reading disability: Left visual field deficit in poor readers. Neuropsychologia 13.83-94.

LEARNING TO SPEAK A SECOND LANGUAGE: WHAT EXACTLY DOES THE CHILD LEARN?

KENJI HAKUTA

Harvard University

Introduction. Research in child second language acquisition has been accumulating at a remarkable rate over the past few years. Most of these studies have focused on certain grammatical features of the language and have attempted to characterize the data in terms of order or stages of acquisition. Grammatical morphemes seem to be a favorite, and Dulay and Burt (1973, 1974b), Bailey, Madden, and Krashen (1974), and Hakuta (1974a) have all made attempts to establish an order of acquisition for these structures. The interrogative structures have been characterized in terms of sequences of development by Ravem (1968), Huang (1971), and by Cancino, Rosansky, and Schumann (1974). The development of negation has been described by Milon (1974) and by Rosansky, Schumann, and Cancino (1974). And Zimin (1973), Dulay and Burt (1974a), and Selinker, Swain, and Dumas (1974) have made attempts at characterizing the types of systematic errors made by second language learners.[1]

While these studies are beginning to give a clearer picture of the learners' patterns of development, very little is yet known about the learning process itself, that is, the way in which children go about learning the structures that they produce. What I would like to report on in this paper is a small set of observations that I have made in studying the acquisition of English as a second language by a five-year-old Japanese girl named Uguisu. These observations, I believe, may give a glimpse of some of the leading edges of a more general process which may be operative in the acquisition of a second language, and possibly a first.

Uguisu, 'nightingale' in Japanese, came to the United States during the period of two years that her father was a visiting scholar at Harvard, and they took residence in North Cambridge in a working-class neighborhood. The children in that neighborhood were her primary source of language input. Uguisu also attended public kindergarten for two hours a day, and later elementary school, but with no explicit tutoring in English syntax. Most of her neighborhood friends were in her same class at school.

Spontaneous speech of about two hours for each biweekly sample was recorded and later transcribed in traditional orthography. She was observed over a period of 60 weeks, from the time she was 5;4, which was five months after her exposure to English began, until the time she was 6;5, when her family returned home to Japan. The first sample represents the point at which she first began spontaneously producing utterances in English.

One of the advantages to a longitudinal study of this nature is that one can perform what might be called a 'micro-analysis' of the data. That is, one can take given structures which appear with a good deal of frequency across samples, and trace the development of the form over time. The profiles of development obtained through such micro-analyses may give a glimpse of some processes involved in the acquisition of language. What follows are profiles of the development of three rather unrelated linguistic forms, all of which I believe have something to tell concerning the nature of language acquisition. The first form involves a rather functionally redundant yet semantically complex feature of English: the indefinite article a, as in a sock. The second form that I shall micro-analyze is the future form be gonna (be going to in more formal adult English), as in I'm gonna fool you and we're gonna play with playdough. And finally, I will discuss wh-embeddings, as in I know how to play hopscotch and I don't know where you are.

The indefinite article a. English has a very complex system of articles, dividing along the dimension of the definite and indefinite.[2] They come under the category of what Brown (1973) has called 'grammatical morphemes', for which obligatory contexts can be established and the child's performance scored for whether or not the morpheme is supplied. Brown in his study of Adam, Eve, and Sarah did not score separately for the definite and indefinite forms of the articles. I, however, did since I was present at every sampling session with Uguisu and was always aware of the context, and I found it possible to identify the obligatory context for the respective forms of the articles in about 90% of the cases. I thus tallied the two separately. For purposes of the present paper, I shall concentrate only on the indefinite form a, but it is of incidental interest to note that both forms attain the 90% criterion set by Brown within one sample of each other, suggesting that the full control of a and the requires learning along similar dimensions. [3] Figure 1 charts the development of the indefinite article a over time. [4] One sees that in no way is there a sudden leap in the usage of the form, but rather a slow and gradual rise in the probability of the morpheme being supplied, eventually settling somewhere above the 90% level. Why this gradual and non-abrupt rise in Uguisu's control of the indefinite article? At least two

FIGURE 1. Acquisition curve for the indefinite article a, scored for percent supplied in obligatory contexts. Samples are biweekly. The number of obligatory contexts for each data point ranges from about 50 to 200.

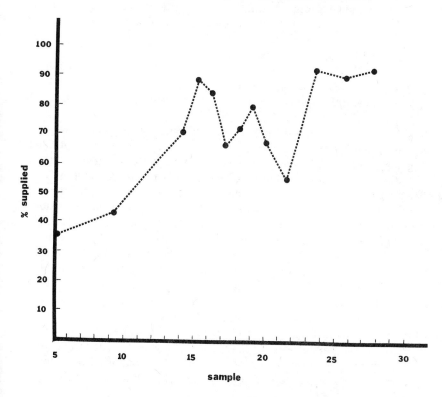

possibilities exist. One such possibility is that what is considered to be the rule for the indefinite article in fact consists of many minute subrules, and that although each individual subrule is learned abruptly, the curve appears to be gradual because they are all 'scrunched' together under one category. A second possibility is that there are certain phonological constraints which make the article more difficult to supply with certain nouns than others.

There is a way to test for such possibilities. One can take a maximally restricted context in which the article is obligatory and score for percent supplied in only that context. Then one can compare the acquisition curve obtained from this analysis with that of Figure 1, that is, the entire range of contexts requiring a, and see how closely they match. Ideally, what one would like to find is a single noun, such as book, which appears frequently in the data. Taking that single noun, one could establish maximally restricted contexts, and score for only those contexts. Unfortunately, I found no such ideal. What I did find, however, was a rather odd but adequate substitute: 'nother, as in Do you have 'nother story?. In earlier samples, Uguisu consistently used 'nother, as opposed to which she gradually began using: a#nother. I am particularly confident that the a in a#nother was productively supplied because Uguisu, though infrequently, also used its variants the#nother and some#nother, as in the following:

The#nother one is, um, Maria.
But some#nother people will catch your children.

All samples were scored for presence/absence of the indefinite article in the context [a/_nother], and the acquisition curve obtained appears in Figure 2, superimposed on the acquisition curve for the entire range of contexts requiring a, which is taken from Figure 1. The profiles of the two curves are strikingly similar, except for the earlier samples (prior to Sample 14) where the percent supplied for the context for [a/_nother] is close to zero. The difference in the earlier samples, I believe, is due to instances where in total contexts, the instances of a which appeared were in fact simple phonological stems of other morphemes, such as in-a or look-like-a, and not necessarily productive. What the foregoing analysis suggests, then, is that even within maximally restricted contexts, the learning involved is not abrupt and sudden but rather a gradual process in which the probability of the article being supplied slowly rises from a zero to a 100 percent.[5] Furthermore, it suggests that the probability, at any given point in time, may very well be constant across the entire range of obligatory contexts for the indefinite article.

Be-gonna. The second form which I wish to micro-analyze is the future form be-gonna. Uguisu began using this form as early as Sample 4, and with high frequency from Sample 9. She produced utterances such as the following:

I gonna make 'nother baseball.
Oh, they gonna kill the fish.

FIGURE 2. Acquisition curve for the indefinite article a in the restricted context a/_nother compared to the entire range of contexts a/_NP, scored for percent supplied in obligatory contexts. Samples are biweekly. The number of obligatory contexts for each data point for a/_nother ranges from 4 to 18, with a mean of 9.

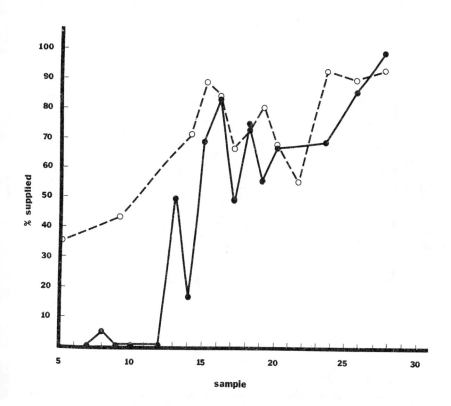

She gonna kill her.
Everybody gonna do it.
We gonna punch you.

Note that the auxiliary be, which is obligatory in adult speech, is missing. She eventually did begin supplying the be, and so I decided to score for percent supplied in obligatory contexts for all samples, tallying separately for the three allomorphs am, is, and are. The results of the scoring appear in Figure 3. For the moment, leave aside the strange downward swoop of the curve for am between

FIGURE 3.　Acquisition curve for the three allomorphs am, is, and are as auxiliaries to the catenative gonna, scored for percent supplied in obligatory contexts. Samples are biweekly. The number of obligatory contexts for each data point is greater than 5, in most cases between 15 and 30.

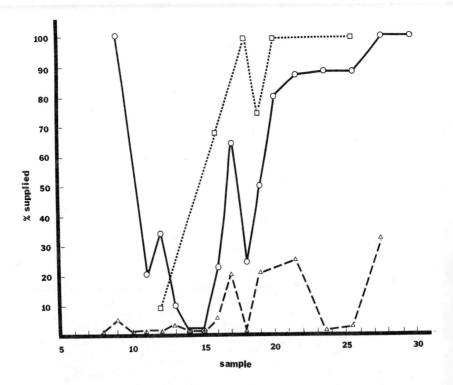

Samples 9 and 14. We shall return to it later. Notice first in Figure 3 that the acquisition curves for the three allomorphs manifest a slow, probabilistic rise, just like the curve observed for the indefinite article in Figures 1 and 2. Also note that the allomorphs am and is

attain the 100 percent level of being supplied, while the allomorph are trails limply, never getting above the 40 percent level.

Why the difference between the different allomorphs of be? This is a rather odd result in light of the fact that Uguisu was quite good with other forms of be, namely the copula and the auxiliary in the present progressive. For the copula, omissions occurred rarely (about 1 percent), and I have argued elsewhere (Hakuta 1974b) that they are what I have called 'prefabricated patterns'. Similarly for the auxiliary, omissions were infrequent, the auxiliary being supplied in well over 95% of the obligatory contexts across all samples. Uguisu produced am, are, and is with equal ease, and so the problem cannot be phonological in nature.

One possibility is that the sequencing of constituents in the input may provide difficulty. That is to say, when a declarative sentence, such as You're gonna try this one, is transformed into the interrogative form, it becomes Are you gonna try this one?, where the auxiliary be is moved out of its normal environment and placed in front of the sentence. Thus:

$$\text{Pro} + \underline{\text{be}} + \underline{\text{gonna}} + \text{VP} \Longrightarrow$$
$$\underline{\text{Be}} + \text{Pro} + \underline{\text{gonna}} + \text{VP}$$

This results in a sequence of constituents where the auxiliary be is in effect omitted from its position between the subject and gonna.[6] It may very well be the case that this provides an erroneous model to the learner. The possibility is reinforced by the observation of Evelyn Hatch (1972) that a good number of the second language learners studied by her students at UCLA followed an 'operating principle' of 'pay attention to the end of utterances and especially to content words'. In accounting for Uguisu's poor performance with are, the explanation on grounds of sequencing of constituents is an intuitively appealing one. One generally asks questions about you and we, such as Are you gonna come with me? or What are we gonna do about this problem?, both of which involve the allomorph are. It seems unlikely that one would ask questions with the subject I, i.e. Am I gonna have a tantrum?. Questions involving a third person singular subject, such as Is he gonna read this paper?, would also be less likely than questions with you and we as subjects.

To test for this possibility, I decided to analyze the interactor's speech[7] taken from two distinct time periods, the first from Samples 7 through 9, and the second from Samples 17 through 22. I shall refer to these two periods as Time I and Time II. I first extracted all utterances involving the form gonna, and then scored them, using as categories the three allomorphs am, are, and is, as to whether they provided a 'good model' or a 'bad model'. A good model was defined as where the be is placed between the subject and gonna, such as We're gonna play with playdough; a bad model as where the be is not between the subject and gonna, but rather preposed, as in What are you gonna do? The percentage of good models over total gonna constructions was computed for Time I and II, and the results appear in Table 1. The results show that at both Time I and Time II, the percentage of good models for are is significantly lower than for am and is. If one accepts the assumption that similar profiles appear in Uguisu's input, and I think it likely, then this analysis suggests that her apparent difficulty with the allomorph are had to do with her attempts to make her speech in effect consistent with what she heard in her input, a process which might be called 'external consistency'.

TABLE 1. Percent of good models over total gonna constructions in interactor speech from two time periods.

	Time I	Time II
am	.80 (15/19)	.95 (18/19)
is	.74 (14/19)	.74 (23/31)
are	.29 (22/75)	.33 (29/87)

Reference is again made to Figure 3 where, as mentioned earlier, there exists a rather strange downward swoop for the allomorph am between Samples 9 and 14. In Sample 9, Uguisu supplied am in all five instances with gonna. Prior to Sample 9, between Samples 4 and 8 when the gonna form was infrequent, Uguisu supplied am in 4 out of 5 instances. By Samples 14 and 15, am was omitted in all 22 obligatory contexts. One can well ask the question: 'Uguisu, what are you doing?' When a presumably correct form becomes deviant over time, one infers that some process of reorganization is going on. One possibility which immediately presents itself is that the function of the form gonna is quite similar to that of other catenatives, have to and wanna. They all signal some form of 'intentionality' or 'imminence' (Brown 1973:318). Of these three catenatives, however, gonna is the only one in which an auxiliary be is required. Did Uguisu have the other forms wanna and have to? Wanna was present from the very first sample; more interestingly, the form have to, though existent infrequently from Sample 5, went through a 'peak usage' between Samples 9 and 12, where approximately 14-15% of her total constructions used this form. This compares to an approximate 4% usage in the later samples. When a form undergoes such overuse, it suggests some process through which the form is being actively 'tried out' by the learner. Interestingly, this period of overuse of have to, which lasted from Sample 9 to 12, corresponds to the period when the downward swoop for am in gonna is observed, between Samples 9 and 14. This observation leads me to speculate that Uguisu was attempting to make her gonna form consistent with her other two catenative forms, wanna and have to, thereby dropping the am in gonna, a process which might be called 'internal consistency'. Uguisu was trying to keep related linguistic forms within her system consistent with one another.

Wh-embeddings and wh-questions. [8] While the notion of 'internal consistency' is still fresh in mind, I shall go on to the next problem of wh-embeddings and wh-questions, which I think speaks more directly to this issue.

As early as Sample 5, Uguisu made the following set of utterances:

I know how to do it.
I know how to do read it this.
I know how to read it this.
I know how to make.
I know how to draw it cat.
I know how to draw (it) butterfly.
I know how to draw it boy.

What appeared at that time to be quite grammatical constructions of embedded how-questions, however, disintegrated over time into forms such as the following, which she produced at the very last session:

First I gotta write it and show you how do you spell 'Debra'.
I know how do you spell 'Vino'.
We only know how do you make it like that.
I know how do you write this.

What one finds here once again is a progression, from presumably grammatical utterances to a deviant form. This progression, from how to to how do you, is also a gradual and not a sudden process. Figure 4 plots the story, and the graph can be read as follows: 'Given the instances when embedded how-questions were used, what percentage took the proper form how to?'[9] Once again, one may well ask the question: 'Uguisu, what are you doing?' A glimpse of the process can be had by looking at other wh-embeddings used by Uguisu. Table 2 gives an exhaustive list of embedded where-questions used by Uguisu. The form starts out with the configuration 'Sentence+ Questions', as in We know where is this. [10] Through a gradual process, the question becomes 'uninverted', as in I don't know where the

FIGURE 4. Proportion of correct <u>how</u> embeddings (how to) over total <u>how</u> embeddings. Biweekly samples are paired.

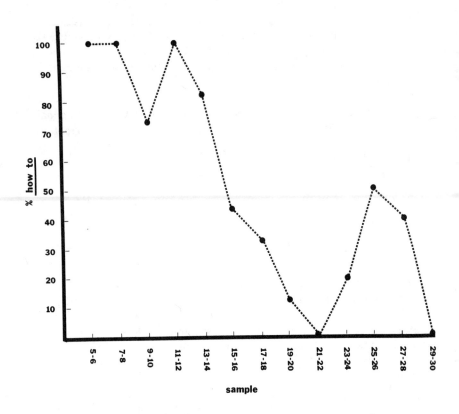

bathroom is, after some redundancy, as in <u>You will see where is your house is</u>. A similar progression is observed with other embedded <u>wh</u>-questions, but with less frequency of occurrence.

The <u>wh</u>-questions produced by Uguisu complete the picture. From the first sample on, Uguisu was able to construct <u>where</u>-questions of the following sort:

Where's purple?
Where is the nose?
Where is potato?

She was also able to construct <u>how</u>-questions of the following sort:

How do you make it bread?
How do you play this?
How do you put it on?

TABLE 2. Exhaustive list of embedded <u>where</u>-questions in Uguisu.

Form*	Sample	Sentence
I	1	I don't know, where is money.
I	7	We know where is this.
I	7	I don't know where is it.
I	10	My father tell me where is here.
I	10	I didn't know, where is, um, doctor's room.
U	11	I know where it is.
I	11	You have to close your eye and you have to see where is it.
U	12	I don't know where she is.
I	13	I don't know where is your house.
I	14	I didn't know where is it.
I	16	You know where is my house.
I	16	You will see the house where is it.
R	16	You will see where is your house is.
R	16	I don't know where is the telephone number is.
R	18	I don't know where is the woods is.
I	18	I know (it) where is it.
U	18	I know where it is.
U	24	I don't know where the bathroom is.
U	26	I know where it is.

*I = inverted; U = uninverted; R = redundant

It seems that Uguisu was forming her <u>wh</u>-embeddings by attaching her <u>wh</u>-question to a sentence, except for the <u>how</u>-embeddings. The gradual progression from the proper form <u>how to</u> into the deviant <u>how do you</u>, then, suggests Uguisu's attempt once again to maintain the internal consistency of her linguistic system. I suppose that, had Uguisu remained in the United States, her now deviant <u>how</u>-embeddings would have returned through a gradual process to the proper <u>how to</u> form, just as her deviant <u>where</u>-embeddings gradually became un-inverted into the proper form. Presumably, the move away from the internally consistent 'Sentence+Question' configuration is motivated this time by some propelling forces toward the maintenance of an external consistency, that is, the input that Uguisu hears.

Concluding remarks. The impression that I hope to have conveyed through the above set of observations is that the process of second language acquisition is a dynamic, fluid process in which the system of the learner is constantly shifting: shifting in a slow and gradual manner either toward the maintenance of an internal consistency within the structures which the learner possesses, or in the direction of an external consistency, where the learner attempts to fit the internal system into what is heard in the input.[11] The phenomena described in this paper may be the edges of some generally overlapping and interacting processes which make occasional appearances in the data. What one needs to know, of course, are the dimensions along which the child comes to maintain the internal or external consistency; one would also like to know what the variables are that make the child 'ready' to make certain changes in the linguistic system at certain periods in the course of development.

Let me conclude this paper with a point which is so easily overlooked. The learner does not sit in a box receiving input of the second language, working at the task of figuring out the grammar of the language day in and day out, generating rules, hypotheses, strategies, and utterances. Language is learned in the context of the environment within which the learner operates, and from that environment the learner learns things other than language as well. The environment may be in the context of playing hopscotch, in the context of routine daily activities, in the context of fighting with a friend over a Tinkertoy piece. What it is that motivates a child to learn language in order to operate within those contexts is clear: the child wants to communicate. What it is that motivates a child to change the form of an utterance, I don't know where is the answer to I don't know where the answer is, is not clear: it needs to be.

NOTES

This research was supported by Grant GSOC-7309150 from the National Science Foundation to Professor Roger Brown.

I thank Professors Roger Brown and Jill de Villiers for suggestions and comments in the preparation of this paper. I also thank Bruce Fraser for helpful stylistic suggestions.

1. There is, of course, conflicting evidence. See Schumann (1975) for a concise, insightful review of some of the studies.

2. See Brown (1973:340-356) and Maratsos (1971) for a detailed discussion of the English article system and its acquisition by L1 children.

3. The full story on the development of articles in Uguisu can be found in Hakuta (in preparation). Relative to other grammatical morphemes, it is worth noting that articles were acquired late by Uguisu.

4. Articles were scored for Samples 14 through 28, since prior to Sample 14, many seeming articles appear to be not segmented morphemes but rather phonological features of verbs (e.g. look-like-a) and prepositions (e.g. in-a). Brown (1973:355) notes similar problems with the analysis of articles in his early samples: 'Before the attainment of the 90% criterion I have found that the child's use of articles cannot support any inferences about his control of semantic and grammatical rules. This is partly because certain seeming articles in earlier samples probably are not organized as separate morphemes at all but are rather features of the pronunciation of particular words.' However, I did score Samples 5 and 9, regardless of whether the seeming articles were unsegmented morphemes or not, and the data points appear in Figure 1.

5. It might be argued that the curve for a/_nother is abrupt, especially between Samples 12 and 16. It should be noted, with regard to this consideration, that each sampling period covers two weeks. Furthermore, it is not until Sample 28 that it attains the 100 percent level. In addition, the n for each sample for the context is relatively small (only those cases with more than four obligatory contexts were included), as the contexts are restricted. Mathilda Holzman (personal communication) suggests that a 'moving average' system for scoring might cut down on random fluctuations due to sampling, and may provide a more reliable, gradual curve although it has not been done for the present paper.

6. Roger Brown (personal communication) points out that in colloquial speech, especially in lower-class speech, the auxiliary is often dropped, to yield You gonna try this one?

7. The interactor varied from sample to sample: in a few cases, I was the only one present; in others, native English-speaking adults were simply asked to 'play' with Uguisu. The profiles of the different interactors, however, were very similar with regard to gonna.

8. Part of the data in this section was reported in Hakuta (1974b).

9. Samples were paired in order to give sufficient sample size, i.e. n > 5, but in most cases, the n was about 10.

10. Evelyn Hatch (1974) reports similar structures of the configuration 'Sentence+Question' in many of the second language learners whom she has studied, from varying L1 backgrounds.

11. Note, incidentally, the analogy between my notion of internal and external consistency and Piaget's notion of assimilation and accommodation. I am heavily tempted to make some generalizations, but feel that at this point with so little data, it's stretching it a bit too far. Future studies, with more emphasis on input, may substantiate this analogy.

REFERENCES

Bailey, N., C. Madden, and S. D. Krashen. 1974. Is there a 'natural sequence' in adult second language learning? Language Learning 24. 235-243.

Brown, R. W. 1973. A first language: The early stages. Cambridge, Mass., Harvard University Press.

Cancino, H., E. Rosansky, and J. Schumann. 1974. The acquisition of English question formation by Spanish speakers. Paper presented at the Linguistic Society of America, Winter meeting, New York.

Dulay, H. and M. K. Burt. 1973. Should we teach children syntax? Language Learning 23. 235-252.

_____. 1974a. Errors and strategies in child second language acquisition. TESOL Quarterly 8. 129-137.

_____. 1974b. Natural sequences in child second language acquisition. Language Learning 24. 37-54.

Hakuta, K. 1974a. A preliminary report on the development of grammatical morphemes in a Japanese girl learning English as a second language. Working Papers in Bilingualism 3. 18-38.

_____. 1974b. Prefabricated patterns and the emergence of structure in second language acquisition. Language Learning 24. 287-297.

_____. In preparation. Becoming bilingual at age five: The story of Uguisu. Senior honors thesis. Dept. of Psychology and Social Relations, Harvard University.

Hatch E. 1972. Studies in second language acquisition. Paper presented at the Third International Congress of Applied Linguistics, Copenhagen.

_____. 1974. Second language acquisition: Universals? Working Papers in Bilingualism 3. 1-17.

Huang, J. 1971. A Chinese child's acquisition of English syntax. Unpublished M.A. thesis, UCLA.

Maratsos, M. P. 1971. The use of definite and indefinite reference in young children. Unpublished doctoral dissertation. Dept. of Psychology and Social Relations, Harvard University.

Milon, J. 1974. The development of negation in English by a second language learner. TESOL Quarterly 8. 137-143.

Ravem, R. 1968. Language acquisition in a second language environment. International Review of Applied Linguistics 6. 175-185.

Rosansky, E., J. Schumann, and H. Cancino. 1974. Second language acquisition: The negative. Paper presented at the Linguistic Society of America, Summer Meeting, Amherst, Mass.

Schumann, J. 1975. Second language acquisition research: Getting a more global look at the learner. Paper presented at the University of Michigan Sixth Annual Conference on Applied Linguistics, Ann Arbor, Mich.

Selinker, L., M. Swain, and G. Dumas. 1974. The interlanguage hypothesis extended to children. Paper presented at the Linguistic Society of America, Summer Meeting, Amherst, Mass.

Zimin, S. 1973. A pilot study of eleven Hebrew speakers' acquisition of English in Boston. Unpublished paper, Program of Applied Psycholinguistics, Boston University.

A NEW APPROACH
TO DISCOVERING UNIVERSAL STRATEGIES
OF CHILD SECOND LANGUAGE ACQUISITION

HEIDI C. DULAY AND MARINA K. BURT

State University of New York at Albany

Introduction. Second language acquisition research today owes a
great deal to the last 15 years of research on first language acquisition, much of which was inspired by Noam Chomsky's views on the
essential role of human cognitive structure in the language learning
process. Were it not for the insightful and laborious work of Roger
Brown, Dan Slobin, Tom Bever, and their colleagues, second language acquisition might not have had a place on this program today.
It is indeed a pleasure to be sharing this Round Table on Languages
and Linguistics with some of the very people to whom we owe many
of our ideas and much of our methodology. We hope that now, after
the benefit of several years of begging and borrowing from first language research, second language acquisition research is ready to
make a contribution in its own right.

The data given in this paper, showing the universality of acquisition
orders of elementary grammatical structures in children, supplements
an earlier study described in Burt and Dulay (1974). The 1974 study,
however, covered only one state (New York) and dealt with 115 children, whereas this paper reports on some 500 children in ten states
across the United States, and presents language variability with respect to the acquisition order of certain structures for different language groups (Spanish and Chinese). The theoretical discussion in
this report is substantially the same as that presented in Language
Learning, Vol. 24, No. 2 (December, 1974), pages 253-278, and is
repeated here almost verbatim through the kind permission of that
journal's editor, Professor H. Douglas Brown. Those interested

in the original study of 115 children in New York are referred to the Language Learning article.

The early work in child second language (L2) acquisition ('early' meaning 5-6 years ago) emphasized the comparison of the developing L2 syntactic structures children produced with the corresponding developing structures children produced in first language acquisition. For example, Ravem (1974) at the University of Essex studied the acquisition of English wh-questions by his Norwegian-speaking son and daughter over a period of four months. He found that the intermediate steps his children went through in the acquisition of wh-questions were generally the same as those that Brown's research children, Adam, Eve, and Sarah went through. That is, the children used structures like Where daddy go? and Where daddy is going? before they produced the mature forms. John Milon (1974) in Hawaii studied the acquisition of English negation by a Japanese-speaking child named Ken over a six-month period. Like Ravem, he found that Ken used basically the same developmental sequence of structure types that Adam, Eve, and Sarah had used in the acquisition of English negation. Daniel Dato (1970, 1971, and this volume), in his study of Spanish second language acquisition by six American children in Madrid, also provided us with evidence of a systematic progression of developing language structures. In a study conducted on Spanish speaking children learning English in the United States (Dulay and Burt 1974a), we found that out of some 513 errors made by 179 children, 86% were the same types of errors that first language learners made in English. Even some perceptual strategies have been found to be similar for first and second language learners.

We believe that we are now at a stage where we can assume that creative construction indeed plays a major role in child second language acquisition, and that we can begin to approach the more interesting and complex question of the precise nature of the process itself.

One of the first ideas that come to mind, especially after the wave of studies that show general similarities between L2 and L1 learners is that L2 learners are somehow obviously different from L1 learners. After all, L2 learners are older, more cognitively developed, and have already learned a language once before. As 'experienced' language learners, they must bring something to the acquisition process that transferred over from their days as L1 learners. Although there is no time to discuss it fully here, we can report that the data indicates that what transfers is not the surface structure of the first language, as has been widely believed. The amount of actual syntactic interference in child second language speech is trivial--barely 5% of the syntactic error types observed. What is transferred--, or revived, if you will, is the general creative process of language learning. This does not mean that the speech produced (or, speech product) is identical for first and second language learners in all respects. Developing structures of L2 learners are more varied and somewhat more sophisticated. For example, second language learners know a language requires certain frills, such as grammatical morphemes. Thus, it is natural that when learning a second language, children should tend to try to use these frills even in the earliest stages of acquisition. The result is error types not typically made by first language learners. For example:

He nots eats
He do hungry

Such examples merely reflect the learner's effort to pay early tribute to certain language requirements, a principle learned through the first language learning experience, or, if you will, the metalinguistic awareness that comes with acquisition experience. The ability to pay such tribute is simply a function of their more advanced cognitive development. That they do so seems to be a function of having learned a language before.

However, it was difficult to part with the L1 research crutch that had been so helpful until now. And indeed, it was not yet necessary; for speculation about the differences between L1 and L2 suggested a manageable research plan to begin to approach L2 acquisition strategies.

After an exhaustive analysis of the semantic and grammatical complexity of the functors in his acquisition studies, Brown (1973b: 255) concluded that 'the order of acquisition is dependent upon relative complexity, grammatical and/or semantic.' In other words, the two major 'determinants of acquisition' for the L1 order were, according to Brown, semantic and grammatical (or 'linguistic') complexity. He defined semantic complexity as the number of major meanings of roughly equal weight expressed by a functor. The greater the number of major meanings, the more semantically complex that functor should be. He defined linguistic complexity in terms of 'derivational complexity': the more transformations required in the derivation of a functor (according to the Jacobs and Rosenbaum (1968) analysis) the more linguistically complex that functor should be.

It seems intuitive that children who are acquiring their first language have to deal with both semantic and syntactic information. However, six, seven, and eight-year-old children learning a second language need not struggle with semantic concepts they have already acquired, such as concepts of immediate past, possession, or progressive action. Thus, one would not expect the semantic complexity of functors already acquired in L1 to be a major determinant of the order of those functors in L2 acquisition. If this is correct, the functor acquisition sequences for L1 and L2 should differ significantly due at least to the absence of the semantic complexity factor in L2. The importance of such a finding would be that conceptual development, at least for those concepts expressed by the functors, could be safely discarded as a major explanatory device for L2 acquisition sequences.

This task involves two steps: (1) a comparison of the L2 and L1 functor sequences, and (2) an examination of the predictions made by Brown's semantic and linguistic complexity factors from the viewpoint of their explanatory power for the L2 sequence obtained.

Comparison of L2 and L1 functor sequences. Fortunately, in a previous study on L2 acquisition order (Dulay and Burt 1974b) 9 of Brown's 14 functors had been included. Thus, we only needed to compare the sequence we had already obtained for L2 with that of Brown, making the appropriate adjustments to include only the 9 functors found in both L1 and L2 studies. Table 1 lists the L1 rank orders obtained by Brown (1973b) and by the de Villiers' cross-sectional study (1973) along with the L2 rank orders we obtained using three different methods of analysis (these methods are described in detail in Dulay and Burt 1974b).

TABLE 1. L1 and L2 orders for 9 functors.

	L1 Rank Order			L2 Rank Order		
	Brown	de Villiers Method I	de Villiers Method II	Group score	Group means	SAI
-ing	1	1.5	2	3	2.5	2.5
Plural	2	1.5	1	4	4	5
Past-irreg	3	3	3	7	7.5	7.5
Possessive	4	5	6	8	7.5	6.5
Article	5	4	5	1	1	2.5
Past-reg	6	7.5	4	6	6	8.5
3rd Person	7	7.5	8	9	9	8.5
Copula	8	6	7	2	2.5	1
Auxiliary	9	9	9	5	5	4

It is obvious from Table 1 that the three L1 rank orders are very similar, as are the L2 orders, but that the former differ significantly from the latter. This difference is clearly illustrated in Figure 1, and the supporting Spearman rank order correlations appear in Table 2. (As the L1 orders are approximately the same, as shown by the Spearman coefficients in Table 2, those obtained by the de Villiers are excluded from the L2-L1 correlations.)

TABLE 2.   Spearman rank order correlation coefficients.

	L1			L2		
	Brown	de Villiers Method I	de Villiers Method II	Group score	Group means	SAI
Brown		.84	.78	.43	.42	.39
de Villiers Method I			.87			
Group score					.98	.89
Group means						.91

FIGURE 1.   Comparison of L1 and L2 acquisition sequences.

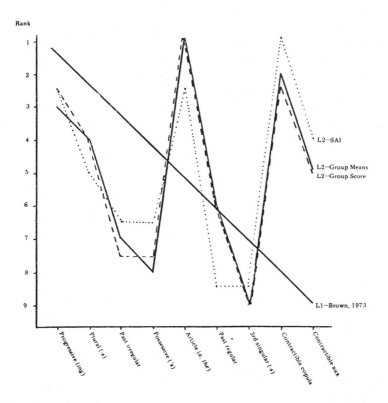

As Table 1 indicates, Past-irregular, Article, Copula, and Auxiliary show the greatest amount of difference: approximately four
ranks between L2 and L1. Except for Past-irregular, which is acquired later in L2, these functors are acquired earlier in L2 than in
L1. The other functor ranks also differ consistently, but the difference
is not as great, i. e. there is a difference of approximately 1-2 ranks
between L2 and L1 for -ing, Plural, Possessive, Past-regular, and
3rd Person. Notice also that this group of functors is acquired later
in L2 than in L1.

The explanatory power of Brown's semantic and linguistic complexity factors for L2. In an effort to account for the L1 acquisition
sequence, Brown (1973b) carried out a detailed analysis of the
semantics and the transformational derivation of each functor in the
sequence. This analysis enabled Brown to order the functors according to their semantic complexity (number of 'major meanings' of
roughly equal weight) and according to linguistic complexity (number
of transformations in the derivation of a given functor based on Jacobs
and Rosenbaum 1968). Our task was simply to see to what extent the
L2 sequence could be predicted by Brown's semantic and linguistic
complexity ordering.

The ordering predictions based on semantic complexity appear in
the left-hand column of Table 3. The column on the right indicates
whether or not each prediction is borne out by the L2 acquisition sequence. That is, say -ing is less semantically complex than Auxiliary
(-ing < Auxiliary). If -ing was acquired before Auxiliary in the L2
sequence, then the semantic ordering prediction (-ing < Auxiliary) is
borne out by the L2 sequence. However, if -ing was not acquired before Auxiliary, then the semantic prediction is not borne out by the
L2 sequence. Table 3 summarizes the extent to which Brown's
semantic complexity ordering could account for the L2 sequence.

Table 3 shows that almost half (4 out of 9) of the semantic predictions were not borne out in the L2 sequence. The L1 sequence, on
the other hand, agreed with all 9 semantic predictions.

Since it appears that semantic complexity is not a major determinant of our L2 order, as it seems to be for L1, it might be reasonable to expect that linguistic (derivational) complexity, the second
major determinant of acquisition proposed by Brown, should predict
much of the L2 order. In this framework, one would expect that linguistic complexity orderings should predict the L2 sequence precisely
where semantic predictions had failed. Brown's linguistic complexity
predictions appear in the left-hand column of Table 4. The column on
the right indicates whether or not each prediction is borne out by the
L2 sequence. As we can see from Table 4, the linguistic complexity
predictions fared little better than those on semantic complexity.

TABLE 3. Semantic complexity in the L2 sequence.

Semantic complexity ordering predictions (< = 'is less complex than')			Borne out (+)/Not borne out (-) in L2 sequence
-ing	<	auxiliary	+
plural	<	3rd person	+
		copula	-
		auxiliary	+
past irreg	<	3rd person	+
		copula	-
		auxiliary	-
3rd person	<	auxiliary	-
copula	<	auxiliary	+
		Totals:	+ = 5
			- = 4
			9

Again, nearly half of the linguistic predictions were not borne out by the L2 sequence. Nevertheless, one might still hope that the linguistic predictions that were borne out by the L2 order would be precisely those involving Copula, Auxiliary, Article, and Past Irregular, as their places in the L2 sequence were not predicted by semantic complexity, and at the same time, their ranks were the most different in L2 and L1.

Unfortunately, this is not the case. Both the semantic and linguistic complexity predictions are almost exactly the same for the four functors whose rank orders were the most different in the L1 and L2 sequences. Table 5 displays this predicament. Table 5 includes only those predictions where L2 and L1 differ and excludes the three predictions involving Possessive since Jacobs and Rosenbaum (1968) did not provide a derivation for the Possessive. It first lists those predictions which are the same in both the semantic and linguistic complexity orderings. The few remaining predictions are unique to linguistic complexity. As we see from the table, all of the semantic predictions are also made by linguistic complexity. These predictions are all borne out by the L1 sequence, but not by the L2 sequence. Of the three predictions made by linguistic complexity alone, two are not borne out by the L2 sequence.

TABLE 4. Linguistic complexity in the L2 sequence.

Linguistic complexity ordering predictions (< = 'is less complex than')			Borne out (+)/Not borne out (–) in L2 sequence
-ing	<	past reg	+
		plural	+
		3rd person	+
		copula	–
		auxiliary	+
Article	<	past reg	+
		plural	+
		3rd person	+
		copula	+
		auxiliary	+
Past irreg	<	past reg	–
		plural	–
		3rd person	+
		copula	–
		auxiliary	–
Past reg	<	3rd person	–
		copula	–
		auxiliary	–
Plural	<	3rd person	+
		copula	–
		auxiliary	+
3rd person	<	auxiliary	–
copula	<	auxiliary	+
		Totals:	+ = 13
			– = 10
			23

TABLE 5.   Differences in L1 and L2 predicted by Brown's
semantic and derivational complexity.

Predictions that are the same in both the semantic and linguistic complexity orderings:			Borne out (+)/Not borne out (−) by:	
			L1	L2
Plural	<	Copula	+	−
Past-irreg	<	Copula	+	−
		Auxiliary	+	−
3rd person	<	Auxiliary	+	−
Predictions made by semantic complexity alone:			Ø	
Predictions made by derivational complexity alone:				
Article	<	Plural	−	+
Past-irreg	<	Past-reg	+	−
Past-reg	<	3rd person	+	−

The linguistic complexity analysis shows with disconcerting clarity
that what we might have inferred from the semantic complexity analysis is invalid, at least in this framework. That is, since both linguistic and semantic complexity yield the same predictions with regard to the differences between the L2 and L1 sequences, we cannot
say that this analysis supports the 'absence of semantic complexity'
hypotheses mentioned earlier. Nor can either 'determinant of acquisition' proposed by Brown explain the L2 sequence obtained. It appears then, that we are still at the beginning of the search for factors
that explain the L2 acquisition sequence.

A new approach. This first unsuccessful attempt to deal with
factors that might explain, at least in part, the observed progression
in child L2 syntax acquisition inspired a rethinking of the notion 'complexity', as well as a search for new research procedures.

'Complexity' and 'strategy'. The notion of complexity in its strict-
est sense refers to characteristics of what is to be learned. That is,

if X and Y are items to be learned, X is more complex than Y if it involves more learning matter than Y. For example, perfect tenses require more morphemes than the simple tenses, and thus are considered more complex. Or, in reading, blends and diphthongs are considered more complex than simple vowels and consonants. Since more complex items involve more increments of learning matter, it is generally assumed that they will be learned later. In other words, the more there is to learn, the longer it must take. Not surprisingly, an inspection of oral language or reading curricula reveals that the more complex items are presented later than the 'simpler' ones. Apparently, then, complexity has become synonymous with lateness of learning. Specifically, if the complexity of X and Y is known, so is their learning sequence. Empirical verification of the learning sequence is, in this view, superfluous.

Research on child language acquisition, on the other hand, has given primary importance to the empirical determination of learning sequences and consequently, careful studies of learning sequence were undertaken. As acquisition orders began to emerge from these investigations, so did attempts to explain them. It is in these explanations that the reliance on complexity again appears. As we have seen, Brown used the notion of linguistic (and semantic) complexity to explain his functor acquisition order. Linguistic complexity was defined in Brown's study as the number of optional transformations in a derivation. To correct some of the difficulties of this metric (such as assuming equal increments of complexity of all transformations), Brown offered a more refined notion of linguistic complexity as a recommendation to future researchers, namely, 'cumulative derivational complexity':

> We do not . . . simply count the number of optional transformations in a derivation, since this procedure involves the generally unwarranted assumption that any one transformation, or some other feature, involves the same increment to complexity of knowledge as any other. In our 'cumulative' sense of complexity a construction $\underline{x} + \underline{y}$ may be regarded as more complex than either $\underline{x}$ or $\underline{y}$ because it involves everything in either of the constructions alone plus something more. (Brown 1973b:406-407)

Although this cumulative notion is certainly an improvement on simple derivational complexity, it still consists entirely of a description of what is to be learned to explain the learning sequence. As Brown (1973b:407) stated: 'If $\underline{x} + \underline{y}$ involves all the knowledge of $\underline{x}$ and $\underline{y}$, each taken alone, how could it fail to be the case that $\underline{x} + \underline{y}$ will be acquired later than its components?' This complete dependence on a description of the target language to explain acquisition order is made quite clear by the reasons Brown gives for any possible failure of his cumulative complexity notion to predict learning sequences:

> . . . the prediction can fail if the analysis of requisite knowledge, grammatical and semantic, is faulty, or if the evidence used to indicate constructional acquisition is insufficient. (Brown 1973b:407)

It is clear that Brown's notions of semantic and linguistic complexity refer explicitly to the analytical description of what is being learned, e.g. a linguist's description of the syntactic and semantic components of the target language. However, one cannot assume that what is more 'complex' (more transformations, features, etc.) in a linguistic description of a language system also prescribes the sequence in which a child acquires a language. It seems reasonable to ask whether a child organizes linguistic data in a different fashion. In other words, the criteria that might be perfectly adequate for a description of a language may not be the criteria the child uses to organize and learn that language. Bever (1970:349) makes a similar point:

> . . . we cannot use preconceived notions about the form of grammar underlying a child's utterances . . . because this would prejudge the sort of fact that we are trying to ascertain by collecting his utterances in the first place.

But this is not the only problem. The reliance of psycholinguists on linguistic descriptions partially explains their great interest in transformational derivations, as well as their impatience with the changes that linguists inevitably make in their descriptions. Chomsky's transformational grammar has been partially susceptible to such reactions from psycholinguists, as the 'ultimate' goal of transformational grammar does involve the description of mental structure. However, Chomsky and Halle (1968) have been very careful to state that before any claim can be made about human cognitive structure or learning strategies, a comprehensive description of language structure must be available. Therefore, they have undertaken the task of providing an empirically adequate description of language. They also emphasize that their choice of this 'first step' has no bearing on the psychological reality of their linguistic descriptions. Rather, it is a decision about which research program they believe might be most fruitful in the search for knowledge about human cognitive structure.

Chomsky and Halle (1968:331) note that:

We have been describing acquisition of language as if it were
an instantaneous process. Obviously, this is not true. A
more realistic model of language acquisition would consider
the order in which primary linguistic data are used by the
child and the effects of preliminary 'hypotheses' developed
in the earlier stages of learning on the interpretation of
new, often more complex, data. To us it appears that this
more realistic study is much too complex to be undertaken
in any meaningful way today . . .

A 'more realistic study' is precisely what we are venturing to
undertake. Although an adequate description of the structure of language is still in the process of being formulated, we feel that its
absence does not preclude a meaningful attempt to specify language
learning strategies. An adequate description of the developing syntactic structures children produce while learning a language should
be an equally fruitful route to the discovery of cognitive structure.
We must, however, caution the reader not to forget the distinction
between a 'first step' and our ultimate goal, i.e. between a description of the speech children produce (product level) and the learning
strategies underlying that speech (process level). In sum, while
Chomsky and Halle focus on a description of the target language(s)
to arrive at universal cognitive structure, we focus on a description
of the developing syntactic structures children produce while learning
a language, to make similar types of inferences.
    The notion of learning strategy as an explanation of acquisition
cannot rely on a description of what is to be learned. Rather, it
assumes that the cognitive mechanisms a child innately possesses
make an independent contribution to the learning process. These
mechanisms have certain definable characteristics that cause the
child to use a limited set of hypotheses to deal with the knowledge he
is acquiring. No matter how accurately that knowledge may be
described or analyzed into its elements by language scholars, the
child will organize and learn it in the manner and order in which his
cognitive apparatus specifies. The specification of these principles
of mental organization is our long-range goal.
    The 'learning strategy' approach is not new. It has been used,
for example, by Bever and Slobin in their first language acquisition
research. Bever (1970:280-281) has discussed 'perceptual strategies'
in the concept of their role in determining the universal structure of
language:

. . . linguistic structure is itself partially determined by the
learning and behavioral processes that are involved in acquiring and implementing that structure. . . . Thus, some formally
possible linguistic structures will never appear in any language
because no child can use them. In this way the child's system
for talking and listening partially determines the form of linguistic structure . . .

For example, such findings as children's interpretations of reversible passives as active sentences yield Strategy D: Any Noun-
Verb-Noun (NVN) sequence within a potential unit in the surface
structure corresponds to 'actor-action-object' (Bever 1970:298).
Bever uses this information together with results of sentence processing experiments on adults to account for the pervasive NVN word
order of English syntax. This strategy, however, cannot account for
the structure of languages with other word orders, such as Japanese
which is an SOV language. In fact, L1 acquisition studies have shown
that children in the very earliest stages of learning use the word order
of the language they are learning (Kernan 1969 and Blount 1969), whatever it may be. This indicates that Strategy D is only a description of
the 'product' of the interaction between a child's perceptual mechanisms and primary linguistic data, not a specification of a universal
cognitive strategy. (Bever's general thesis, however, is one of the
most provocative advanced recently.)
  Slobin (1971) also proposes strategies referred to as 'operating
principles' which he suggests children use to process adult speech.
For example:

Operating Principle A: Pay attention to the ends of words
   (Slobin 1971:335)
Operating Principle C: Pay attention to the order of words
   and morphemes (Slobin 1971:348)
Operating Principle D: Avoid interruptions or rearrangements
   of linguistic units.

He arrives at these operating principles by looking at how 'communicative intent' is expressed by children learning different first languages, and drawing generalizations about children's developing syntax from these data. Slobin calls these generalizations 'universals'
from which he then infers 'operating principles'. For example, he
finds that 'post-verbal and post-nominal markers are acquired
earlier than prenominal markers' (Universal A, Slobin 1971:334),
hence, he infers Operating Principle A. In our framework Slobin's
'universals' are generalizations about the product level, and his

'operating principles' are statements that presumably refer to the process level.

Two rather serious drawbacks become apparent in Slobin's approach. First, an accurate specification of 'communicative intent' does not exist, which Slobin recognizes when he states that 'what is needed is a taxonomy and coding scheme for pre-linguistic intention' (Slobin 1971:324). Second, his operating principles and universals are presented as a list, in which the relation of the principles to each other, if there is one, is left unspecified. There is no attempt to provide criteria predicting when certain principles apply and when they do not. This is especially significant when two apparently conflicting principles are applicable in the production of a certain structure. For example, in English L1 acquisition, children regularly produce utterances such as No Daddy go, or Wear mitten no. In these constructions they seem to be using Operating Principle D as they do not interrupt the NVN sequence. However, the above constructions violate Operating Principle C as they have obviously not paid attention to the proper placement of the negative morpheme.

A similar problem emerges when we encounter cases that appear to disconfirm a certain operating principle. For example, Operating Principle A seems to be violated in English L1 acquisition, where functors attached to the ends of words are regularly omitted by L1 learners (e.g. past -ed, 3rd person singular -s, etc.) even after several prepositions have been acquired. However, such disconfirming cases need not necessarily constitute disconfirmation of the existence of a particular operating principle. Rather, if operating principles were placed in their proper perspective, such cases would provide the evidence necessary to specify under what conditions certain 'principles' apply or do not apply.

Incidentally, Operating Principle A cannot speak to the acquisition of prefixing languages such as Navajo. Thus, paying attention to the ends of words would not help Navajo children acquire their functors. Yet there is no evidence we know of that Navajo children acquire their morphological structure later than children acquiring suffixing languages, such as Turkish.

From the foregoing discussion, it has become obvious that a description of universal second language learning strategies is indeed a long-range goal. Nevertheless, in pursuit of this goal, two observations may be helpful.

(i) The description of acquisition sequences, including those in our own research studies, has consisted of 'rank orders', i.e. given a certain numerical criterion (such as MLU or SAI, or the mean score of a given sample of subjects for a functor), functors are ranked according to the decreasing (or increasing) numerical value of the chosen criterion. This results in a linear sequence, say, from 1 to

11 (or 14). Such linear descriptions of acquisition order go hand in hand with the linear explanations that have been offered for such orders. In other words, the use of rank orders increases the tendency to think of syntax acquisition as an additive process. The converse may also hold, namely, if one thinks of acquisition as the addition of increments of linguistic material, one would probably set out to look for rank orders in children's emerging syntax.

(ii) The notion 'acquisition strategy' (operating principle) refers to cognitive operations that are presumably universal. If this is their status, then strategies must be able to account for an enormous body of diverse facts about children's developing syntax. For example, a strategy must be able to account for the acquisition of both suffixing and prefixing languages, or of languages with different basic word order such as NVN (SVO) or NNV (SOV). Furthermore, strategies must not contradict each other in terms of what children are observed to do within a given language. As just discussed, most of the recently suggested strategies seem to fall short of universality, in the sense that there is much acquisition data they cannot explain, or that contradicts their predictions. It seems that the formulation of strategies has been too dependent on the description of the observed facts about children's developing syntax. While the description of the product (e.g. acquisition sequences or errors) is useful for the discovery of a learning strategy, it is not sufficient, and may even be misleading.

The following is a response to these two observations.

An alternative to rank orders: Acquisition hierarchies. Rank orders imply additive explanations of the learning process (such as derivational complexity). Our methodological alternative to this approach is to look for 'groups' of functors that are acquired together and that are ordered. If such groups of functors can be found, a search for the underlying characteristics that define each group and set it apart from others would become possible. Professor Marcus Lieberman of Harvard University introduced us to a recent development in measurement that does just that. The method is applicable to studies on acquisition orders, and also solves some of the problems inherent in cross-sectional design for developmental studies. The use of large samples has not been too popular in language acquisition research. However, with the new and increasing evidence of variability among individual children studied, it may be helpful to look at larger samples. It would permit us to look at both common trends, or if you will, universal orders of development, as well as variability in an efficient manner.

The method is formally called the 'Ordering-Theoretic-Method' by its authors (Bart and Krus 1973); but, for short, it is also known as the 'tree method' (following its origin in mathematical tree theory).

Other methods of measurement, such as Guttman scaling, 'invariably assume that the trait measured is linearly ordered and can be measured with a single additive model' (Bart and Krus 1973:201). The tree method, on the other hand, assumes that there is a logical relationship among items; and it is designed to determine those relationships.

The relationship worked out in the version of the method presented here is that of 'X is a prerequisite to Y'. For our purposes, it is stated as: 'the acquisition of functor X precedes the acquisition of functor Y'.

In order for the method to be used to score interrelated items, binary coding is necessary; that is, the items must be scorable as correct or incorrect with values of 1 and 0, respectively. Accordingly, functors were treated as items for which a child received a 1 if the functor had been acquired and a 0 if it had not been acquired. A functor is acquired if it is used 90% correctly given at least three obligatory occasions per child for a given functor. (See Dulay and Burt 1974b:45-46.) Thus if a child scored 90 or higher on a given functor he received a 1 for that functor, but if he scored 89 or less he received a 0 for that functor.

The requirement for positing a relationship between a set of items, say, for positing the acquisition of Case before Copula is as follows: The acquisition of Case precedes the acquisition of Copula if and only if the disconfirming response pattern--Case = 0 (not acquired); Copula = 1 (acquired)--does not occur. It is the number of such 'disconfirmatory response patterns' that comprises the test of the relationship. If there were more than a tolerable number of disconfirmatory response patterns (6% of the total), the relationship would not hold. A detailed description of the data analysis appears in Bart and Krus (1973) and Dulay and Burt (1974b).

We used the tree method on three separate samples totalling 536 children: 55 Chinese-speaking children from New York's Chinatown, 60 Spanish-speaking children from Brentwood, New York, and 421 children from 10 states in the United States (Arizona, California, Colorado, Florida, Illinois, Massachusetts, New York, Oregon, Texas, and Washington). The data was collected using an expanded version of the Bilingual Syntax Measure (Burt, Dulay, and Hernández 1975), which is primarily a testing instrument, but because it systematically elicits 'natural' speech from children containing a range of syntactic structures, it can also be used for the efficient gathering of speech data for basic research of this type. The findings are illustrated in Figure 2.

The labels for the grammatical items in Figure 2 are very precisely defined grammatical structures (see Dulay and Burt 1974b and Burt, Dulay, and Hernández 1975 for a specification of these items).

FIGURE 2.

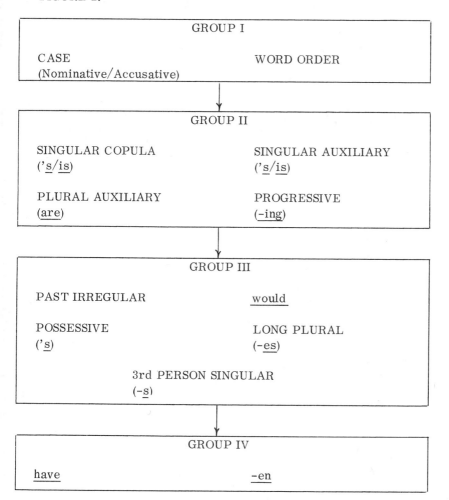

For example, Case here includes only nominative and accusative pronoun forms in simple sentences with simple subjects. It does not include sentences like She and I are leaving. The Possessive is mostly the elliptical possessive such as the dog's, rather than the dog's food.

The chart shows that the items in Group I are acquired before all the items in the Groups below. Items in Group II are acquired after those in Group I, but before those in Groups III and IV, etc. The reverse is also true. Namely, the acquisition of items in Group IV implies the acquisition of the items in Groups I-III.

These ordering relationships obtained for all three of our samples, including Chinese and Spanish-speaking children, for a total of 536 children across the United States, in the process of learning English as a second language.

If there are universal characteristics of the creative construction process in child second language acquisition, these findings seem to reflect them. Of course, it is possible, within this framework, to expect that second language acquisition hierarchies may vary depending on the type of target language exposure available to the second language learner. All of the subjects in our sample were exposed to the natural English speech of their peers. There are other environments where children are exposed only to a list of vocabulary words and a predetermined sequence of syntactic structures via classroom drills and dialogues. The resulting acquisition hierarchy might be quite different from that resulting from the exposure to much of the target language system, as in exposure to natural speech. Likewise, exposure to natural speech of adults only might also result in a hierarchy different from the one we obtained. Very little is known about the effects of such different types of language learning environments on the shape of the child's speech product.

The tree method also reveals variability. For example, comparing the Spanish and Chinese trees (New York samples) revealed the differences illustrated in Figure 3. For the Spanish-speaking children, Article preceded all the other items in Group III. However, for the Chinese-speaking children, Article did not precede Possessive. Twelve percent of the Chinese children disconfirmed that relationship, while 0% of the Spanish children did. Thus, Article is not included in the 'universal' order shown. For the Chinese children, an order obtained for Progressive and Plural, but it did not obtain for the Spanish-speaking children. Thus the Progressive-Plural relationship is not part of the 'universal' hierarchy either.

Implications for future research. The ultimate value of the tree analysis lies in its potential to uncover the sorts of empirical facts needed before one can begin to specify with any confidence the nature of language acquisition strategies. Of course, empirical facts of any sort are of little interest if not placed within a theoretical framework. The above discussion of complexity and strategy thus focused on two distinct approaches to the nature of language learning. In the first approach, one accepts the notion of complexity as the primary explanation of language learning and thus relies on variables that are linear (or additive) to explain acquisition phenomena; that is, variables that can be broken down into units, the number of which determines learning sequence. The more units there are in a particular item to be learned, the later that item will appear in the learning

FIGURE 3.

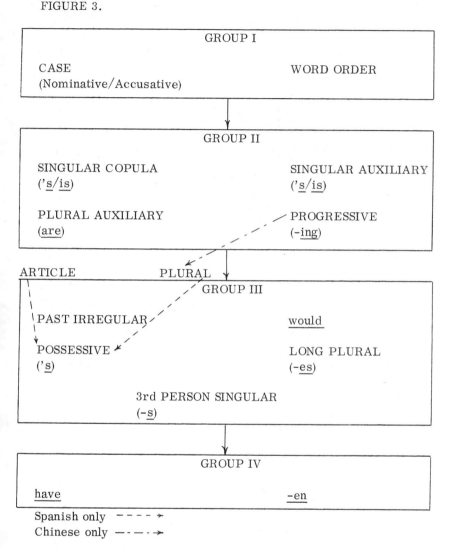

Spanish only - - - - ➤
Chinese only —· — ·· ➤

sequence. This approach relies totally on descriptions of what is to be learned, and assumes that learning strategies correspond perfectly to those descriptions, i.e. descriptions of what adult native speakers know about their language.

The second approach does not assume this perfect correspondence between learning process and learning matter and thus it must rely on variables that have to do with criteria for the cognitive organization of linguistic data (language acquisition strategies). There is no reason to assume that the nature of these criteria is additive, nor that the description of the target language (learning matter) is the most productive source of explanations of the progression of structures language learners produce. One might instead begin to explain acquisition orders by searching for critical characteristics of those parts of syntax that children produce in a predictable order. For example, a characteristic such as 'X's are exceptions to a general rule (syntactic, phonological, or semantic)', as in the four structures studied by C. Chomsky (1969), might be among those that define a late group of structures. A group that is acquired earlier might be defined by characteristics that are not directly related to those that define a late group, such as 'Y's express a basic semantic relation'. Notice that such characteristics do not rely on 'preconceived notions about the form of grammar underlying a child's utterances' (Bever 1970:349), nor are they in any way increments or units of an overriding variable. Rather, they are characteristics that emerge from the particular aggregation of structure that children produce at a particular point in the acquisition process. In sum, critical characteristics are those features (or attributes) of syntactic structures that distinguish each group of structures in an acquisition hierarchy from any other group in the hierarchy. It seems that such characteristics may provide a rich empirical source from which language acquisition strategies might be inferred.

If this line of reasoning is correct, and if its potential is to be realized, then specific kinds of empirical data which are not yet available, become necessary.

First, acquisition hierarchies of English syntactic structures that are of a higher level than functors must be obtained. The presence of such structures within an acquisition hierarchy should make the relationship among items in a group more apparent than it is now.

Second, effects of native language phonology and semantics on second language acquisition must be clarified along with the relationship of these aspects of the acquisition of syntax in a second language.

Third, information on the acquisition hierarchies in second languages other than English would offer important insights concerning the accuracy of critical characteristics that are based only on English syntax acquisition, and would add new dimensions that English alone could not offer. Characteristics that define corresponding groups in the acquisition hierarchies of two or more languages should be related in some significant way that would strongly indicate the shape of universal language learning strategies.

Fourth, within a given language second language acquisition hierarchies may vary depending on the type of exposure available to the second language learner. For example, if the child is exposed only to a list of vocabulary words and a predetermined sequence of syntactic structures via classroom drills and dialogues, the resulting acquisition hierarchy might be quite different from that resulting from the exposure to much of the target language system, as in exposure to natural speech. Likewise, exposure to natural speech of adults only might also result in a hierarchy different from that resulting from exposure to peer speech in the target language. Thus data collected in immersion programs in Canada, where only the teacher speaks the target language fluently, might reveal a different acquisition hierarchy than data collected in United States bilingual programs where non-English speaking children interact with English speaking peers (as well as an English speaking teacher). Very little is known about the effects of such radically different types of language learning environments on the shape of child's speech product.

Studies such as these, as well as all of our own work, are predicated on the belief that we cannot borrow learning theories that have been developed for other fields (such as the training of animals or the treatment of non-normal human beings) without first verifying their applicability to second language learning. Rather, the rigorous and systematic observations of the speech and environments of children (and adults) learning a second or foreign language should be the basis for the adoption and refinement of general learning theories, and perhaps for the development of a particular theory for second language acquisition. Further, it seems that the description of languages, which is the domain of theoretical linguistics, must be put into proper perspective. Linguistic description tells us 'what' the student should ultimately learn and is therefore a valuable research tool. However, a linguistic description does not tell us 'how' a language is learned.

From the second language acquisition research studies that have been conducted to date, a rough framework seems to be emerging. There is general consensus that the second language learner (the child in particular) gradually reconstructs the target language system using certain cognitive strategies that remain as yet unspecified. The crucial assumption in this view is that the learner is active in the learning process, not a passive receptacle of knowledge. Precisely how the learner acts upon language data is the question this framework addresses.

While the creative construction process is not directly observable, its characteristics can be inferred from adequate descriptions of the learner's developing language (interlanguage), accompanied by an adequate description of the language input the learner receives. Unique characteristics of certain types of language input may well affect the shape of the learner's interlanguage. The relationship in Figure 4 illustrates the framework within which specific data on either environment or speech product take on significance.

FIGURE 4.

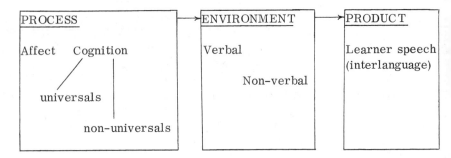

Data on learner speech product includes: acquisition hierarchies or sequences (Milon 1974, Hatch 1974, Hakuta 1974, Dulay and Burt 1973, 1974b, this article, and one in press); error types (Selinker 1972, Richards 1972 and 1972, Corder 1967 and 1971, Dulay and Burt 1972 and 1974a); characteristics of developing structures (Hatch 1974, Cancino et al. 1974, Ravem 1968 and 1970, Milon 1974); frequency of structure types actually produced, with or without errors (Schachter 1974).

Data on language input includes: source of input, e.g. native or nonnative speaking peers, teachers, parents, siblings, etc.; types of input, e.g. natural speech, pattern drills, etc.; frequency of structures in input language; length of exposure; dialect.

The inferences about the creative construction process that can be made from such data might refer either to universal strategies of the L2 acquisition process, or to variations in learning style, where a 'learning style' (Hatch 1974) might well be a particular selection of processing strategies used by a language learner.

In sum, rigorous descriptions of the many aspects of the developing speech of language learners, together with equally rigorous descriptions of the nature of the language the learner hears, should reveal some of the secrets of the creative construction process in second language learning.

These kinds of findings, which provide the type of empirical support necessary to suggest with confidence the major role of creativity in child second language acquisition, may be of only passing interest to many of you who are generative linguists or first language acquisitionists. The creative aspects of language have comprised the basic premises of the work undertaken in both these fields for the last two decades. This, however, has not been the case for second language acquisition research, a field that has the unique responsibility of responding to the vast number of school programs that are in the business of teaching English as a second language to millions of children. Most of the teaching methods and materials in use today are still based on the diametrically opposite tenets of habit formation. Therefore, the importance of a strong empirical statement in support of a creative construction process in child second language acquisition cannot be overemphasized, nor can the important task of making the findings clear and available to the educational establishment be neglected. [1]

NOTES

Permission to reproduce figures and tables in this paper is acknowledged as follows: Tables 1 through 5, and Figure 1: From Language Learning, Vol. 24, No. 2, December, 1974.

1. See Dulay and Burt (in press) for a discussion of the instructional implications of these findings.

REFERENCES

Bart, W. M. and D. J. Krus. 1973. An ordering-theoretic method to determine hierarchies among items. Educational and Psychological Measurement 33.291-300.

Bever, T. 1970. The cognitive basis for linguistic structures. In: Cognition and the development of language. Edited by J. R. Hayes. New York, John Wiley and Sons, Inc. 279-352.

Brown, R. 1973a. Development of the first language in the human species. American Psychologist. February. 97-102.

_____. 1973b. A first language. Cambridge, Mass., Harvard University Press.

Burt, M. K., H. C. Dulay, and E. Hernández. 1975. Bilingual syntax measure. New York, Harcourt Brace Jovanovich, Inc.

Cancino, H., E. Rosansky, and J. Schumann. 1974. Testing hypotheses about second language acquisition: The copula and negative in three subjects. Working Papers on Bilingualism, No. 3, 80-96. Toronto, Ontario Institute for Studies in Education.

Chomsky, C. 1969. The acquisition of syntax in children age 5 to 10. Cambridge, Mass., MIT Press.

Chomsky, N. 1968. Language and mind. New York, Harcourt Brace Jovanovich, Inc.

_____ and M. Halle. 1968. The sound pattern of English. New York, Harper and Row.

Corder, S. P. 1967. The significance of learner's errors. International Review of Applied Linguistics 5.161-69.

_____. 1971. Idiosyncratic dialects and error analysis. International Review of Applied Linguistics 9.

de Villiers, J. and P. de Villiers. 1973. A cross-sectional study of the acquisition of grammatical morphemes in child speech. Journal of Psycholinguistic Research 2.

Dato, D. P. 1970. American children's acquisition of Spanish syntax in the Madrid environment: Preliminary edition. United States, H. E. W., Office of Education, Institute of International Studies, Final Report, Project No. 3036, Contract No. O. E. C. 2-7-002637.

_____. 1971. The development of the Spanish verb phrase in children's second language learning. In: The psychology of second language learning. Edited by Pimsleur and Quinn. Cambridge, England, Cambridge University Press.

Dulay, H. C. and M. K. Burt. 1973. Should we teach children syntax? Language Learning 23.245-258. Reprinted in: Handbook for ESL teachers. Edited by R. L. Light and M. Gutierrez. New York, New York State Department of Education.

_____. 1974a. Errors and strategies in child second language acquisition. TESOL Quarterly 8.2.

_____. 1974b. Natural sequences in child second language acquisition. Language Learning 24.37-53. Reprinted in: Working Papers on Bilingualism. Toronto, Ontario Institute for Studies in Education.

_____. 1974c. You can't learn without goofing: An analysis of children's second language errors. In: Error analysis: Perspectives on second language acquisition. London, Longman. 95-123.

_____. In press. Creative construction in language acquisition and education. New York: Harcourt Brace Jovanovich.

Hakuta, K. 1974. A preliminary report on the development of grammatical morphemes in a Japanese girl learning English as a second language. Working Papers on Bilingualism 3.1-17. Toronto, Ontario Institute for Studies in Education.

Hatch, E. 1974. Second language learning-universals? Working Papers on Bilingualism 3.1-17. Toronto, Ontario Institute for Studies in Education.

Jacobs, R. A. and P. S. Rosenbaum. 1968. English transformational grammar. Waltham, Mass., Blaisdell Publishing Company.

Kernan, K. T. and B. G. Blount. 1966. The acquisition of Spanish grammar by Mexican children. Anthropological Linguistics. Vol. 8, No. 9.1-14.

Milon, J. 1974. The development of negation in English by a second language learner. TESOL Quarterly 8.

Ravem, R. 1968. Language acquisition in second language environment. International Review of Applied Linguistics 6.175-185.

Ravem, R. 1974. The development of wh-questions in first and second language learners. In: Error analysis: Perspectives on second language acquisition. Edited by J. Richards. London, Longman.

Richards, J. 1971. Error analysis and second language strategies. Language Sciences 17.

_____. 1972. Social factors, interlanguage, and language learning. Language Learning 22. 159-188.

Schachter, J. In press. An error in error analysis. Language Learning 24. 2.

Selinker, L. 1972. Interlanguage. International Review of Applied Linguistics 10. 209-231.

Slobin, D. 1971. Developmental psycholinguistics. In: A survey of linguistic science. Edited by William Orr Dingwall. College Park, Md., University of Maryland.

Swain, M. 1972. Bilingualism as a first language. Unpublished doctoral dissertation. University of California at Irvine.

ON PSYCHOLINGUISTIC UNIVERSALS
IN CHILDREN'S LEARNING OF SPANISH

DANIEL P. DATO

Georgetown University

In recent years intensive research on first- and second-language
development has significantly increased the understanding of language
learning. Linguists, psychologists, and others have studied the acquisition of a wide range of languages (Slobin 1973) to explore the
existence of properties that appear to be common to all languages.
In order to provide a broader perspective of the developmental process and of the nature of psycholinguistic universals, some investigators have compared normal native-language acquisition with the
development of language that is delayed or deviant in some way because of hearing impairment (Fry 1966), mental retardation (Lenneberg et al. 1964), extreme social and psychological deprivation
(Curtiss et al. 1974; Fromkin et al. 1974), and other types of deviance (Menyuk 1964, Morehead and Ingram 1973, Kessler 1973).
Other investigators have begun to provide descriptions of second-
language learning by children (Dato 1966, 1970; Ravem 1968; Ervin-
Tripp 1974; Dulay and Burt 1974) and adults (Krashen 1973) and
make comparisons with the process by which children acquire their
first language. We can all agree that this multi-faceted approach to
studying language acquisition has resulted in considerable insight
into the problems of the nature and function of language. It must be
pointed out, however, that most of these investigations have been
done on English either as a native language or as a second language.
    There is no question that the search for psycholinguistic uni-
versals requires comprehensive research on many languages in
order to provide dimensions that English alone cannot offer.
Meaningful comparisons of structures and functions of widely

divergent languages acquired in various learning situations are critically needed to indicate certain strategies in universal language learning. This paper attempts to contribute to the need for descriptions of the learning of languages other than English. While certain structures are similar in both Spanish and English, especially within the framework of Indo-European grammar, they are sufficiently different so that valuable insights about the nature of psycholinguistic universals can be obtained from studying how Spanish is learned. The purpose of this presentation is twofold: (1) to describe how children randomly learned certain aspects of Spanish syntax as a second language (L2), and (2) to compare these findings with data on the acquisition of the same structures by monolingual children who speak Spanish as a native language (L1).

1. The Madrid Study

Submitted as a final report to the U.S. Office of Education in 1970 under the title, 'American children's acquisition of Spanish syntax in the Madrid environment', the Madrid Study approached second-language learning research in a manner similar to that of many native-language investigations which were being conducted in the 1960's. That children become successful bilingual speakers in a relatively short time has been attested in the numerous diary reports and anecdotal accounts of persons traveling with their families to foreign countries. Thus, studying the process by which children with no previous exposure to a second language become fluent in that language in a relatively short time provides a telescopic view of language development that is highly accelerated. Let me draw an analogy with the technique of time-lapse photography employed by the botanist who may obtain an overall picture of plant development by taking pictures of his plant periodically, say, every few hours, from the time of germination of the seed to the time of its full bloom, and then viewing all the pictures in quick succession as though they comprised a motion picture sequence. The underlying strategy of the Madrid Study, therefore, was to periodically 'take pictures' or make recordings of the child's linguistic capabilities in Spanish, starting from the time when he could say nothing in Spanish to the time when he could communicate adequately in Spanish with native speakers of that language.

1.1 Data collection. A significant aspect of the Madrid Study is the method of data collection. In the past much data has been provided by 'extrapolation' techniques in which the investigator would select subjects from various age levels and then extrapolate from one age level to the next, thereby obtaining a view of language development on an 'apparent time' basis (Menyuk 1963, Gonzalez 1970). This approach to data collection contributes significantly to a general understanding of language acquisition which still has many gaps. However, even more critical is the need for developmental data representing the continuous, overall learning process from the time of no previous exposure to the language until the time when communicative competence is achieved. Furthermore, this type of information should be obtained from an adequate number of children. The Madrid Study attempted to obtain this kind of developmental data that would provide representative second-language learning behavior by a sufficient number of subjects.

1.2 Subjects. Following a one-year pilot study with Michael, the investigator's son, age 4, a group study was conducted the following year involving eight subjects: four 6-year-olds, three 8-year-olds, and one 2-year-old. In addition, the subject from the pilot study, then 5 years old, continued to provide data. In this presentation data from Michael, another boy and two girls will be used for comparison with data on the acquisition of Spanish as a native language. In selecting the subjects care was taken to include only those children with no previous knowledge of Spanish whose parents wanted their children exposed maximally to the new language and culture during their stay in Madrid. All subjects arrived in Spain with their families at approximately the same time.

1.3 Sampling techniques. Sampling techniques included recordings of the children in the following situations: (1) with a trained Spanish-speaking research assistant who elicited speech from children through the use of pictures, questions, spontaneous conversation, and story telling; (2) supervised play indoors with one or more Spanish children participating in appropriate games (Brown and Fraser 1963). Twenty to twenty-four recordings were made of each child over a ten-month period, averaging about one every two weeks for approximately 30 to 45 minutes each, providing a total of about ten hours' sampling for each child.

1.4 Grammatical analysis. The grammatical structures described in the Madrid Study included the noun phrase, the verb phrase, imperatives, interrogatives, and embeddings (Dato 1970, 1971). In this paper I deal with only certain aspects of the noun phrase and the verb phrase which I use to contrast children's second-language learning of Spanish with children's acquisition of Spanish as a native language. A study of the developing noun phrase described within the framework of transformational grammar (Chomsky 1965, Stevens 1966, Falk 1968) may serve as an example of the type of linguistic analysis that was used to account for the sequencing of various structures.

2. The noun phrase

2.1 Structure of the noun phrase in adult Spanish. I shall assume that the deep structure of every Spanish sentence includes a noun phrase (NP), even though it may not appear in the surface structure.

In this treatment of NP I use phrase structure rules to describe the various components of this constituent as they exist in adult Spanish and then indicate the order in which these components emerge in the data.

The model for the structure of NP in Spanish may be written:

$$NP \rightarrow (Det) \; N \; (S')$$

According to this rule NP may consist of a single noun (N), or a combination of N with either one or both of the elements determiner (Det) and embedded sentence (S'). Det, which could be an article (Art), a demonstrative (Dem), or a possessive (Poss), may be optionally combined with a limiting adjective (LAdj), here defined as an adjective which relates N to its environment in terms of ordered relations, amount, or quantity. The rule for Det is:

$$Det \longrightarrow \begin{Bmatrix} Art \\ Dem \\ Poss \end{Bmatrix} \; (LAdj)$$

S' could be a noun modifier including a descriptive adjective, prepositional phrase, clause, or even a complete sentence. NP may be preceded by a preposition or joined with other NP's with or without the use of conjunctions.

In this treatment of NP the following elements are considered:

N	noun
Art	article
Dem	demonstrative
Poss	possessive
Adj	descriptive adjective
LAdj	limiting adjective
Prep	preposition
PPh	prepositional phrase
Adv	adverb
Pro	pronominalization
S'	embedding

I shall describe each of these components in the order in which they were first observed in various forms and combinations, in the learning process by the most productive subject, Michael, and then compare the order of structures observed in his output with that of three other subjects. Only those features of nouns and determiners that are clearly observable in the syntactic structure of NP will be considered here.

2.2 Development of NP in Michael's Spanish

2.2.1 In the first two recordings of Michael's Spanish, NP appears mostly as an individual noun in utterances like:

chocolate	'chocolate'
castillo	'castle'

which may be written in terms of the formula:

NP $\longrightarrow$ N

2.2.2 Beginning complexity in NP structures is indicated by the insertion of Art, used in short phrases like un momento 'a moment', un casa, intended for una casa 'a house' and even in front of words he doesn't know in Spanish, such as un [ráy], intended for 'a ride'. The rule for NP is thus expanded as:

NP $\longrightarrow$ Art N

2.2.3 During the early phase in the child's learning, Spanish utterances were found which may be interpreted as either a NP consisting of a demonstrative (Dem) plus N, or as a pivot-type construction similar to those discussed in recent native-language studies (McNeill 1966, Ingram 1968).

esto avión (for: este avión)	'this airplane'
esa casa	'that house'
este allí	'this there'

If one assumes the child intended an utterance such as esto avión for Este avión es mío 'This airplane is mine', or for Quiero este avión 'I want this airplane', then esto may be interpreted as a demonstrative and the entire utterance as NP functioning either as subject or direct object.

If, on the other hand, one assumes that a copula (Cop) was intended, then the demonstrative esto could be interpreted as a pronominalized subject and consequently, utterances of this type could be considered pivot-like constructions. As a result of this interpretation of NP as a pronominalized demonstrative, the rule for generating this type of NP structure may be written as follows:

NP ⟶ Dem (N)

2.2.4 During this same period Michael produced the utterances:

dos soldados	'two soldiers'
las dos semanas	'the two weeks'

where the use of a limiting adjective (LAdj) before N is observed. Since the Art before LAdj appears to be voluntarily deletable, these structural features may be combined in the following rule:

NP ⟶ (Art) LAdj N

2.2.5 Also observed at this time is a construction involving conjoined NP's:

los ojos y las manos	'the eyes and the hands'

which may be described as:

NP ⟶ Art N y Art N

Thus, by the end of the fifth recording, Michael's competence to generate NP elements may be stated cumulatively with the rule:

$$NP \longrightarrow \begin{Bmatrix} Art \\ Dem \end{Bmatrix} (LAdj)\ N\ (\underline{y}\ NP)$$

2.2.6 Recording number 6 is notable for the occurrence of several different prepositions:

a mí	'to me'
de España	'from Spain'
en tu casa	'in your house'

The use of these prepositions may be interpreted as the creation of a prepositional phrase:

PPh ⟶ Prep NP

where:

Prep ⟶ de, a, en

2.2.7 The possessive determiner (Poss) is expressed in the phrase:

mi libro   'my book'

which may be formulated:

NP ⟶ Poss N

2.2.8 In the following example PPh is used as a modifier of another NP:

¿los sellos de mi libro?   'the stamps from my book?'

These structures may be combined into a single rule, as follows:

NP ⟶ NP PPh

2.2.9 In recordings 6, 7, and 8 these utterances are observed:

la otra pequeña   'the other small one'
tienes mucho   'you have a lot'
un grande   'a big one'

in which an optional deletion rule for N is being applied. The structure of these NP's may be stated:

NP ⟶ Art LAdj (N) Adj

2.2.10 In previous recordings the descriptive adjective came before the noun, as in muy grande bota for bota muy grande 'very large boot'. In recordings 8, 9, and 10, there are indications of the child's awareness of the concept of the adjective placement rule in which descriptive adjectives generally follow the nouns they modify:

la dibujo grande (for: 'the big drawing'
el dibujo grande)

The rule showing adjective placement may be stated:

NP ⟶ Art N Adj

Some cases of the adjective coming before N probably represent influence from the child's native English:

los grandes orejas (for: 'the big ears'
las orejas grandes)

2.2.11 The adjective in Michael's NP's may also be modified by an adverb. Although one example of this type of construction occurs earlier,

un muy grande bota (for: 'a very big boot'
una bota muy grande)

it isn't until recording 10 that the modified adjective <u>after</u> the noun is observed, as in:

puerta arriba muy grande   'very big door upstairs'

The use of an adverb such as <u>muy</u> to modify the adjective changes the rule to read:

NP ⟶ Art N Adv Adj

At this point, with the tenth sampling of Michael's Spanish, the cumulative structure of NP may be written as follows:

$$NP \longrightarrow \begin{Bmatrix} (Art) \\ (Dem) \\ (Poss) \end{Bmatrix} \; (LAdj) \; N \begin{Bmatrix} (Adv) \\ (PPh) \end{Bmatrix} \; (Adj)$$

Although the data does not contain any examples of NP with all of the components shown in this rule, it is assumed that the child has the competence to generate this type of structure. Later on, in fact, all these elements are included in a single NP structure.

2.2.12 In recording 11, there are utterances in which NP is modified by a relative clause:

la caballo que tienes   'the horse that you have'
(for: el caballo que tienes)

which may be formulated as:

NP ⟶ Art N S'

The question of relative clauses, indicated here as embedded sentences, is discussed in detail in the Madrid Study (Dato 1970). In this discussion on NP's, mention is simply made of their occurrence.

2. 2. 13 In the twelfth sampling one can observe the use of a special type of limiting adjective, <u>todo</u>, which precedes the entire NP:

todos los dibujos	'all the drawings'
todas las partes	'in all places'

This construction may be formulated:

NP ⟶ <u>todo</u> Det N

2. 2. 14 In recording 13 a pronominalized adjective followed by a PPh may be observed, as in:

un poco de éste   'a little of this'

This structure can be written:

NP ⟶ Art LAdj PPh

In this same sampling are found more embeddings, including some in the form of infinitives:

déjame scribir (for:	'Let me write. '
Déjame escribir)	
no se puedo pasar (for:	'You can't pass. '
No se puede pasar)	

Also at this time, NP shows a pronominalized LAdj indicating the deletion of a noun:

uno de esos   'one of those'

Observe that in this example the pronominalization involves the deletion of a count noun, whereas the utterance <u>un poco de esto</u> includes the pronominalization involving the deletion of a mass noun.

2. 2. 15 In this same sampling one can find noun modifiers both preceding and following the noun simultaneously, as in:

un grande castillo muy alto   'a very high big castle'
(for: un castillo grande y muy
alto)

which may be written:

NP ⟶ Det LAdj N Adv Adj

In recordings 14, 15, and 16, there are more examples of embedded sentences:

ves la dibujo que pinto   'You see the drawing I'm making.'
(for: Ves el dibujo que
pinto)
en un sitio donde se toma   'in a place where you drink water'
agua

2.2.16 In this same recording there are examples of infinitives followed by nouns, as in the utterances:

¿Quieres ver vaqueros?   'Do you want to see cowboys?'
Quiero ver indios.   'I want to see Indians.'

which may be written as follows:

NP ⟶ S'

Further development takes place also in the production of NP's containing embedded sentences. A final structure observed in a later recording is especially complex:

uno muy grande que tenía   'a very big one that had meat'
carne

The combined rule representing all the NP structures discussed thus far is:

$$NP \longrightarrow (Det)\ (LAdj)\ N \begin{Bmatrix} (Adv) \\ (PPh) \\ (S') \end{Bmatrix} (Adj)\ (\underline{y}\ NP)$$

I shall now summarize the various NP structures treated in this section for the purpose of comparing the order of learning of Michael's output with that of the other subjects. Chronological order may be shown by numbering each of Michael's NP structures to correspond with the paragraphs in our text which discuss these structures. In order to make a meaningful comparison of the development of NP constituents among all subjects, I have found it useful to characterize the structure rules in terms of basic learning processes. In effect, this characterization represents a further degree of abstraction of the structure rules which are, in turn, abstract descriptions of actual utterances. In this way an overall perspective of the learning of NP components among all subjects may be obtained. While the actual number of the recording, indicated in parentheses after each example, provides a general picture of the development of NP for each subject, it is not as significant as the observed chronological order of structures as they emerge in the recorded samples.

TABLE 1.   First occurrences of various NP structures in all children

2.2.1 Single word	2.2.2 Creation of NP; Det N
NP ⟶ N	NP ⟶ Art N
M: castillo (1)	M: un casa (2)
O: caballo (1)	O: una caballo (1)
N: perros (1)	N: un niño (1)
S: puerta (1)	S: una torre (1)
2.2.3 Creation of NP; Det N	2.2.4 Creation of NP; LAdj N
NP ⟶ Dem (N)	NP ⟶ (Art) LAdj N
M: esto (2)	M: las dos semanas (5)
O: esta indio (1)	O: ¿más caballos? (1)
N: y esto (1)	N: pequeños zorras (1)
S: esta vez (2)	S: mucho poquito español (1)
2.2.5 Compounding; NP y NP	2.2.6 Use of preposition with NP
Det N y Det N	PPh ⟶ Prep Np
M: los ojos y las manos (5)	M: a mí (6)
O: dos muchachas y dos muchachos (11)	O: en casa (3)
N: un gato y un perro (1)	N: con los dos (1)
S: la Niña, la Pinta y la Santa María (2)	S: en la luna (1)
2.2.7 Creation of NP; Poss N	2.2.8 NP plus modifying PPh
NP ⟶ Poss N	NP ⟶ NP PPh
M: mi libro (6)	M: los sellos de mi libro (6)
O: mi mamá (2)	O: un beso a su mamá (5)
N: mi hermano (1)	N: una casa de coches (4)
S: mis zapatos (5)	S: una estrella de Russian (5)

TABLE 1. Continued

2.2.9 Use of two elements before N; optional deletion of N	2.2.10 Adjective postposition
NP ⟶ Art LAdj (N) Adj	NP ⟶ Art N Adj
M: la otra pequeña	M: la dibujo grande (9)
O: el otro (7)	O: un lápiz negro (6)
N: otro roto (6)	N: un pato feo (4)
S: un grande gato poquito (15)	S: un castillo moro (13)
2.2.11 Adverb modifying adjective	2.2.12 Embedding: Adjectival
NP ⟶ Art N Adv Adj	NP ⟶ Art N S'
M: puerta arriba muy grande (10)	M: la caballo que tienes (11)
O: un plato muy grande (17)	O: una gatitos que están en la cama (12)
	N: una cosa que es azul (9)
	S: el bajarillo que haces (18)
2.2.13 Use of todo	2.2.14 Use of partitive mass noun
NP ⟶ todo Art N	NP ⟶ (Art) LAdj PPh
M: todos los dibujos (12)	M: un poco de éste (12)
O: todo eso cosas (7)	O: un poquití así de arroz (4)
N: todo el personas (18)	N: mucho más de estos (6)
S: todo el libro (12)	S: uno de éste (5)
2.2.15 Modifiers both before and after N	2.2.16 Embedding: Infinitive plus direct object
NP ⟶ Art LAdj N Adv Adj	NP ⟶ S'
M: un grande castillo muy alto (14)	M: Quiero ver indios. (16)
	O: No quiero hablar. (8)
S: un grande gato poquito (15)	S: Quieres ver a pájaros. (1)

2.3 Discussion of the comparative development of NP

Since it is difficult to abstract from Table 1 any systematic pattern of learning, a comparison of the observed order of occurrence of NP structures in all subjects is presented in Table 2. Symbols used here are abbreviations of those appearing in Table 1. Thus, 1, 2, etc. represent the structure listed as 2.2.1, 2.2.2, etc. Unfortunately, because of wide variations among the children in the pace of learning, cross-column comparisons based on the actual recording number are

not very useful. However, Table 2 does provide a clearer indication
of the order of appearance of NP structures for each child, thus
facilitating more meaningful comparisons in the discussion below.

TABLE 2. Comparison of the observed order of occurrence of
noun phrases in four subjects

Recording	M	O	N	S
1	1	1, 2, 3, 4	1, 2, 3, 4, 5, 6, 7, 16	1, 2, 4, 6
2	2, 3	7		3, 5
3		6		
4		13	8, 10	
5	4, 5	8		7, 8, 14
6	6, 7, 8	9	9	
7		12, 14	14, 16	
8	9	16		
9	10		12	
10	11			
11	12	5		
12	13, 14	11		13
13				10
14	15			
15				9, 15
16	16	10	13	12

The processes involved in the development of NP may be characterized in terms of the number, combination, positioning, and complexity of its individual components. The following comments summarize my observations about the development of NP. (1) The

earliest NP's appear as single-word utterances, usually N or a pro-nominalized demonstrative. (2) Short NP's appear next, usually of two, three, or even four words; in these phrases N is combined with one of four different kinds of prenoun elements: Dem, Art, Poss, or Adj. There are a number of two- and three-word constructions re-sembling those found in first-language acquisition; whether or not these pivot-like structures constitute an identifiable stage in second-language learning requires a great deal more research. (3) As more components are added to NP, the number of combinatory possibilities increases. This development, however, is generally limited to N and any elements preceding N. (4) The concept of placing adjectives and other modifiers after N in Spanish is generally learned after the de-velopment of the Det element is established. (5) Compounding may occur after or concurrently with the post-positioning of N modifiers. The coordinate conjunction y 'and' is used almost exclusively. (6) The use of prepositions results in the creation of PPh which may be observed early in the data of some of the children. However, the modification of N or NP by a PPh appears in the data only after the concept of post-noun modification is well established. The first prepositions are en 'in', de 'of', and a 'to'. (7) Although the place-ment of modifiers after N is learned by all children, there is no evi-dence that any of the subjects can distinguish the contrastive uses of the small number of adjectives which, depending upon meaning, may either follow or precede N. (8) The development of post-position modification provides the most significant indicator of linguistic competence. There appears to be a definite progression of these modifiers: (a) single adjective, (b) adjective modified by an adverb, (c) prepositional phrase, (d) compounding of adjectives, (e) embedding of infinitives and relative clauses.

On the basis of grammatical analysis of NP, and other subsystems including the verb phrase, interrogatives, imperatives, and embed-dings, these findings supported the various hypotheses posited for this research.

The hypothesis which stated that there would be significant differ-ences in the incidence of base and transformed structures in the sam-ples of children's language behavior at different time intervals was substantiated. This meant that at different time intervals, that is, with each successive recording or series of recordings, there were significant differences in the incidence of base and transformed structures. This was supported by the occurrence of a number of short, simple utterances during the early recordings which became progressively more complex in terms of the number of required transformations.

The hypothesis which explored the significant difference in the incidence of base and transformed structures in speech samplings from individual to individual was also substantially upheld. The data showed sufficient conformity in the order of occurrence in which these structures were observed.

A further hypothesis implied a similarity in the results of the learning of one 4-year-old with that of the three 6-year-olds.

Because of the high positive correlation among the 6-year-old subjects in the chronological order of their learning of structures and functions, there is reason to suspect that second-language learning under certain environmental conditions follows a systematic pattern of development. Furthermore, because of the similarities between the results of the 6-year-olds and those of the 4-year-old, there is the implication that the learning of a second language may follow similar psycholinguistic rules within certain broad age limits, regardless of the specific age. An important question that may be asked now is: How do these findings compare with data on the acquisition of Spanish as a native language?

3. Acquisition of Spanish as a native language

Studies of the acquisition of Spanish as a native language are very rare. Besides the investigation by Kernan and Blount (1966), who devised a Berko-type (Berko 1958) test of morphological and syntactic growth in Mexican children, there are three studies, to my knowledge, that involve data relating directly or indirectly to the learning of Spanish as a native language. They are studies by González (1970), Martínez-Bernal (1972), and Toronto (1972).

Martínez-Bernal conducted an experimental study for developing a bilingual diagnostic language test, using findings on the monolingual acquisition of Spanish and English. In her investigation she focused attention on the acquisition of noun phrases of varying degrees of length and complexity as well as other aspects of the morphological systems, including verb tenses. Using data from the Kernan and Blount study (1966) and the Madrid Study (1970), she selected and ordered grammatical elements for testing. In her method of testing, she used a task involving parallel sentence production in which the experimenter (E) and the subject (S) look at pairs of pictures together. E models a sentence to go with one of the pictures, and S applies parallel structures to go with the other picture. For example, E says: Es la taza verde. 'It's the green cup.' and S should say: Es el libro rojo 'It's the red book.'

After presenting 17 items to a large sampling of children, ages 5 to 8, from the levels of kindergarten, first and second grades, the results indicated the following order of difficulty in constructing and combining the various components of the Spanish noun phrase. In order to make a comparison this data has been placed alongside the order of observed noun phrase structures taken from the Madrid Study, as seen in Table 3.

TABLE 3. Comparison of Dato's observed order of development and Martínez-Bernal's order of difficulty of items in Spanish noun phrases

Order	Dato Structure Rule	Martínez-Bernal Structure	% Correct
1.	N	N	94
2.	Det N	Dem N	86
3.	Dem (N)	Det N	81
4.	(Det) LAdj N	Det N S'	80
5.	Det N y Det N	N Adj	76
6.	PPh --→ Prep NP	Adj N	72
7.	Poss N	Det N Adj	69
8.	Np PPh	Det N Adj PPh	60
9.	Det LAdj (N) Adj	Det Adj N	53
10.	Det N Adj	Det N Adj y Adj	45
11.	Det N Adv Adj	Det N Adj S'	45
12.	Det N S'	Dem N Adj	44
13.	Todo Det N	Todo Dem N	20
14.	(Det) LAdj PPh	Det N PPh S'	14
15.	Det LAdj N Adv Adj	Det N Adj y Adj PPh	11
16.	NP-→ S'	Det N Adj PPh S'	0

A preliminary comparison of these two sets of data suggests that the sequence of NP structures observed in a longitudinal descriptive analysis like the Madrid Study parallels appreciably the order of difficulty found in an experimental study on bilingual children. A tentative conclusion reached by Martínez-Bernal is that the subjects appear to be acquiring both English and Spanish in substantially the same way as children who are monolingual in each language. It seems that neither Spanish nor English is a second language for these children.

One of the few descriptive studies done on the acquisition of Spanish as a native language was completed by González in 1970. The purpose of this study was to provide information for use as guidelines for Spanish curriculum designers and use in preschool programs for Spanish-speaking children. He described the performance of 24 children between the ages of 2 and 5 from Texas who had a conversational proficiency in Spanish.

Speech samples used in his study represent utterances in each of the following age groups: 24, 30, 33, 36, 42, 48, 54, and 60 months. The grammatical analysis treated the various sentence types, verb tenses, interrogatives, imperatives, and other structures, including the order and frequency of occurrence. Even though González used only three children from each of the age groups cited, he argued that his study provided a set of tentative norms for language development. From the structures that González studied, the verb tenses will be used to make a comparison. The order of difficulty of the verb tenses investigated by Martínez-Bernal will also be compared as seen in Table 4.

TABLE 4. Comparison of the observed order of development of Spanish verb tenses by Dato and González, and the order of difficulty by Martínez-Bernal

| Order of development: | | Order of difficulty: |
Dato	González	Martínez-Bernal
1. present indicative	present indicative	present indicative
2. present perfect	preterite	preterite
3. preterite	present progressive	present subjunctive
4. future (ir a + infinitive)	future (ir a + infinitive)	future (ir a + infinitive)
5. present progressive	present subjunctive	past subjunctive
6. imperfect	imperfect*	present perfect
7. present subjunctive	present perfect*	future (inflected)
8. future (inflected)	past subjunctive	conditional
9. past subjunctive	future (inflected)*	
10. conditional	conditional*	
*According to González (1970:148) these tenses were not completely established at the age level indicated, although they appeared in the order indicated.		

Comparison of the Spanish verb tenses indicates complete agreement on the early use of the present indicative. The overall sequence of tenses, although not conclusive, shows evidence that the preterite and future using ir a plus infinitive emerge soon afterwards. The Dato and González studies concur on the relative order of the present subjunctive while on the occurrence of the present perfect they do not. However, the inflected future, the past subjunctive, and the conditional in all three studies are uniformly among the last tenses to appear. It must be pointed out that González (1970:148) makes a distinction between the earliest occurrences of a tense in his data and what he calls the establishment of that tense.

Also in general agreement with these findings on the development and use of Spanish verb tenses is the study by Toronto (1972), who used the González data as one of his principal sources for determining significant developmental hierarchies in Spanish syntax. Based on the developmental sentence scoring procedures devised by Laura Lee (1966) and Lee and Canter (1971), Toronto's purpose was to devise a developmental sentence scoring procedure to diagnose language deviance among Spanish-speaking Mexican-American children between the ages of 3;0 and 5;11. Of the grammatical categories used: indefinite pronouns, personal pronouns, primary verbs, secondary verbs, conjunctions and interrogatives, Toronto stated that the verbs represented the most effective syntactic hierarchy for discriminating and separating age groups. That this is the case lends greater significance to the existence of the similarities that have just been observed in the comparison of verb tenses in these studies.

4. Summary

In this paper I have described the process by which several American English-speaking children of different ages acquired certain aspects of Spanish syntax in random fashion while living in a natural Spanish-speaking environment. After having presented data suggesting that children of differing ages under certain conditions learn a second language using similar psycholinguistic strategies, I made some preliminary comparisons with data relating to the acquisition of Spanish as a native language. While it is tempting to hypothesize the existence of psycholinguistic universals in children's learning of Spanish observed in these learning situations, it is too soon to draw such conclusions on the basis of these few studies. Certain similarities, however, can be pointed out between the two learning situations as observed in the data relating to noun phrases and verb tenses. The need for further research on both first- and second-language learning of Spanish is obvious. It would be fruitful to compare not only the relationship between first- and second-language learning, but also the relationship between first-language acquisition by normal children and that of children who, for any number of reasons, show deviance in their language development. These different research strategies would not only provide a clearer perspective of how Spanish in particular is learned, but would also add to the growing number of L1 and L2 studies that are needed in a wide range of diverse languages in order to obtain an understanding of psycholinguistic universals.

REFERENCES

Berko, J. 1958. The child's learning of English morphology. Word 14.150-77.

Brown, R. and C. Fraser. 1973. The acquisition of syntax. In: Verbal behavior and learning: Problems and processes. Edited by C. N. Cofer and B. Musgrave. New York, McGraw-Hill.

Chomsky, N. 1965. Aspects of the theory of syntax. Cambridge, Mass., MIT Press.

Curtiss, Susan, V. Fromkin, S. Krashen, D. Rigler, and M. Rigler. 1974. The linguistic development of Genie. Lg. 50.528-554.

Dato, Daniel P. 1966. Una base psicolingüística para el estudio del aprendizaje de español por niños de habla inglesa. Filología Moderna. Madrid, Universidad de Madrid.

_____. 1970. American children's acquisition of Spanish syntax in the Madrid environment. Preliminary ed. U.S. Department of Health, Education and Welfare, Office of Education, May.

_____. 1971. The development of the Spanish verb phrase in children's second-language learning. In: The psychology of second language learning. Edited by P. Pimsleur and T. Quinn. Cambridge, Cambridge University Press.

Dulay, H. and M. Burt. 1974a. Natural sequences in child second language acquisition. Language Learning 24.37-53.

_____. 1974b. A new perspective on the creative construction process in child second language acquisition. Language Learning 24.253-278.

Ervin-Tripp, S. 1974. Is second language learning like the first? TESOL Quarterly 8.111-127.

Falk, Julia S. 1968. Nominalizations in Spanish. Studies in linguistics and language learning. Vol. V. Seattle, University of Washington Press.

Fromkin, Victoria A., S. Krashen, S. Curtiss, D. Rigler, and M. Rigler. 1974. The development of language in Genie: A case of language acquisition beyond the 'critical period'. Brain and Language 1.81-107.

Fry, D. B. 1966. The development of the phonological system in the normal and deaf child. In: The genesis of language. Edited by F. Smith and G. A. Miller. Cambridge, MIT Press.

González, Gustavo. 1970. The acquisition of Spanish grammar by native Spanish speakers. Doctoral dissertation, The University of Texas at Austin.

Ingram, D. 1968. An approach to writing grammars for child language. Working Paper No. 1, Scottish Rite Institute for Childhood Aphasia at Stanford University, August.

Kernan, K. T. and B. G. Blount. 1966. The acquisition of Spanish grammar by Mexican children. Anthropoligical linguistics. Vol. 8, No. 9.1-14.

Kessler, C. 1973. Postsemantic processes in children with language delay. Paper presented at the annual meeting of the Linguistic Society of America, San Diego.

Krashen, S. 1973. Lateralization, language learning, and the critical period: Some new evidence. Language Learning 23. 63-74.

Lee, Laura L. 1966. Developmental sentence types: A method for comparing normal and deviant syntactic development. Journal of Speech and Hearing Disorders 31. 311-330.

_____ and S. M. Canter. 1971. Developmental sentence scoring: A clinical procedure for estimating syntactic development in children's spontaneous speech. Journal of Speech and Hearing Disorders 36. 315-340.

Lenneberg, Eric H., I. A. Nichols, and P. F. Rosenberger. 1964. Primitive stages of language development in mongolism. Disorders of communication 43. Research publications, Association for Research in Nervous and Mental Diseases. Baltimore, Maryland, Williams and Wilkins.

Martínez-Bernal, Janet A. 1972. Children's acquisition of Spanish and English morphological systems and noun phrases. Doctoral dissertation, Georgetown University.

McNeill, D. 1966. Developmental psycholinguistics. In: A psycholinguistic approach. Edited by F. Smith and G. Miller. Cambridge, Mass., MIT Press.

Menyuk, P. 1963. Syntactic structures in the language of children. Child Development 34. 2. 407-22.

_____. 1964. Comparison of grammar of children with functionally deviant and normal speech. Journal of Speech and Hearing Research 7. 107-121.

Morehead, D. and D. Ingram. 1973. The development of base syntax in normal and linguistically deviant children. Journal of Speech and Hearing Research 16. 330-352.

Ravem, R. 1968. Language acquisition in a second language environment. International Review of Applied Linguistics 6. 2. 175-185.

Slobin, D. 1973. Cognitive prerequisites for the development of grammar. In: Studies of child language development. Edited by C. A. Ferguson and D. Slobin. New York, Holt, Rinehart and Winston.

Stevens, Claire E. 1966. A characterization of Spanish nouns and adjectives. Studies in linguistics and language learning. Vol. II. Seattle, University of Washington Press.

Toronto, A. 1972. A developmental Spanish language analysis procedure for Spanish-speaking children. Doctoral dissertation, Evanston, Illinois, Northwestern University.

PIAGETIAN EQUILIBRATION PROCESSES IN SYNTAX LEARNING

RUTH V. TREMAINE

University of Ottawa

Abstract. The implications for a theory of syntax learning of certain findings drawn from a study of bilingual children are examined in the light of Piaget's theory of cognitive development. In the study, Piagetian operational intelligence and the comprehension of English and French syntax, defined in terms of Fillmore's case grammar, were assessed in 60 English-speaking children learning French through a school curriculum. The results indicated that some aspects of syntax are acquired by the same abilities Piaget describes as operational intelligence. It is argued that the equilibration processes Piaget posits to explain cognitive growth could be considered as learning principles in child language, alternatives to those of behaviorist psychology.

In recent years, the term 'learning' has fallen into disrepute among developmental psycholinguists. The titles of books and research articles on child language reflect this trend: language is not 'learned', it either 'develops', or to use the even more noncommittal term, it is 'acquired'. These studies have concentrated on describing what children of various ages say and understand, and have generally ignored the crucial question of how children arrive at this knowledge. I am aware that behaviorist learning principles cannot explain the child's gradual construction of adult syntax, as they cannot explain most other abilities and characteristics of children. Nonetheless, the simple view that maturation is something that happens independently of practice and acquired experience is no longer tenable. The environment plays a role in physiological maturation as well as in maturational abilities such as language and intelligence. Language may not be learned by the principles of association, reinforcement and generalization, but it is somehow learned and experience plays a role.

Jean Piaget's theory of cognitive development suggests a new way of thinking about learning which could be extended to language learning. Logico-mathematical structures, for example, are both learned and not learned, in the usual sense. They are learned in the sense that actions on the environment and the experiences resulting from them are absolutely necessary. They are not learned in the sense that they are constructed from the actions themselves, not from environmental stimuli. Equilibration, or autoregulation processes, appear to be the mechanisms involved, not reinforcement and association.

This paper focuses on the implications for a theory of syntax learning of certain findings drawn from a larger study reported in detail elsewhere (Tremaine 1975). Some aspects of the design and results of the study will be presented briefly as they come up in my argument, but space does not permit a full description.

The study was mainly concerned with analyzing how the comprehension of syntax in bilingual children is related to the development of Piagetian operational intelligence. The purpose of the study was not to demonstrate that language and intelligence are closely related during development--a fact which few people would argue--but to see what could be learned from an analysis of this kind about the processes or learning principles which underlie maturational abilities.

I tested the hypothesis that when children learning a second language reach the stage of concrete operations, comprehension of the syntax of their two languages improves dramatically. This entailed a subject sample whose age range would straddle the well documented average age of the onset of concrete operations. The 60 children chosen were between the ages of 6 and 10 (average age about 8), came from English-speaking homes, and were learning French at school in grades 1, 2, or 3. Half of the children in each grade were enrolled in a French immersion curriculum--all subjects at school were taught in French--and the other half were enrolled in what will be called the 75-minute curriculum--that is, they were exposed to 75 minutes of French instruction per day. The subjects, therefore, were chosen to fit a balanced design with three factors: sex, grade, and curriculum (see Table 1). The curriculum and grade factors were treated as amount-of-exposure-to-French factors. That is, curriculum was an intensity factor and grade was a time factor of exposure to French.

The children were given two series of tests over a six-week period at the end of the school year. With one series, concrete operational thought was assessed by means of five Piagetian tasks. The other series assessed comprehension of English and French syntax defined in terms of case grammar. [1]

TABLE 1. Number of subjects by grade, sex, and type of curriculum
(N=60)

	Grade 1		Grade 2		Grade 3	
	M	F	M	F	M	F
French immersion	5	5	5	5	5	5
75-minute	5	5	5	5	5	5

The Piagetian tasks were seriation, numeration, conservation of
mass, weight, and solid volume, chosen so that they would vary in
difficulty, but all would be within the grasp of at least some of the old-
est children. Seriation and numeration are two Piagetian tasks which
explore how children understand the relations between ordination and
cardination in the development of the number concept. In the numeration task, for example, the child's ability to attribute cardinal value to
an ordinal series is tested, as is his ability to manipulate the series
as a set of classes. The other three tasks (conservation of mass,
weight, and solid volume) assess the child's understanding of the in-
variance of certain attributes of objects when their shapes are variously
transformed. Performance on each of the five tasks was classified as
operational, or nonoperational, according to Piaget's classical criteria.

The structures tested in the syntactic comprehension tests were ones
which the literature suggested were late-developing, and which could
be interrelated through Fillmore's (1968, 1971) case grammar and se-
quenced from simple to complex. They represented syntactic relations
between the agentive, objective, source, goal, and benefactive cases,
in various combinations and in simple and embedded sentences.

The tests were adapted from a study done by Kessler (1971) on the
acquisition of syntax in English-Italian bilingual children. This study
is of special interest since Kessler found, among other things, that
the comprehension of an interrelated set of syntactic structures common to Italian and English follows a maturational sequence much like
that of operational thought. That is, the order of acquisitions in both
languages showed a sequential, cumulative pattern ranging from simple
to complex structures when these structures were defined in terms of
Fillmore's case grammar. The study also showed that structures
shared by the two languages have a parallel development--that is,
children made the same kind of errors in both languages and the pattern of these mistakes was also approximately the same for the two
languages. However, as is the case for concrete operational intelligence, the order of acquisitions could be defined for the group but this
order did not necessarily hold for any one child.

The tests that Kessler constructed were apparently tapping those aspects of language we call linguistic universals. One purpose of our study, therefore, was to see whether the order of acquisitions for Italian and English would also hold for French and English. This involved a series of analyses which are peripheral to my topic here, although it should be mentioned that Kessler's findings were generally replicated.

In my opinion, the major obstacle in recent years to doing research relating operational intelligence to syntax has been the lack of an instrument detailed enough to assess a broad spectrum of linguistic competence, and sensitive enough to those aspects of language we call linguistic universals.

With some modifications, Kessler's (1971) tests were adapted to assess comprehension of English and French syntax. Briefly, comprehension of a syntactic structure was tested by means of having the child point to one of three pictures representing a spoken phrase or sentence. These pictures were of some action, situation, or object which could be conveyed through a line drawing. Two of the pictures represented the syntactic contrast tested, and the third was a neutral item. The child showed his comprehension of a structure by choosing the correct alternative from a contrasted pair. Table 2 lists the surface manifestations of syntactic structures tested in this fashion.

For the active structure, for example, the child would hear the sentence 'the boy hits the ball' and see a set of three pictures, one representing a boy hitting a ball, another showing a ball hitting a boy, and a third picture representing an irrelevant situation. Later on in the test, the child would hear 'the ball hits the boy' and see the same set of pictures. Each structure listed in Table 2 was tested by means of two contrasts, or four items, presented at random intervals during the test.

Note that some of the structures tested were relatively complex. The for/to contrast, for example, is not the normal word order in English or French, but it is possible in both languages. In case grammar terms, this contrast represents a shift in the rank order of the subject selection hierarchy and therefore should be more difficult to comprehend than a sentence with the normal order.

There was both an English and a French version of the picture test, as well as an auditory test which assessed comprehension of synonymity within and between languages. The whole test series took about an hour and fifteen minutes to administer to each child, not of course at one sitting. Performance was analyzed in terms of correct items and in terms of types of errors within a variety of subtests, such as inflectional categories, syntactic structures, comprehension of synonymity within languages, between languages, total scores for English and for

TABLE 2. Surface manifestations of syntactic structures tested by means of contrasted picture representations

Syntactic contrast	Example
1. for/to	the girl brings the ball for the baby to the mother/the girl brings the ball for the mother to the baby
2. reflexive/reciprocal	the boys see themselves/the boys see each other
3. passive	the boy is hit by the ball/the ball is hit by the boy
4. relative clause	the baby on the table eats the cake/ the baby eats the cake which is on the table
5. possessive x of y	the king of the castle/the castle of the king
6. comparative adjective	the car is longer than the truck/the truck is longer than the car
7. from/to	the cat jumps from the table to the floor/the cat jumps from the floor to the table
8. noun/adjective	the dog with a big ball/the big dog with a ball
9. direct/indirect object	the boy brings the mouse to the cat/ the boy brings the cat to the mouse
10. subject/indirect object	the baby gives the ball to the girl/ the girl gives the ball to the baby
11. active	the boy hits the ball/the ball hits the boy

French, and so on. Scores on eleven subtests were obtained for each child.

To summarize so far, data were gathered on the children's operational level by means of five Piagetian tasks varying in difficulty. On

each task, the child was classified as operational--that is, his performance exhibited the kind of reasoning characteristic of the stage of concrete operations--or he was classified as nonoperational. Data were
also gathered on the children's comprehension of syntactic structures
common to English and French, structures which also varied in difficulty. Scores on eleven subtests indicated how well the child understood English and French syntax.

The children were then reclassified in each grade and type of French
curriculum according to whether they were operational or nonoperational
on each of the five Piagetian tasks, and the syntactic comprehension
scores were treated as the dependent variable. Loosely speaking, we
wanted to see whether operational level on various kinds of tasks would
predict syntactic comprehension, how the amount of exposure to French
would affect syntactic comprehension, and what was the effect of age on
syntactic comprehension.

One aspect of the way operational intelligence develops should be
mentioned at this point since it has a bearing on the kind of inferences
that can be drawn from the data of the study. Unlike psychometric
indices of intelligence, such as mental age from which IQ's are computed, operational intelligence is not a linear function of age. A
plateau period where performance on Piagetian tasks does not change
is followed by sudden and rapid improvement around the age of seven
or eight, after which little improvement is evident until about age
thirteen, when again dramatic improvement occurs. The difference
in intelligence between operational and nonoperational children, therefore, is not a minor difference. It represents a major change in the
way the child perceives, understands, and interprets his experience
(Piaget and Inhelder 1969, 1971). If there is a significant and consistent difference in the way children who have reached the stage of
concrete operations comprehend their native language as well as a
second language which they are in the process of learning, this would
imply that the rules and learning processes descriptive of concrete
operational thought may also be descriptive of the syntax of operational children.

My first hypothesis was that children classified as operational
would perform significantly better on each of the eleven syntactic
subtests than children classified as nonoperational. This hypothesis
involved 65 independent analyses of variance, multivariate and uni-
variate, 62 of which supported the hypothesis. When the effects of
grade and type of curriculum were statistically removed, the same
trend persisted. That is, even when the effects of exposure to
French were removed, operational children performed significantly
better in English and French.

These findings suggested the interpretation mentioned a moment
ago, that the same abilities are involved in the comprehension of

syntax and in operational thought. Put another way, the rules and learning processes which govern performance on Piagetian tasks also seemed to govern performance on the syntactic comprehension tests, both English and French.

To explore this interpretation further, I then did a principal components/principal axis factor analysis of all the variables in the study, 22 of them. A clearly interpretable factor pattern emerged after varimax rotation, which seemed to support my hypothesis. Two of the Piagetian tasks and most of the syntactic comprehension subtests loaded significantly on the same factor, which accounted for most of the variability. This factor logically suggested that the syntax of English and French is comprehended by the same abilities needed for certain types of concrete operational thought. As Kessler (1971) concluded in her study of bilingual children, the languages of the bilingual child are not encoded separately, at least those aspects that have to do with the comprehension of forms analogous at the deep structure level. I can now add that operational thought is not encoded separately from syntactic comprehension. This finding I believe is the most important one of the study. The analyses just described were part of a larger set leading to this conclusion.

For example, another series of analyses allowed a test of an interesting hypothesis suggested by Lambert and Tucker (1972) regarding the strategies children may use in learning a second language. In their longitudinal study of English-speaking children learning French through an immersion program in Quebec, they expressed astonishment at how easily these children transferred skills learned through the medium of the French language to tests conducted in English. Lambert and Tucker suggested that this transfer of skills between languages may have been due to a more abstract form of learning independent of the language of training. They speculated that a form of 'incipient contrastive linguistics' is practiced by children. That is, when a child is exposed to a second language, he compares the vocabulary and syntax of the two languages and actively searches for equivalents which he does not know. This translation and search process would not only allow him to learn the second language, but would also increase the knowledge of his native language.

Following this kind of reasoning, it was predicted that the more exposure our subjects had to the French language, the better would be their comprehension of English syntax.

It will be recalled that amount of exposure to French was defined in terms of an intensity factor (French immersion or 75-minute curriculum) and in terms of a time factor (grades 1, 2, or 3). We then did the appropriate analyses of variance to see whether comprehension of English syntax improved with amount of exposure to French. Both the time and intensity factors were found to be significant, although they did not interact. As expected, comprehension of English syntax improved in successively higher grades. The interesting finding was that children in the French immersion curriculum comprehended English syntax significantly better than children in the 75-minute curriculum.

To isolate the effect of intensive exposure to French from the possibly confounding effects of age and intelligence, a series of analyses of covariance was then done. In other words, since both grade level and operational level influenced syntactic comprehension, we wanted to see whether intensive exposure to French alone could account for this facilitative effect on English syntax. The results showed that it clearly did.

This finding was unexpected, since at first glance it seemed to contradict much of the recent research on child language. This research has shown how notoriously hard it is to train a child to use adult-like syntax or to accelerate the acquisition of syntax. And here it was found that intensive exposure to a second language, not even deliberate training, accelerated syntactic comprehension of the mother tongue. How can this effect be explained?

By extending and amplifying the conclusions reached in the previous analyses, that the same abilities or learning processes are involved in the learning of syntax and in the learning of concrete operations, I believe an explanation is possible.

While Piagetian research has shown that it is impossible to train operational thinking in children younger than five years, there are cases in which such training is possible. When the child is in the intermediate stage between pre-operational thought and the stage of concrete operations, that is, between the ages of about 6 and 8, it is possible to bring him to a more mature way of thinking either by deliberate training or by certain kinds of social interaction (e.g. Elkind and Flavell 1969, Silverman and Geiringer 1973). At this intermediate stage, it seems that cognitive structures are quite vulnerable to environmental effects. Or rather I should say relatively vulnerable, since both before and after this stage, children are utterly sure of themselves and will not be coerced into another way of thinking.

This self-confidence takes a turn for the worse in the intermediate stage. Children begin to give self-contradictory answers under environmental pressure. For example, one moment the child will say that a plasticene ball now contains more plasticene because it is rolled into a long shape, and the next moment he will say that it contains less plasticene because now the sausage is 'so thin'.

It could be that exposure to French facilitated English syntax because many of the subjects were, for one type of reasoning or another, in the intermediate stage. That is, during the age period when concrete operations are trainable, syntactic comprehension proved to be trainable also. The phenomenon that Lambert and Tucker (1972) called 'incipient contrastive linguistics' may have been the sort of equilibration processes Piaget posits to explain the growth of operational thought.

This interpretation of the results implies several interrelated ideas. First, it implies that exposure to French facilitated English because the abilities which underlie syntactic comprehension are very similar and are drawn upon when the child tries to understand either his native language or another language he is in the process of learning. Second, these abilities are the same ones implicit in the concrete operations.

A simple diagram will clarify the points I wish to make.

FIGURE 1. Cognitive 'abilities'

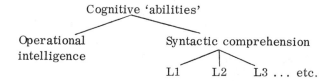

Although Figure 1 is in the form of a hierarchical tree, no hierarchies are implied in the processes represented. Rather, the tree structure is meant to illustrate the direction of our inductive reasoning, from bottom to top, which led us to posit an identity of the learning processes underlying operational intelligence and language. From the data of this study and others it can be assumed that the same, as yet undefined, cognitive 'abilities' or processes are tapped when children are presented with certain tasks, such as tests of syntactic comprehension and operational intelligence. L1, L2, L3, etc. represent, loosely speaking, the deep structures of languages which are comprehended by the same cognitive abilities implicit in operational thought. Or in Piaget's terminology, L2 was assimilated to L1 structure. But L2 structure was different enough to force an accommodation of L1 structure, that is, a modification or change in the direction of greater 'stability'. In other words, environmental intervention at L2 (intensive exposure to French) influenced L1 (English) for two reasons: because the same abilities are involved and because the children were in the intermediate, 'unstable' stage.

This interpretation further implies that operational intelligence would be facilitated by intensive exposure to French during the intermediate stage. Unfortunately, it was not possible to analyze this effect for reasons of experimental design.

In considering Figure 1, another hypothesis immediately suggests itself, namely, that around the age of eight, new abilities become available which allow the child to comprehend adult-like syntax which was previously understood partially or inconsistently. The question then arises: what types of structures can operational children comprehend which nonoperational children cannot, or at least not consistently?

The study provided some data on this question. For example, nonoperational children performed much worse on syntactic contrasts which violated the normal order of cases, such as the for/to contrast, the passive structure, or structures which involved complex embedding such as the comparative adjective (see Table 2). Operational children, on the other hand, comprehended these structures almost perfectly. The question now arises, what are those new cognitive abilities which explain the difference in performance?

If one turns to Piaget's recent theoretical writings, it is possible to give at least a tentative, speculative answer to some of the questions I have raised regarding syntax learning. In his radical synthesis of the theories of cognitive and biological growth, Piaget (1971) reinterprets in cybernetic terms the processes by which children achieve operational thought. These writings suggest that we look for two major phases in syntax learning.

The first phase, coinciding with pre-operational intelligence, defines a period where a kind of serial processing is dominant, not serial in the sense of stimulus and response chains, but serial in the sense of feedback loops. The child adjusts his understanding of the world, including the linguistic world, after he has experienced failure in applying his knowledge. This trial and error process, or what others have called hypothesis testing, is characterized by an active search for and experimentation with rules of construction. Rules are discovered, overgeneralized, and then adjusted. During this phase, learning a syntactic rule is probabilistic, progresses by a series of approximations, and can be described as inconsistency in rule application. The equilibration processes involved are those of retroactive control, in the usual cybernetic sense of corrections and modifications in case of error. The learning process, therefore, is a succession of regulations, and in this sense it involves serial processing.

During the second phase of syntax learning, coinciding with concrete operational thought and beginning around the age of eight, a different type of processing is dominant. Equilibration no longer involves feedback and correction 'after the event', so to speak, but complete reversibility which carries out the function of 'precorrecting, avoiding, or eliminating errors', a kind of regulation of regulations (Piaget 1971:210). The effect of this kind of processing can be seen in the way operational children comprehend syntax. Structures involving rank shift in the hierarchy of cases and complex embedding, for example, were understood quite easily. Through reversibility principles, structures can be perceived as identical even when certain aspects are transformed or serially rearranged.

In conclusion, I think the study showed that the similarity between operational intelligence and syntactic comprehension is not just an isomorphism. The likeness is to be found not between syntactic structures and logico-mathematical concepts, but in the learning processes which underlie both. It could be called a similarity, but there are cogent reasons for thinking of it as an identity.

NOTE

1. Detailed descriptions of assessment procedures and how performance on the Piagetian test series and the syntactic comprehension test series was analyzed can be found in Tremaine (1975).

REFERENCES

Elkind, D. and J. H. Flavell, eds. 1969. Studies in cognitive development. Toronto, Oxford University Press.

Fillmore, C. J. 1968. The case for case. In: Universals in linguistic theory. Edited by E. Bach and R. T. Harms. New York, Holt, Rinehart and Winston.

_____. 1971. Some problems for case grammar. In: Georgetown University Round Table, 1971. Edited by Richard J. O'Brien, S.J. 535-556.

Kessler, C. 1971. The acquisition of syntax in bilingual children. Washington, Georgetown University Press.

Lambert, W. E. and G. R. Tucker. 1972. Bilingual education of children. Rowley, Mass., Newbury House.

Piaget, J. 1971. Biology and knowledge: An essay on the relations between organic regulations and cognitive processes. Chicago, University of Chicago Press.

_____ and B. Inhelder. 1969. The psychology of the child. New York, Basic Books.

_____. 1971. Mental imagery in the child. New York, Basic Books.

Silverman, I. W. and E. Geiringer. 1973. Dyadic interaction and conservation induction: A test of Piaget's equilibration model. Child Development 44. 815-820.

Tremaine, R. V. 1975. Syntax and Piagetian operational thought: A developmental study of bilingual children. Washington, Georgetown University Press.

THE ACQUISITION OF KNOWLEDGE
BY CHILDREN EDUCATED BILINGUALLY

G. RICHARD TUCKER

McGill University

Abstract.   In this paper, I have looked back at a portion of the data
that we have collected from one group of children participating in the
'St. Lambert' bilingual program.   Specifically, I have examined the
pupils' mastery of content material during the period from kindergarten to grade 5 when they were studying arithmetic, science, and
social studies in French, their second language.   The data suggest
that the children do attain the anticipated level of content mastery;
and, in addition, that they develop a functional knowledge of two major
world languages.

Almost ten years ago, in September, 1965, the South Shore Protes-
tant Regional School Board began its first experimental French 'immersion' classes for a group of English-speaking kindergarten children.   This project, designed to promote functional bilingualism
through a policy of home and school language switch, was initiated
by the Board on an experimental basis in response to numerous requests from parents living in the community of St. Lambert, Quebec.
The program, which started out with two kindergarten classes in one
school during 1965-66, has expanded throughout the South Shore system.   During the 1974-1975 school year, this program is being offered
from kindergarten through grade 9.   This year approximately 40 percent of all eligible kindergarten pupils have enrolled in an immersion
program on the South Shore.

The kindergarten curriculum has been left largely to the discretion
of the participating teachers.   They stress the development of vocabulary and passive comprehension skills in French along with other traditional kindergarten activities.   They use a direct native language

approach, in contrast to the second language methods typically used to teach French to English-speaking children. At the end of the kindergarten year, the children are assessed through direct observation by teachers and evaluators; but no attempt has ever been made to test them formally. By the end of the school year, most have built up an extensive recognition vocabulary and use single French vocabulary items as well as occasional short sentences. Productive skills vary considerably from one child to the next; but all are able to comprehend, without difficulty, simple children's stories as well as their teacher's directions.

At the grade 1 level, reading, writing, and arithmetic are introduced exclusively via French. No attempt is made to teach the children to read in English, and parents are specifically urged not to do so in the home. In grade 2, two daily 35-minute periods of English Language Ar are introduced. The rest of the curriculum remains essentially the same, with reading, writing, arithmetic, and elementary science being taught via French. The amount of instruction via English is increased gradually and by grade 8 approximately 70 percent of the curriculum is taught in English with the balance in French.

At the request of the Board authorities and the Minister of Education of the Province of Quebec, members of the Language Research Group at McGill (see Lambert and Tucker 1972) were asked to formally evaluate the program. The progress of the pupils in a pilot experimental class and in a follow-up experimental class has been compared each year with carefully selected control classes of French children instructed via French and English children taught via English. The control classes were selected from schools in comparable middle-class neighborhoods. In view of the well-documented influence of social class on language and intellectual development, and since the number of students involved was relatively small, considerable care was taken to equate the experimental and control classes on nonverbal intelligence and socio-economic factors.

No attempt whatsoever was made to preselect or screen children for the experimental classes on the basis of IQ or other variables; thus both the pilot and follow-up classes (in fact, all subsequent classes) contained children with a wide range of IQ and even had a few pupils with recognized perceptual-motor or language disabilities (see Bruck, Rabinovitch and Oates 1975).

We have now been following these two separate experimental groups of children, the pilot and follow-up classes, since they began their formal schooling. Thus far, after nine years, we are satisfied that this novel program of second language teaching has not resulted in any native language or subject matter (for example, arithmetic, science, or social studies) deficit. Nor does there appear to be any cognitive retardation attributable to participation in this program. In summary, the experimental pupils as a group appear to be able to read, write, speak, understand, and use English as well as youngsters instructed via English in the conventional manner. In addition, and at no apparent cost, they can also read, write, speak, and understand French in a way that English pupils who follow a traditional FSL program never do. These children have acquired a mastery of the basic elements of French phonology, morphology, and syntax; and they have not developed the inhibition which so often characterizes the performance of the foreign or second language student (Bruck, Lambert and Tucker 1974; Bruck, Lambert and Tucker, in press; Lambert and Tucker 1972; Lambert, Tucker and d'Anglejan 1973).

The acquisition of content material via a second language

The pilot and follow-up experimental classes are now enrolled in grades 9 and 8 respectively, and we continue to monitor their progress. Recently, as the immediate need for program evaluation has become less pressing, we have begun to re-examine our accumulated data in some detail. For example, last year I investigated the development of English and French reading skills by the follow-up group of experimental pupils (Tucker, in press).

We have long been aware that the type of program evaluation typically carried out, in which a group of experimentally instructed pupils is compared with one or more groups of traditionally instructed pupils, may mask some of the fascinating and important variation among the individuals involved. Thus, although the experimental pupils, as a group, have developed far greater facility in French than English pupils who have followed a typical FSL program, it is nevertheless the case that there does exist a wide range of variation in the performance of the experimental pupils.

The aim of this paper is to continue this mode of ancillary evaluation by examining what I have here called somewhat over zealously the acquisition of 'knowledge' in a second language. Specifically, I propose to examine the performance of the follow-up experimental pupils on tests of mathematics, social studies, and science at grades one, three, and five. I shall focus special attention on the results of those tests which were administered to the pupils at a time when they had studied the particular content subject only in French--their second language.

Performance in grade one (1967-68). The follow-up group comprised thirty-eight pupils in grade one. They had received all instruction, including the development of reading and other readiness skills, via French at the kindergarten and grade one levels. That is, all content material was taught to these pupils via their second language. As mentioned, the experimental pupils and comparable groups of

English children attending an English-medium school and French children attending a French-medium school were given an extensive battery of tests at the end of each academic year.

The results of the 'Arithmetic Concepts' section of the Metropolitan Achievement Test (MAT) are of particular interest at this grade level. The performance of the experimental pupils, as a group, did not differ significantly from that of the English control pupils (F = 0.91; 2, 75 df; NS). Thus, the experimental pupils who had studied arithmetic only in French performed as well on a standardized English-language test of arithmetic skills as a comparable group of pupils who had studied arithmetic in English, their native language. The performance of both groups fell between the 75th and 80th percentile on national norms. Apparently, the concepts which they learned through French were well assimilated in such a way that they were available for use in either French or English.

I have calculated several Pearson product-moment correlations with the data from the experimental pupils. There was a significant, positive correlation between the pupils' total English ability, as measured by four subtests of the MAT, and their arithmetic skills (r = .563; N = 35; p = .001); as well as marginally significant relationships between the Lorge-Thorndike test of intelligence and their arithmetic skills (r = .327; N = 37; p = .048); and the Raven Progressive Matrices (nonverbal) test with arithmetic skills (r = .328; N = 36; p = .051).

The pupils were not given a standardized arithmetic test in French at this grade level, nor were they formally tested in science or social studies.

Performance in grade three (1969-70). The experimental class comprised thirty pupils at the grade three level.[1]

As I have already mentioned, the members of the experimental class first began to receive English instruction in grade two with two daily 35-minute periods devoted to English Language Arts. At the grade three level, the English Language Arts program was continued, and in addition art, music, and physical education were taught in English. The core content subjects, however, continued to be taught exclusively in French.

Once again, we compared the arithmetic performance of the experimental pupils in English with that of the English control group; and, also at this grade, using another test, with the norms for French-speaking children studying under the auspices of the Commission des Ecoles Catholiques de Montréal (CECM).

The performance of the experimental pupils on the English-language MAT did not differ from that of the English control group on either the 'Arithmetic Computation' subtest (F = 0.57; 1, 50 df, NS) or the Arithmetic Problem Solving subtest (F = 0.13; 1, 50 df; NS). Once again, it must be remembered that the experimental children had received all of their formal instruction in mathematics via French. Likewise, on the French-language Test de Rendement en calcul, the experimental pupils stood at the fifth stanine. Thus, their class average was at the same level as that of approximately 60 percent of the French-speaking grade three youngsters in Montreal. In addition, I calculated a series of Pearson product-moment correlations which are summarized in Table 1. I was very interested to see that there were significant, positive correlations between the pupils' performance on the Test de Rendement en calcul and MAT computation ($r = .807$; $N = 24$; $p = .001$) as well as between their Calcul performance with MAT problem solving ($R = .779$; $N = 24$; $p = .001$). In addition, as the summary table shows, there were significant positive correlations between language skill per se in English or in French and the relevant English or French language arithmetic tests as well as between nonverbal intelligence and the various arithmetic tests.

TABLE 1. Summary of correlations performed at grade three level

Variable		Variable					
		1	2	3	4	5	6
1.	MAT (Total English)	–	.689**	.559**	.510**	(a)	(a)
2.	MAT (Computation)		–	.823**	(a)	.807**	.609**
3.	MAT (Problem Solving)			–	(a)	.779**	.424*
4.	Test de Rendement en Français				–	.648**	(a)
5.	Test de Rendement en calcul					–	.489*
6.	Ravens Progressive Matrices						–
*Indicates that $p < .05$							
**Indicates that $p < .01$							
(a)Indicates that this correlation was not calculated							

These data, limited as they may be, do suggest that relatively bright pupils who study arithmetic exclusively in their second language will perform well when tested either in their language of instruction or in their mother tongue, and likewise that those students who perform well on arithmetic tests administered in their second language will also perform well on tests given in their native language. Conversely, those pupils who perform poorly on arithmetic tests administered in their second language will also tend to perform poorly on tests given in their mother tongue. Furthermore, the data suggest that relatively 'slower' students will perform relatively poorly when tested either in their language of instruction or in their mother tongue. Thus, we find no evidence to suggest that the performance of these students who have studied arithmetic via French has been affected in any unusual manner--

except that they can effectively utilize French, in contrast to their anglophone peers.

However, it is appropriate to add that the results of a multiple regression analysis in which I attempted to predict students' scores on the MAT Computation test revealed that only 76 percent of the variance was accounted for by a knowledge of the students' performances on the Raven Progressive Matrices, the total-English component of the MAT, the Test de Rendement en français and the Test de Rendement en calcul and 69 percent for the MAT Problem Solving test.

Performance in grade five (1971-72). The experimental class comprised twenty-seven pupils at the grade five level. They had studied arithmetic, science, and geography in French at the grade four level and these same subjects as well as history in French at the grade five level. In grades four and five, approximately 65 percent of the pupils' class time was spent in French with about 35 percent in English.

At the grade five level, the experimental pupils did not perform so well as the English control pupils on the MAT 'Arithmetic Computation' subtest ($F = 7.70$; 1, 41 df; $p < .05$) or on the MAT 'Problem Solving' subtest ($F = 6.48$; 1, 41 df; $p < .01$). It is difficult to account for this unusually poor performance in arithmetic which placed the pupils at the 25th and 30th percentiles respectively on the two subtests. Parenthetically, I should add that we intensified our testing of the pupils' arithmetic skills at the grade six level. We found that they did not differ from English control pupils on either the MAT or the Stanford Diagnostic Arithmetic Test. The experimental group's poor performance at the grade five level, then, must be attributed to a number of 'performance' factors such as inattention, fatigue, or sheer boredom resulting from the annual testing.

At the grade five level, we also administered a standardized English-language science test and social studies test. On the MAT 'Science' subtest, the experimental class performed similarly to the English control pupils ($F = 1.24$; 1, 43 df; NS), even though all of their formal training in science had been conducted in French. Likewise, they performed no differently from the English control pupils on the MAT 'Social Studies' subtest ($F = 0.86$; 1, 43 df; NS). Thus, despite their anomalous performance in arithmetic, which was apparently a transitory drop off, we concluded that the experimental pupils were able to comprehend, store, retrieve, and utilize material first presented to them via French in either French or English.

We also gave the experimental pupils the Test de Rendement en Mathématiques developed by the CECM. On this French-language test, the pupils scored, as a group, at the fifth stanine, which meant that they performed as well as approximately 60 percent of the French-speaking children in Montreal.

I again calculated a series of Pearson product-moment correlations which are summarized in Table 2. Notice, once again, the consistently high, positive correlations between the pupils' measured English performance and Computation skills (r = .701; N = 25; p = .001), problem solving ability (r = .714; N = 25; p = .001), mastery of science concepts (r = .687; N = 26; p = .001) and social studies skills (r = .654; N = 26; p = .001). Likewise, there were high positive correlations

TABLE 2. Summary of correlations performed at grade five level

Variable	Variable							
	1	2	3	4	5	6	7	8
1. MAT (Total English)	–	.701**	.714**	.687**	.654**	(a)	.621**	(a)
2. MAT (Computation)		–	.866**	.325	.562**	.626**	(a)	.694**
3. MAT (Problem Solving)			–	.292	.567**	.581**	(a)	.805**
4. MAT (Science)				–	.603**	.380	(a)	.392*
5. MAT (Social Studies)					–	.459*	(a)	.548**
6. Raven Progressive Matrices						–	(a)	.561**
7. Test de Rendement en français							–	.537**
8. Test de Rendement en calcul								–
*Indicates that p <.05								
**Indicates that p <.01								
(a)Indicates that this correlation was not calculated								

between the experimental pupils' performance on the Test de Rendement en Mathématiques and their MAT Computation skills (r = .694; N = 26; p = .001) and Problem Solving ability (r = .805; N = 26; p = .001). The data once again seem to suggest that these bilingually-educated pupils who have studied core-content material from grades one through five exclusively via French have mastered the material and are now able to use this information in either French or English.

It is once again appropriate to add that the results of a multiple regression analysis in which I attempted to predict students' scores on the MAT Computation test revealed that only 59 percent of the variance could be accounted for by a knowledge of the students' performances on the Raven Progressive Matrices, the total-English component of the MAT, the Test de Rendement en français and the Test de Rendement en calcul (and 76 percent for the MAT Problem Solving test; 56 percent for the MAT Social Studies test; 43 percent for the MAT Science test).

Performance in grade seven (1973-74). The follow-up experimental class comprised twenty-one pupils at the grade seven level. At this grade level, they moved from the St. Lambert Elementary School to the Chambly County Regional High School. French continued to be used as a medium of instruction for about 30 percent of their program. At this level, mathematics and social studies were taught in English; but the science course was taught in French. At the grade six level, however, these pupils had studied mathematics and social studies in French; but their science course was taught in English. Our evaluation took a somewhat different direction at this grade level as we became more interested in assessing the development of functional bilingualism within the context of the 'early immersion' program (see Bruck, Lambert and Tucker 1975). For this reason, we did not administer standardized tests in various content areas during our normal spring testing period. We concentrated, instead, on assessing the facility with which the experimental pupils could understand, read, and write French in a variety of contexts. I would like to add anecdotally, however, that according to the reports of teachers and the principal, the pupils following this experimental program continue to perform approximately at grade level despite the fact that the majority of their early education had taken place in a second language.

Discussion

What generalizations, if any, can we draw from the data which I have just presented? First, it seems clear that the bilingual education experience of this particular group of middle-class, English-speaking Montrealers has left no enduring symptoms of confusion or retardation in their mastery of basic arithmetic, science, or social studies concepts. That is, for this group of youngsters and many others who have subsequently enrolled in similar programs in Montreal, we have found no evidence of any continuing deficit which might conceivably be attributed to following a curriculum in which the second language is used as the initial medium of instruction and in which initial reading training and readiness activities occur in this second language.

How well do the data which I have reported reflect the results or observations collected by other researchers? Unfortunately, the other contemporary North American bilingual programs which have been carefully evaluated were started relatively recently, and so it is not yet possible to take the same retrospective look at the children's performance. The recent research, however, does seem to complement the findings from the St. Lambert project. Swain (1974), for example, has been associated with the evaluation of a number of French-English bilingual programs for English-speaking youngsters in Ontario, and has concluded that a lack of exposure to formal English study until the grade two or three or even four level does not in any way adversely affect the capacity of students to master English skills when they are finally introduced. Cameron, Feider, and Gray (1974), working in New Brunswick, have reported a spontaneous transfer of reading skills to the children's native language, English, as a result of immersion instruction in French. In the United States, Cohen

(1974) reports a similar transfer for Anglo students enrolled in a Spanish-immersion program. Presumably, a similar transfer of content material can also be expected in these programs.

In this paper, I have tried to look back at a portion of the data that we have collected from the follow-up experimental group of children who have been participating in the 'St. Lambert program' of home and school language switch. I have tried to look specifically at the pupils' mastery of content material during that period when they were studying arithmetic, science, and social studies in French--their second language. My purpose in this focused re-examination has been to provide some data which are relevant to the concerns that many educators and parents express concerning the cumulative effects of participation in such programs. They worry that their children may not achieve the same level of content mastery as other English-speaking children who follow the traditional English program of instruction.

The data which I have presented must, of course, be interpreted cautiously. They must be interpreted cautiously because they are based on the results of a series of standardized tests which should always be carefully scrutinized. Furthermore, the data are based on only one group of children from a particular socio-economic and ethnolinguistic background in the community of St. Lambert, Quebec. Nevertheless, the data suggest that children who study in a second language for a large portion of the school day do attain the anticipated level of content mastery which they are able to demonstrate when tested in either the second language or their mother tongue. Furthermore, the correlation matrices at grades three and five reflect a pattern typically seen with monolingually educated children--positive relationships among IQ, basic language skills, and various other factors such as tests of arithmetic, science, or social studies.

From my perspective, then, the single most noteworthy aspect of this paper is that I have nothing unexpected to tell you. A group of children have attended school, albeit a somewhat special program, for a number of years; and the one conclusion we can draw is that they seem perfectly normal. In closing, I would like to return to the very important question posed by Susan Ervin-Tripp at the meetings of the 1970 Georgetown University Round Table (Ervin-Tripp 1970). Essentially, she asked how is it that the Canadian immersion experience seems to have been so successful while the typical [English] immersion programs for Chicanos and other minority-group Americans have been so unsuccessful? Her answer (1970:313-314) to that question remains appropriate to this day:

Since the overt linguistic circumstances seem entirely parallel, it seems to me the differences are social. In the Montreal environment, English-speaking children have no sense of inferiority or disadvantage in the school. Their teachers do not have low expectations for their achievements. Their social group has power in the community; their language is respected, is learned by Francophones, and becomes a medium of instruction later in the school. In the classrooms, the children are not expected to compete with native speakers of French in a milieu which both expects and blames them for their failures, and never provides an opportunity for them to excel in their own language.

Under these, perhaps ideal, conditions, children who follow a program of home and school language-switch in Montreal do master basic arithmetic concepts; they do master basic science concepts; they do master basic social studies concepts--that is, they do acquire knowledge--and, in addition, they develop a functional knowledge of two major world languages.

NOTES

The preparation of this paper was supported, in part, by grants from the Canada Council and the Defense Research Board to W. E. Lambert and G. R. Tucker.
1. Note that although the number of students participating in the follow-up experimental group drops from year to year, the classes at each grade level were still regulation size. The varying N reflects the fact that we have included in our yearly testing only those children who have participated in the program from its inception.

REFERENCES

Bruck, M., W. E. Lambert, and G. R. Tucker. 1975. Assessing functional bilingualism within a bilingual program: The St. Lambert project at grade eight. Paper presented at TESOL convention, Los Angeles, 1975.
_____. 1974. Bilingual schooling through the elementary grades: The St. Lambert project at grade seven. Language Learning 24: 2.183-204.
_____. In press. Cognitive and attitudinal consequences of bilingual schooling: The St. Lambert project through grade six. International Journal of Psycholinguistics.
Bruck, M., M. S. Rabinovitch, and M. Oates. 1975. The effects of French immersion programs on children with language disabilities--a preliminary report. Working Papers on Bilingualism, Ontario Institute for Studies in Education 5.47-86.

Cameron, A., H. Feider, and V. Gray. 1974. Pilot evaluation of French immersion grade one in Fredericton, New Brunswick. Spring, 1974. Interim report to the Board of Education, Mimeo.

Cohen, A. D. 1974. The Culver City Spanish immersion program: The first two years. The Modern Language Journal 58.95-103.

Ervin-Tripp, S. 1970. Structure and process in language acquisition. Georgetown University Round Table on Languages and Linguistics 1970 (GURT 1970). Edited by James E. Alatis. Washington, D.C., Georgetown University Press. 313-353.

Lambert, W. E. and G. R. Tucker. 1972. Bilingual education of children. Rowley, Mass., Newbury House.

Lambert, W. E., G. R. Tucker, and A. d'Anglejan. 1973. Cognitive and attitudinal consequences of bilingual schooling: The St. Lambert project through grade five. Journal of Educational Psychology 65.141-159.

Swain, M. 1974. French immersion programs across Canada: Research findings. Canadian Modern Language Review 31.117-129.

Tucker, G. R. In press. The development of reading skills in a bilingual education program. In: Western Washington symposium on learning. Edited by F. Aboud and S. Smiley.

COMPARISONS AND CLASS-INCLUSION

ELIZABETH F. SHIPLEY

University of Pennsylvania

One of Piaget's tenets is that cognitive development in areas other than language is relatively independent of language mastery. Such a belief has methodological implications for the study of the child: it implies that all kinds of cognitive competence can be probed with verbal tasks. One asks the child a question; and if the child fails to respond correctly, it is a sign of cognitive deficiency. I argue that linguistic considerations have a role in the assessment of cognitive competence, specifically in what is known as the 'class-inclusion task', and I report on two studies that support this argument. These results do not attack the assumption that language development and cognitive development in other areas are independent. However, they do suggest that caution is needed in the interpretation of verbal tasks that are offered as indices of non-linguistic cognitive competence; and, further, that we must not forget the hypothetical nature of the assumption that language mastery and non-linguistic cognitive development are independent.

Piaget claims to take from logic the nature of the adult's organization of concepts. The structure is that of hierarchical classification which is characterized by 'norms of reasoning to which the subject himself conforms' (Inhelder and Piaget 1964:48). One of the norms, and the last to be mastered, is class inclusion: 'A class A (or A') is included in every higher ranking class which contains all its elements, starting with the closest, B: A=B-A' (or A'=B-A) and AxB=A, which amounts to saying that all A are "some" B' (1964:48).

Psychologically, for Piaget, class-inclusion involves conservation of the whole:

. . . in the case of true inclusion, B, the larger class, does not exist only when its constituent parts, A and A′, are actually united . . . [but] . . . it continues to encompass them, and it conserves its identity, even when these are dissociated . . . be it in space or even in thought . . . (1964:49, 50).

Logically, mastery of class-inclusion is dependent upon mastery of reversible operations; namely, the addition and subtraction of classes: $B=A+A'$ and $A=B-A''$.

Mastery of class-inclusion is manifest in two ways: 'The conservation of the whole and the quantitative comparison of whole and part' (1965:117). These two characteristics have been explored with two behavioral indices. The first index involves the ability to answer correctly and to justify the answer to questions of the form 'Are all females adults?'. This is said to indicate mastery of the 'all-some' relation. The second index, usually called the class-inclusion task, involves the ability to compare class with subclass, for example, to answer correctly questions of the form 'Are there more children or more girls?'

The typical Piagetian class-inclusion task involves presenting the child with five toy dogs and three toy cats and asking 'are there more dogs or more animals?' Young children consistently respond 'dogs'. According to Piaget, the young child is unable to 'conserve' the class of animals, so he 'reduces' the class of animals to cats and replies as if he were asked 'Are there more dogs or more cats?'

If we grant that the child is comparing part-and-part, rather than part-and-whole as requested in the class-inclusion task, two separate theoretical questions arise: (1) why doesn't the child compare the whole with the part; and (2) why does he compare the part with another part? Any theoretical attempt to explain failure on the class-inclusion task should also explain the children's consistent behavior when they fail.

Piaget accounts for failure in the class-inclusion task by postulating an inability to conserve the whole. He posits a 'reduction' of whole-to-part to explain the consistent error. But does the reduction of the whole B to the part A′ follow from Piaget's model? In fact, nothing in the possible properties of non-graphic collections (1964:48) said to be formed by 'pre-conservers' implies the reduction of a destroyed superordinate class to a subclass. Further, Inhelder and Piaget (1964:106) mention other possible errors, suggesting that they themselves do not see the reduction error as a necessary consequence of failure to conserve. We must tentatively regard the reduction hypothesis as an ad hoc explanation of the child's performance.

There are other problems with Piaget's analysis. For instance, adults also have difficulty with the class-inclusion question (Klahr and

Wallace 1972; Winer 1974), although not to the same degree as young children. The adult's difficulty is inconsistent with Piaget's position that failure is due to the child's lack of mastery of the logical relations of class-inclusion.

Now let us consider a grammatical restraint that may be relevant to performance in the class-inclusion task. In a theoretical discussion of hierarchical organization in the lexicon, Bever and Rosenbaum (1971) hypothesize certain restrictions on comparative constructions. They state that constructions are grammatical 'just in case a comparing noun neither dominates nor is dominated by a compared noun in the Be hierarchy' (1971:593). Thus, the sentences

(1) A gun is more deadly than a pistol.
(2) A pistol is more deadly than a gun.

are ungrammatical because gun dominates pistol in the hierarchy specified by the verb Be (a pistol is a gun), while both

(3) A cannon is more deadly than a pistol.

and

(4) A pistol is more deadly than a cannon.

are grammatical because neither noun dominates the other in the Be hierarchy. (It is not the case that a cannon is a pistol nor that a pistol is a cannon.)

Let us translate this constraint into class nomenclature. Gun names the individual elements of a class, pistol names the individual elements of one subclass of guns, and cannon names elements of another subclass of guns. The two subclasses, one of pistols and the other of cannons, do not over-lap; they are coordinate classes within the gun hierarchy. Elements identified only as members of the class of guns cannot be compared with elements of a subclass of guns; a gun cannot be compared with a pistol or a cannon. This restriction on the comparison of elements of a class and elements of one of its subclasses renders ungrammatical a variety of comparative constructions, for example,

(5) A person is taller than a woman.
(6) Which is stronger: a rabbit or an animal?

These constructions all refer to distributive comparisons of classes, that is, comparisons of properties possessed by each individual element of a class. Relevant to my analysis of the class-inclusion task,

I conclude that the distributive comparisons of elements of a class and elements of a subclass are ungrammatical.

The examples of grammatical comparative constructions presented here all contain nouns which refer to elements of coordinate classes. Do all grammatical distributive comparisons involve coordinate classes? According to Bever and Rosenbaum, they do not. However, the answer is not completely obvious. Certainly distributive comparisons are usually of coordinate classes. This can be demonstrated by considering open-ended comparisons.

(7) Apples are more tart than _____.

(8) Rats are more frightening than _____.

(9) Airplanes are faster than _____.

One tends to complete such statements with coordinate classes from well established lexical hierarchies--pears, mice, boats. Less common completions also seem to imply some hierarchy; for example, rats are more frightening than ice-storms among the natural hazards of some challenging environment. A more extensive analysis of comparisons and of hierarchies is needed to determine if all comparisons involve coordinate classes.

However, it does not matter for our present purposes whether the nature of the process of distributive comparison is such that coordinate classes are always involved in some way, or whether distributive comparisons are simply very frequently of coordinate classes. In either case we have a strong expectation that coordinate classes are involved. I conclude, therefore, that the distributive comparisons usually involve coordinate classes.

Let us now turn to comparison on the basis of collective properties --properties possessed by a class as a whole. Properties such as numerosity, physical extension, weight, monetary value, and usefulness can be the basis of collective comparison. However, with the exception of numerosity, both collective and distributive comparisons can be made on the basis of these properties. Yet we seldom find constructions that are taken to be ambiguous with respect to the kind of comparison, collective or distributive. For example, the following is taken distributively, even though, logically, it could be either a distributive comparison or a collective comparison.

(7) Adults weigh more than children.

is interpreted as

(8) An adult weighs more than a child.

although logically it could be interpreted as

(9) The total weight of all adults in the world is greater than the total weight of all the children.

Additional information (special wording) is necessary to signify that the comparison is between classes, for example, that the class consisting of all adults is compared to the class consisting of all children.

Constructions which are potentially ambiguous as to the nature of the comparison (collective or distributive) are interpreted as distributive comparisons without indications to the contrary. In this sense, distributive comparisons are more 'basic'.

Collective comparisons differ from distributive comparisons in that superordinate class and subclass can be compared. For instance, we can say

(10) The girls alone do a better job than all the children together.
(11) What do you want: the whole newspaper or just the sports section?

Note that these examples of collective comparisons (10 and 11) have syntactic signs that they are collective comparisons. Not only is information given about classes (all the children, the whole newspaper), but also given about class relations (the girls alone, just the sports section). If the collective comparison signs are omitted, for example,

(12) Girls do a better job than children.
(13) What do you want: the newspaper or the sports section?

we tend to reinterpret these as a distributive comparison of elements of coordinate classes (big girls and little children); or we assume the speaker is talking nonsense or making a feeble joke (claiming that sports are not news).

One type of collective comparison, numerosity, cannot be misinterpreted as a distributive comparison. However, statements of numerical comparison of class and subclass usually manifest signs of collective comparison even though such signs are redundant. We say

(14) There are more children all together than just the boys.

rather than

(15) There are more children than boys.

and we say

(16) Which is more: all the animals or just the dogs?

rather than

(17) Which is more: the animals or the dogs?

If we do not provide redundant information that a superordinate class and one of its subclasses are being compared, we tend again to compare coordinate classes, so that (15) may be taken as a comparison of little children and big boys or (16) as a comparison of dogs and other animals.

The class-inclusion question in English is usually worded

(18) Are there more animals or more dogs?

This wording is contrary to standard English usage in that (a) signs that the comparison is collective are omitted, and (b) indications of the class relations are missing. Thus the class-inclusion question has anomalous wording.

Let us now summarize the previous discussion and formulate an account of children's erroneous performance in the class-inclusion task. First, distributive comparisons of classes are linguistically more basic than collective comparisons of classes, as seen by the fact that collective comparisons require more elaborate wording. From this we predict that over-generalizations, if they occur, are of properties of the more basic distributive comparisons to collective comparisons. Second, distributive comparisons of class and subclass are ungrammatical, while collective comparisons of class and subclass are grammatical. We hypothesize that young children over-generalize this constraint on comparison of class and subclass from distributive comparisons to collective comparisons. Thus, collective comparison of class and subclass will be ungrammatical for these subjects. Finally, distributive comparisons are usually of coordinate classes in some hierarchy. We hypothesize that the tendency to compare coordinate classes is also over-generalized from distributive to collective comparisons; hence these young subjects will erroneously compare coordinate classes in the class-inclusion task. These effects are intensified by the fact that the class-inclusion question has an anamalous form; the usual redundant signs that indicate that the numerical comparison is a collective comparison are omitted. Basically, we hypothesize that erroneous class-inclusion performance is due to over-generalization of: (a) grammatical constraints and (b) expectations of comparison of coordinate classes.

I would like to mention briefly two well known phenomena in psycho-linguistics that are relevant to this argument and then to report two empirical studies that offer support for the grammatical constraints hypothesis.

First, it is consistently found in developmental psycholinguistics that rules descriptive of the speech and comprehension of children are over-generalized. Rules which describe a limited set of instances are applicable more widely than is appropriate. Over-generalizations found in children's speech (Ervin 1964) include noun inflections (children say dogs, cats, but also feets), and verb inflections (doed, breaked). Overgeneralized rules are also found in children's comprehension. For instance, the order actor-verb-object is sometimes taken to apply to both active and passive sentences (Fraser et al. 1963). The boy hit the girl and The boy was hit by the girl are taken as synonomous. In general the over-generalization is from the more common and the more uniform to the rarer, more complicated instance. Hence, in the case of comparisons we expect generalizations from distributive comparisons to collective comparisons rather than vice versa.

The second phenomenon concerns the tendency of the listener to interpret ungrammatical material in accord with his own grammar. Natural speech includes very many sentence fragments and syntactic anomalies; yet listeners understand. They impose grammatical structure on speech in the service of comprehensibility. A number of studies bear on this issue, e.g. parents' systematic expansions into grammatical sentences of children's telegraphic, elliptical speech (Brown and Bellugi 1964); subjects' reinterpretations of semantically implausible compounds as plausible ones, in spite of the task requirements (Gleitman and Gleitman 1970).

Further and more explicitly, as C. Chomsky (1969:2) reports of her experimental subjects:

. . . we find that the children do in fact assign an interpretation to the structures that we present to them. They do not, as they see it, fail to understand our sentences. They understand them, but they understand them wrongly.

This description is applicable also to the class-inclusion non-conservers; they too understand wrongly.

Empirical support for the grammatical constraints explanation of the young child's consistent failure in the class-inclusion task was sought in a variety of ways.

In the first study we exposed young children to ungrammatical structures involving distributive comparisons. We asked five-year-olds questions involving comparison of elements of a class and elements of one of its subclasses. For example, we asked:

(19) Which is taller: a person or a woman?
(20) Which is stronger: a rabbit or an animal?
(21) Which is sweeter: a lemon or a fruit?

No child balked at these questions, every child answered readily. If the child offered a justification for his answer, it usually indicated he was comparing elements from coordinate classes. For instance, when asked if a person or a woman is taller one child replied: 'A person--'cause my daddy's a person and he's bigger than my mommy'. Another child, when asked about the relative strength of a rabbit or an animal, selected 'an animal, 'cause elephants are stronger than rabbits and dogs are (too)'.

After some intervening tasks the experimenter returned to these ungrammatical questions and asked if there was anything 'funny' or 'odd' or 'strange' about them. Most children denied there was anything odd about the questions, although one child did volunteer that 'a woman and a person are the same thing'. Apparently the young child consistently misinterprets these ungrammatical questions as grammatical ones and the misinterpretations usually, if not always, involve interpreting the questions as a comparison of elements from coordinate classes.

The parallel to performance in the class-inclusion task is obvious. In both cases the child readily answers a different question from the one posed by the experimenter. In both cases the child compares coordinate classes rather than superordinate class and a subclass. The parallel seems sufficiently compelling to conclude that the same factor, namely, the child's grammar, determines performance in both tasks.

The second study varied the wording of the class-inclusion question. As noted above, the form of the class-inclusion question is anomalous.

(22) Are there more animals or more lions?

We worked with a group of children who could not answer correctly in the Piagetian class-inclusion task and asked them questions in which the wording was the usual wording for a collection comparison.

(23) Which is more: all the animals or only the lions?

One-third of the children who could not answer the class-inclusion question correctly when presented in the first form, <u>lions</u> or <u>animals</u>, were able to answer correctly when the conventional wording for a collective comparison was used, <u>all the animals</u> or <u>only the lions</u>. We apparently were able to get the children to think collectively and hence to weaken the effect of the over-generalization from distributive comparisons by a change in wording.

In sum, we have suggested that the constraints that render un-grammatical the distributive comparison of class and subclass are over-generalized by young children to collective comparisons and that the tendency to compare elements of coordinate classes in distributive comparisons is also over-generalized to collective comparisons. As a consequence the young child consistently misinterprets the Piagetian class-inclusion question, which involves comparison of class and sub-class, as a question about coordinate classes. Support for this argu-ment comes from these two studies. First, when young children are asked analogous questions about distributive comparisons, e.g. to compare a rabbit and an animal, they also consistently misinterpret the question as referring to coordinate classes--rabbits and other animals. Second, when the conventional wording for a collective com-parison is used in the class-inclusion task, the question is often inter-preted correctly.

In conclusion, first, and most specifically, the class-inclusion task is not an index of hierarchical classification as Piaget has main-tained; instead it reflects inappropriate grammatical restraints. Secondly, the results reported here suggest that if one is uncom-fortable about the verbal aspects of some purported measure of cog-nitive sophistication, one might profitably concentrate on the verbal nature of the task which could account for the child's misleading per-formance. And finally, and most generally and most obviously, verbal transmission of knowledge and verbal tests of knowledge are valid only if the techniques are appropriate to the grammatical sophistication of the learner. In the case of young children we should beware of assum-ing that the child understands in the same way that the adult under-stands.

REFERENCES

Bever, T. G. and P. S. Rosenbaum. 1971. Some lexical structures and their empirical validity. In: Semantics. Edited by Danny D. Steinberg and Leon A. Jakobovits. 586-599. London, Cambridge University Press.

Brown, R. and U. Bellugi. 1964. Three processes in the child's acquisition of syntax. Harvard Educational Review 34:2.133-151.

Chomsky, Carol. 1969. The acquisition of syntax in children from 5 to 10. Research Monograph Series No. 57. Cambridge, Mass., MIT Press.

Ervin, S. M. 1964. Imitation and structural change in children's language. In: New directions in the study of language. Edited by E. H. Lenneberg. Cambridge, Mass., MIT Press.

Fraser, C., U. Bellugi, and R. Brown. 1963. Control of grammar in imitation, comprehension, and production. Journal of Verbal Learning and Verbal Behavior 2. 121-135.

Gleitman, L. and H. Gleitman. 1970. Phrase and paraphrase. New York, W. W. Norton.

Inhelder, B. and J. Piaget. 1964. The early growth of logic in the child. New York, W. W. Norton.

Klahr, D. and J. G. Wallace. 1970. An information processing analysis of some Piagetian experimental tasks. Cognitive Psychology 1. 358-387.

Piaget, J. 1965. The child's conception of number. New York, W. W. Norton.

Winer, G. A. 1974. An analysis of verbal facilitation of class-inclusion reasoning. Child Development 45. 224-227.

FATHERS AND OTHER STRANGERS:
MEN'S SPEECH TO YOUNG CHILDREN

JEAN BERKO GLEASON

Boston University

The decade of the 70's in child language research looks very different from that of the 60's. The years of formalism yielded a great deal of information on the order in which various linguistic structures are acquired by children, and hinted at the presence of linguistic and cognitive universals. At the same time, very little was said about the actual process of acquisition; the child was seen as a miniature grammarian testing out his linguistic hypotheses, which had to be innate because no child could be expected to make order out of the jumble of decadent performance surrounding him. Now, as Molière's Dr. Sganarelle would say, 'Nous avons changé tout cela'.[1] A number of studies, beginning with small papers in Susan Ervin-Tripp's laboratory at Berkeley and including the work of Patricia Broen, Juliet Phillips, Catherine Snow, Helen Remick, and others in various countries have shown that mothers' speech to children learning language appears to be an ideal teaching language, one that is characterized by well-formedness, simplicity, repetition, and other design features that appear to facilitate the child's prehension of the system, all delivered at half the rate of adult-adult speech. Moreover, mothers have been shown to adjust the length and complexity of their utterances to conform to the child's gradually emerging competence. The theoretical onus on the child has thus been considerably lightened as language acquisition has come to be viewed as an interactive process involving both the child and a sensitive adult.

Now that it is known that mothers' speech to young children has special input features, it is important to determine if these features are limited to mothers' speech or if they are in a more general sense

characteristic of adult language to young children. There are obvious
practical consequences: with family roles changing and the advent of
daycare, the question of whether or not non-mothers are able to provide the kind of linguistic environment that may be crucial to the interactive development of language becomes increasingly significant.
Catherine Snow answered part of the question when she showed that
women who were not themselves mothers had in their speech to children the same modifications as mothers. But men's language has remained a mystery: to date there have been essentially no published
studies of men's speech to children. In fact, for a while there was
some question as to whether there was such a thing as men's speech
to children: in a study of fathers' speech to their 3-month-old infants,
Rebelsky and Hanks found that fathers spent an average of only 37.7
seconds a day engaged in this activity. Perhaps many fathers share
the sentiments of Nikolai in War and Peace, who regarded infants as
nothing more than a lump of flesh and only became interested in them
when they reached the age of a year or 15 months and began to talk.
At any rate, fathers do talk to their children, as do other males, and
the nature of that language is the topic of our current investigation.

The primary data examined comes from two male and two female
daycare teachers in a small daycare center at a large university in
Cambridge, Massachusetts, and from three mothers and three fathers
at home with their children, mostly at the dinner hour. The home
samples are part of a study conducted by Gary Kriedberg, a student
at Boston University. We have also looked at another comparative
study of mothers' and fathers' speech that was conducted at the Boston
Graduate School of Education by Audrey Stein. Stein compared the
stories that mothers and fathers in five families made up for their
children in response to a picture book. The children were all of preschool age, and the families were visited twice; on each occasion one
parent showed the child the book and made up a study to go with the
pictures. Stein found that in the storytelling situation the mothers'
and fathers' language were similar in terms of mean length of utterance and mean preverb length, both measures of complexity, as well
as in other adult-child register features, like repetitions, expansions,
and expatiations. But the mothers produced significantly more speaker
changes (turns), exclamations, and questions, as well as other indices
of the close mother-child relationship, while the fathers tended to involve the child less and to be less 'tuned in' to what the child was trying to say or was interested in. It was clear, however, that despite
these differences, the fathers' speech in this storytelling situation contained special modifications for children.

The home and daycare samples cover various nonexperimental
loosely structured activities, like eating dinner or having juice and
crackers and playing in the playground. Kriedberg compared the

fathers' and mothers' speech at home along a number of dimensions, and we compared the female with the male daycare teachers. This report describes some findings of Kriedberg's home study, where the parents occupy different roles, and terminates with results from the daycare study, where females and males occupied essentially the same roles.

The mothers and fathers at home all simplified their speech when addressing their children. Their mean preverb length and mean length of utterance within each family were quite similar, although the fathers' MLU was less closely tied to that of the child than was the mothers': mothers used less complex speech with their younger children and produced longer, more complex utterances when addressing the older of their two children. In one family, where the younger child by two years was a girl, the father nonetheless directed longer utterances to her than to his son. This is perhaps a reflection of the fact that there were large differences between fathers and mothers in the types of sentences they produced: fathers' language was filled with direct imperatives, especially to their sons. Since imperatives have zero preverb length this contributes to the shorter average length of father-son utterances. In the home samples, fathers produced significantly more imperatives than mothers. Fathers also produced more threats and more jocular names, names that had a pejorative undertone, like dingaling, especially to their sons. One additional difference between fathers and mothers, which has not been quanti- fied, was that fathers seemed to employ some fairly rare lexical items, like telling a two-year-old that he is being aggravating. Like the mothers', the fathers' speech was essentially limited to the here and now, and was clearly a register especially marked for talking to children, but because of the imperatives, threats, and affection- ately insulting names, the fathers' language 'felt' qualitatively differ- ent from the mothers' language. Finally, the fathers' language clearly demarked their role within the family: a father playing with his small son, for instance, might break off the game to send the child to his mother to have his diaper changed.

While the mothers and fathers had a number of differentiating features in their language, male and female daycare teachers pro- duced language that was quantitatively and qualitatively very similar.[2] The mean length of utterance of the five longest utterances for each was computed; the females averaged 14.9 and the males averaged 14.8. Repetition rates for the males were higher than for the females: males averaged 31 percent repetitions, while females' speech contained 24 percent repetitions. Again, we note anecdotally some unexpected lexical usage by males: one teacher asked a child if she found some- thing intimidating. The child was in a class of 3-year-olds. But the topic of discourse for males and females is very much in the present, and both males and females are concerned with the child's immediate needs, as is evidenced by the following excerpt from the transcript:

> Male teacher: (to Jenny) Does Jenny want to go to the toilet? Do you want to go to the toilet? (to Michael) Did you go to the potty after nap?

Here the language of this male teacher is filled with baby talk features, and the concern is one that in many homes is the exclusive province of mothers, but within the daycare center male and female teachers accepted responsibility for attending to the children's immediate needs, and their language reflects this.

There are two main features that distinguish between the language of the male and female daycare teachers. The first is in the use of the child's name. In a sample of 100 utterances, males called the child by name an average of 32 times. Women did so only one-fourth as often. These vocatives were used about as often in noninitial as in initial position.

TABLE 1. Daycare teachers' use of child's name, per 100 utterances

Teacher	Initial position	Noninitial position	Total vocatives
Mr. B.	12	19	31
Mr. J.	20	12	32
Ms. S.	1	4	5
Ms. L.	6	4	10

The second quantifiable difference between the language of female and male teachers was in sentence type: males again used more imperatives than females, but that has to be seen in light of the fact that the females' speech was singularly devoid of direct imperative constructions: they averaged 2 percent. Males averaged only 11 percent, which is a smaller proportion of imperatives than mothers use at home, and in a different universe from the fathers.

TABLE 2. Percentage of utterance types

	Imperatives	Declaratives	Questions
Fathers (N=3)	38.33	33.33	28.67
Mothers (N=3)	19	52	29
Male teachers (N=2)	11	47	42
Female teachers (N=2)	2	48	50

One important point to note in discussing differences between teachers and parents is that the teachers were dealing with someone else's children. Parents are also aware that they cannot speak as strongly to their children's friends as to their own children. When some children were interviewed about how they felt about the way adults talk to them, one 9-year-old girl volunteered that when she went to a friend's house 'my friend's mother is always much nicer to me than she is to her own child.'

Thus, one of the variables to be taken into account in studying language addressed to children is that adults have separate ways of talking to their own children and to other people's children. This must be added to other variables like sex of adult, sex of child, age of child, the topic, and the setting.

In the setting of the home, mothers and fathers do not produce identical speech, although fathers' speech has many of the formal characteristics of mothers' speech. But fathers are not as well tuned-in to their children as mothers are in the traditional family situation. They do not have to learn to attend to subtle signals from the child, and frequently have no penalty to pay for any lack of attention: someone else cleans up the accidents. On the other hand, there are probably serious and far-reaching good effects that result from the fact that traditional fathers are not quite so sensitive to the needs and intentions of their children. Toward the end of A First Language (p. 412), Roger Brown speculates about why children bother to learn the adult linguistic system at all, since the evidence indicates that their mothers understand them, whatever their needs, and are rarely even conscious of gross syntactic deficiencies on the part of the child. One reason must surely be that children possess deep, inner--epigenetic, if you will--drives to acquire and integrate adult knowledge and adult competence in all of their behaviors. Another, simpler, motivating force is to be found at the dinner table and in the playground: children have to learn to talk to their fathers and other strangers, and these people are not tuned in to them in the warm, sensitive way their mothers are. In Stein's storytelling situation, the fathers sometimes misunderstood what the children said. They also concentrated on telling an interesting story, while mother spent more time interacting with the child, asking questions, making sure he or she understood. The children had to exert themselves more for the fathers, and try harder to make themselves both heard and understood. In this way, fathers can be seen as a bridge to the outside world, leading the child to change her or his language in order to be understood. Of course, children without fathers also learn to talk, but the opportunity to try out new linguistic skills on someone not as intimate as your mother but closer than a stranger may be one of the hitherto unrecognized benefits of coming from an intact family. Perhaps the first step outward toward the outside world and the one that necessitates sharpening linguistic skills is the one in which you try to tell your father what happened while he was away.

While this may describe families that maintain the traditional model, there are many families that no longer conform to this model, and it may well be asked what are the linguistic consequences of shared parental nurturant roles and of daycare with both male and female caretakers. Until now, all of the studies of input language to children have been studies of women's speech. It was possible that child language register was limited to females and that males were incapable of producing appropriate speech--if any speech at all--when addressing young children. Our data, and the small studies I have referred to, indicate that the important features of adult-child speech are found in the language of both fathers and non-fathers when addressing young children. This is not to say that men and women, fathers and strangers, all talk alike when dealing with young children, but rather that the important features of simplicity, well-formedness, repetition, and immediacy are present in the language of all of them. At home with their own children, fathers frequently are cast into the role of disciplinarian. Their language contains more direct imperatives, while the mothers tend to couch their imperative intent in question form. Avoidance of direct imperatives appears to be a general feature of women's language in our society. The fathers also use more imperatives when speaking with their sons than with their daughters, and they use more gruff affectionate terms toward the little boys: little girls are rarely called <u>dingaling</u>, <u>nutcake</u>, or <u>tiger</u> by their fathers. The heavy use of imperatives to the boys gives the impression that in our society males become accustomed early on to taking orders, and, if their fathers provide role models, to giving them.

The male and female daycare teachers were not as different from one another as were fathers and mothers at home. The differences that did exist, however, were in the same direction, the greater use of imperatives by males, for instance. But at the same time, daycare males, like females, expressed many of their requests in question form and tended to state social rules in an impersonal and non-threatening way. The following excerpt from the transcript indicates how one male daycare teacher handled a child transgressor:

Mr. B: Mickey, do you know what the rule is? When someone screams and says they want to get up, you don't hold them down. Mickey, we don't hold people down when they say they want to get up. You were holding Sarah down and she kept saying she wanted to get up. Okay. So the next time someone says, 'excuse me, I want to get up', you let them up.

By contrast, a father at home, faced with a much less serious situation, expressed himself as follows:

> Mr. X: Anthony, stay out of here before I break your head.
> Don't go in there again or I'll break your head.

Both men's utterances are clearly marked as adult-child register: The child is called by name frequently and there are numerous repetitions, but the father is threatening and imperative, while the daycare attendant speaks in an understated, very explicit, and rather 'preachy' way that is perhaps itself an example of schoolteacher register. This is especailly true of the 'we don't's' where 'we' really means 'you'. Finally, it would appear that while the traditional father at home may not be attuned to the immediate needs of his child and may speak to that child in a gruff, imperious way, this is not at all the case where the male shares the nurturant role, as in the daycare center, and, presumably, by extension, in those families that share child care duties. The male daycare teachers' speech is singularly devoid of the kinds of threats that have been seen emanating from the traditional fathers at home. In the use of imperative constructions there is no overlap between home and school samples. In fact, mothers at home produce more imperatives to their children than do males in the daycare setting.

While the language of fathers at home has the same basic syntactic features as the language of mothers, it is distinguished from mothers' speech to children along lines that are connected with the father's role, both as authority figure and as one who is not called upon to be completely sensitive to the needs and intentions of the child. Traditional fathers are not primary providers of nurturance, nor are they called upon to be sensitive to the signals that indicate that nurturance is called for.

In the daycare center male and female teachers occupy the same role and many of the differences that have been noted between mothers and fathers disappear. Male daycare teachers' speech to young children is more like the language of female daycare teachers than it is like that of fathers at home, even though it contains some markers characteristic of male speech in general. While the greater use of imperatives might indicate that males are more 'controlling', it is difficult to explain why men call children by name so much more frequently than women do. The use of the child's name at the beginning of an utterance may also be an attention-getting or controlling device, but utterances frequently terminated with the child's name as well. One possibility is that the use of the child's name is a marker employed by males more frequently than females to indicate that they are speaking in adult-child register; females rely upon other devices, such as varied or exaggerated intonation patterns, to accomplish the same end. Even if one cannot see the addressee, one can usually guess correctly that a woman is talking to a child if she employs exaggerated or singsong intonation; under the same circumstances, if one hears a man call the addressee by name several times over a short period of time, one can also guess that he is speaking to a child.

It is probably possible to find other differences in the language of male and female daycare attendants, but the similarities in their language in terms of MLU, preverb length, topic of discourse, and repetitions are striking. If the small daycare sample we have seen is in any way typical, we can take assurance from the fact that daycare teachers' speech is very like mothers' speech: both female and male daycare teachers appear to provide children with the kind of linguistic input that now is considered necessary for the development of language. Men, as well as women, modify their speech when addressing young children, and where the men occupy a nurturant role they become increasingly sensitive to the needs and intentions of the children.

NOTES

1. Molière, Le médecin malgré lui, Act II, Scene 4: 'Cela était autrefois ainsi: mais nous avons changé tout cela, et nous faisons maintenant la médecine d'une méthode toute nouvelle.'

2. The daycare data was tape recorded and transcribed by Elsie Zanger, and analyzed by Georgene Robinson. I am grateful to them both.

REFERENCES

Bates, Martha. 1973. Mother's and father's speech to children. Unpublished paper, Boston University.

Broen, Patricia. 1972. The verbal environment of the language learning child. American Speech and Hearing Association monograph 17. Washington, D.C.

Brown, Roger. 1973. A first language. Cambridge, Harvard University Press.

Drach, Kerry. 1969. The language of the parent: A pilot study. Working papers, No. 13, Language Behavior Research Laboratory, University of California, Berkeley.

Farwell, Carol. 1973. The language spoken to children. Papers and reports on child language development, Vols. 5 and 6. Stanford University.

Gleason, Jean Berko. 1973. Code switching in children's language. In: Cognitive development and the acquisition of language. Edited by T. E. Moore. New York, Academic Press.

Kobashigawa, B. 1969. Repetitions in a mother's speech to her child. Working papers, No. 14, Language Behavior Research Laboratory, University of California, Berkeley.

Kriedberg, Gary. 1975. Hail to the chief. Unpublished paper, Boston University.

Moerk, Ernst. 1972. Principles of interaction in language learning. Merrill Palmer Quarterly 18. 229-258.

Pfuderer, Carol. 1969. Some suggestions for a syntactic characterization of baby-talk style. Working papers, No. 14, Language Behavior Research Laboratory, University of California, Berkeley.

Phillips, Juliet. 1973. Syntax and vocabulary of mothers' speech to young children: Age and sex comparisons. Child Development 44. 182-185.

Rebelsky, Freda and C. Hanks. 1971. Fathers' verbal interaction with infants in the first three months of life. Child Development 42. 63-68.

Remick, Helen. 1972. Maternal speech to children during language acquisition. Paper presented at the International Symposium on First Language Acquisition, Florence, Italy.

Snow, Catherine. 1972. Mothers' speech to children learning language. Child Development 43. 439-465.

Stein, Audrey. 1973. An analysis and comparison of mothers' and fathers' speech to children in a story-telling situation. Unpublished paper, Boston University School of Education.